December 21, 2001

The Honourable A. Anne McLellan
Minister of Justice
Justice Building
4th Floor, East Memorial Building
Wellington Street
OTTAWA ON K1A 0A6

Dear Minister:

In accordance with section 5(1)(c) of the *Law Commission of Canada Act*, we are pleased to submit this Report of the Law Commission of Canada on Close Personal Adult Relationships.

Yours sincerely,

Nathalie Des Rosiers
President

Gwen Boniface
Commissioner

Alan Buchanan
Commissioner

Roderick Wood
Commissioner

Bernard Colas
Commissioner

Table of Contents

Executive Summary

Introduction

Canadians enjoy a wide variety of close personal relationships – many marry or live with conjugal partners while others may share a home with parents, grandparents or a caregiver. The diversity of these relationships is a significant feature of our society, to be valued and respected. For many Canadians, the close personal relationships that they hold dear constitute an important source of comfort and help them to be productive members of society.

The law has not always respected these choices, however, or accorded them full legal recognition. While the law has recently been expanding its recognition beyond marriage to include other marriage-like relationships, it continues to focus its attention on conjugality. The Law Commission believes that governments need to pursue a more comprehensive and principled approach to the legal recognition and support of the full range of close personal relationships among adults. This requires a fundamental rethinking of the way in which governments regulate relationships.

The Diversity of Personal Adult Relationships

The diversity of personal relationships formed by Canadian adults is not a new phenomenon. Alongside the nuclear family centred on the conjugal couple, there have always been a variety of other living arrangements, including adult siblings sharing a home, widows and widowers forming blended families and multi-generational households. While domestic relationships appear to have become more diverse over the past thirty years, it may simply be that public awareness has increased as a result of the increased availability of statistical data. For example, the 2001 census was the first time that Statistics Canada collected data on same-sex unions. Many non-conjugal relationships are still largely invisible in mainstream social science research. As well, we have only limited information about relationships where adults are economically, emotionally and even physically interdependent, but do not share a residence.

Conjugal Relationships

A majority of Canadians form a conjugal union at some point in their lives. While the marriage rate has declined steadily since 1971, marriages still constitute a predominant choice for opposite-sex conjugal unions. Nevertheless, opposite-sex cohabitation – whether as an alternative to marriage, as a prelude to marriage or as a sequel to marriage – is a growing phenomenon that now has widespread social acceptance.

There is as yet no census data or reliable studies on the number of lesbian and gay couples living together in Canada. The available data from small-scale studies suggests that gays and lesbians form enduring conjugal relationships in numbers comparable to the population as a whole. It appears that a significant minority of Canadian households consists of same-sex couples.

Non-Conjugal Households and Non-Conjugal Relationships

A substantial minority of Canadian households involves adults living alone, lone-parent families or adults living together in non-conjugal relationships. Households centred around a conjugal relationship may also include other adults with no conjugal ties to the couple, such as relatives or close friends. In addition, adult children are often returning home to live with their parents, principally for financial reasons caused by unemployment or the need to complete their education.

The concept of the economic family encompasses all relatives living in the same household, regardless of how they are related. Adult siblings living together form the largest component of this group.

We know little about non-conjugal relationships between non-relatives, since the 1996 census did not differentiate between same-sex conjugal relationships and non-conjugal relationships between non-relatives. We do know that "families of friends" can be of great importance, particularly within the gay and lesbian communities and among older adults, especially older women.

Persons with Disabilities and Their Caregivers

People with disabilities have the same range of close personal relationships as other Canadians. They are spouses, friends, lovers, parents, aunts, uncles and so on. Unlike most other Canadians, many people with disabilities are also in close personal relationships that are characterized at least in part by personal care or support that is related to their disabilities. Over 90 percent of persons with disabilities live in their own homes. The vast majority must develop relationships of support with paid and non-paid caregivers for their basic survival and well-being.

The available data shows that women continue to provide the bulk of caregiving on an unpaid basis. Numerous studies have shown that supports to individuals with disabilities and their families are often insufficient. This situation puts stress on family members who are expected to compensate for gaps in formal care in their unpaid role as caregivers. The extent of their caregiving responsibilities can take a major toll on caregivers' economic security and physical, emotional and psychological health. Inadequate social support of caregiving has an impact not only on caregivers but also on the well-being of the person receiving care and, just as importantly, on the quality of the relationships between caregivers and those receiving care.

Canadians have always formed a diverse array of personal adult relationships. Recognizing and supporting personal adult relationships that involve caring and interdependence is an important state objective. In the past, many policies were framed to apply only to married persons. Governments have taken important steps forward in recent years by extending rights and obligations to persons who are living in non-marital relationships, whether same-sex or opposite-sex. But this extension of rights and obligations has maintained the legal focus on conjugal relationships. A more principled and comprehensive approach is needed to encompass the full range of Canadians' close personal adult relationships.

Fundamental Values and Principles

Equality and autonomy are the two most important values that governments need to consider in framing policies that recognize and support personal adult relationships. State regulation of personal relationships should also seek to enhance other values: personal security, privacy and religious freedom, while pursuing legitimate government objectives in a coherent and efficient manner.

Governments must respect and promote two kinds of equality. **Relational equality** seeks to equalize the legal status among different types of relationships. Legislation like the federal government's *Modernization of Benefits and Obligations Act* largely eliminated distinctions between these two groups. However, by focusing only on conjugal couples, it entrenches unequal legal treatment of conjugal and non-conjugal relationships which may share the functional characteristics of emotional and financial interdependence. The principle of relational equality requires more than equal treatment of conjugal couples.

The concept of **equality within relationships** seeks to overcome unequal distributions of income, wealth and power, much of it based on historic inequality between men and women, or the lack of state support for persons with disabilities.

The value of **autonomy** requires that governments put in place the conditions in which people can freely choose their personal relationships. While governments should discourage the formation of abusive relationships, they should not create financial or other kinds of pressure to discourage relationships without reference to their qualitative attributes. The state should therefore remain neutral with regard to the form or status of relationships and not accord one form of relationship more benefits or legal support than others.

Personal security – whether physical, psychological or economic – enhances the ability of individuals to make healthy choices about entering or remaining in relationships. The state has a role to play in ensuring physical security within a relationship as well as economic security outside the relationship.

Healthy personal relationships are founded on candour and trust; they can flourish only if we are confident that our intimate thoughts and acts will not be discovered by or revealed to others. To promote the **privacy** that is necessary to such relationships, the state should avoid establishing legal rules that require intrusive examinations into, or forced disclosure of, the intimate details of personal adult relationships, unless the relationship involves violence or exploitation. Privacy rights must be balanced, however, and in some circumstances must give way to compelling objectives such as the state interest in prosecuting and preventing crime, including the commission of crimes involving domestic violence and abuse.

Contemporary Canadian understandings of **religious freedom** and equality require that the state not take sides in religious matters. The history of marriage regulation in Canada has thus been characterized by a progressive uncoupling of religious and legal requirements, reflecting a growing emphasis on the separation of church and state in a secular and pluralistic political community. Our current understanding of religious freedom requires that laws and policies, including those that regulate personal adult relationships, pursue objectives that can be defended in secular rather than religious terms. **Coherence** requires that laws have clear objectives, and that their legislative design corresponds with the achievement of those objectives. This would avoid reliance on marital status in a law whose objectives do not necessarily relate to marriage.

The **efficiency** of a law, policy or program may be measured by how effective it is, for example, in reaching its intended beneficiaries and whether it can be administered without undue costs or delays. Perfect coherence may not be achievable if the costs of administering a specifically targeted law are prohibitive.

A comprehensive approach to the recognition and support of personal adult relationships should be guided, first and foremost, by the values of equality and autonomy. In addition, state policies should protect and advance personal security, privacy and religious freedom, and they should seek to accomplish legitimate state objectives in a coherent and efficient manner. Proposed laws and the operation of existing laws should be carefully scrutinized to eliminate any detrimental effects on these values and principles.

Reconsidering the Relevance of Relationships

It is time to try to imagine a legislative regime that more effectively accomplishes its goals by relying less on whether people are living in particular kinds of relationships. The Law Commission proposes a new methodology for assessing any existing or proposed law that employs relational terms to accomplish its objectives. It consists of four questions.

First Question: Are the objectives of the law legitimate?

If not, should the law be repealed or fundamentally revised?

Second Question: Do relationships matter?

If the law's objectives are sound, are the relationships included in the law important or relevant to the law's objectives?

Third Question: If relationships matter, can individuals be permitted to designate the relevant relationships themselves?

Could the law allow individuals to choose which of their close personal relationships they want to be subject to the particular law?

Fourth Question: If relationships matter, and self-designation is not feasible or appropriate, is there a better way to include relationships?

If relationships do matter, and public policy requires that the law delineate the relevant relationships to which it applies, can the law be revised to more accurately capture the relevant range of relationships? This question applies where it is not possible to individualize rights and responsibilities, nor to allocate them on a basis of self-designation. Where the state must ascribe rights and responsibilities to achieve its objectives, it would be preferable to more carefully tailor laws to take into account the functional attributes of particular relationships.

The Report recommends that Parliament apply this four-step methodology in the development and implementation of all future law and programs. In Chapter Three, this methodology is applied to a variety of federal statutory provisions that rely on relational status. Examples are drawn from the *Marine Liability Act*, the *Canada Labour Code*, the *Immigration Act*, the *Canada Evidence Act*, the *Employment Insurance Act*, the *Bankruptcy and Insolvency Act*, the *Bank Act*, the *Income Tax Act*, the *Old Age Security Act* and the *Canada Pension Plan*.

The Report considers statutory provisions where the law makes presumptions based on relational status in order to achieve objectives that are not necessarily or exclusively connected to the targeted relationships. For example, under the *Employment Insurance Act*, employees who are related to their employer must prove their employment was similar to an arm's length relationship in order to be eligible for employment insurance, a burden of proof that is difficult for them to satisfy in practice. If the purpose of the provision is to guard against sham employment contracts set up just to claim benefits, it should do that by examining the features of any employment contract, not just those among family members.

Fraudulent preference provisions in the *Bankruptcy and Insolvency Act* and conflict of interest provisions in the *Bank Act* similarly target only family members. In so doing, they miss capturing all persons who may be receiving preferential treatment from a bankrupt person or a bank officer because of a personal relationship that is outside the family categories defined in those Acts. The Report recommends amending these provisions to reduce the emphasis on certain types of relationships.

Canada Evidence Act

In the section on the *Canada Evidence Act*, the Report considers the limits on spousal testimony in criminal trials. There are two basic problems with the current regime. First, it can lead to the exclusion from the trial process of relevant and probative evidence in circumstances where the state's interest in discovering the truth outweighs the relational interests at stake. Second, in circumstances where the relational interests at stake do outweigh the state's interest in discovering the truth, the law protects only marital relationships. Clearly there are other personal relationships that are worthy of legal protection. As a result, a consensus exists that the law in this area needs to be reformed.

The Report recommends removal of the common law rule that a spouse of the accused is not a competent witness for the Crown. Regarding non-compellability, the Report recommends an amendment to the *Canada Evidence Act* that would enable judges to excuse a witness from having to testify if he or she objects to testifying, has an ongoing close personal relationship with the accused, and the judge finds that the harm that would be caused to the witness or to the relationship by having to testify outweighs the desirability of admitting the testimony. Finally, it recommends replacing the marital communications privilege with an amendment to the *Canada Evidence Act* that enables judges to prevent the divulgence of a confidential communication if the witness has a close personal relationship with the accused at the time the communication was made, and the need to protect and promote candour and trust in close personal relationships outweighs the desirability of admitting the testimony.

Income Tax Act

Income tax has been used extensively as an instrument for delivering government subsidies and transfer payments to individuals. Therefore, the income tax legislation provides an excellent prism through which to examine the role of government in regulating close personal adult relationships. As a preliminary matter, the Report recommends retaining the individual as the basic unit for the calculation of income tax.

The Report goes on to look at some specific tax provisions that rely upon relational status. For example, in the area of dependent relative and spouse and common-law tax credits, the Report determines that the *Income Tax Act* could more accurately capture the range of relevant relationships. As a result, the Report recommends that Parliament replace the *Income Tax Act's* spouse and common-law partner tax credit with enhanced or new programs that more carefully target caregivers and children for direct income support. The Report also recommends that Parliament extend the tax credits for dependent relatives so that they can be claimed by any taxpayer who has provided financial or caregiving support to a person who is dependent by reason of age, disability or illness, without reference to relationship status, and that it consider extending income assistance to caregivers by making dependants' credits refundable or by delivering direct grants outside of the tax system. It further recommends that Parliament consider providing income support, by way of direct grants or refundable tax credits, to disabled people to enable them to hire or purchase the supports they require.

As a second example, the Report concludes that, while the rollover rules for transfers of property between spouses and common law partners serve valid objectives, the provisions should be extended to all persons living together in economically interdependent relationships. This would make the targeted relationships more relevant to the objectives of the provisions: reducing the intrusiveness of the tax system in the lives of those with close personal relationships and encouraging the redistribution of property.

Other legislative provisions examined through the lens of the Commission's four-step methodology include provisions setting out eligibility for compensation for the accidental death or injury of a family member in the air or at sea; entitlement to caregiver leave or bereavement leave under the *Canada Labour Code*; income security programs under the *Old Age Security Act*; survivor's benefits under the *Canada Pension Plan*, and family sponsorship under the *Immigration Act*. In each of these cases, comparison of the objectives of the legislation with the means used to achieve them reveals that the provisions could be better tailored to achieve their aims more coherently.

In considering how state regulation can recognize and support close personal relationships in a more principled and coherent manner, the first task is to clarify the objectives of laws that take relationships into account and determine whether they are valid. The next question is whether relationships are relevant to those objectives. If not, the law should eliminate reliance on relational considerations and individualize the rights and responsibilities in question.

In those areas where relationships are relevant to the legislative objectives, we analyzed whether it is possible to allow individuals rather than governments to choose the relevant relationships. In other contexts, we suggested that some limits be placed on these choices, restricting self-selection to a limited range of relationships.

Where self-selection is not workable, we considered alternative ways for governments to include relationships in legislation and provided examples where relational definitions could be redrawn to cover the full range of relevant relationships.

The Legal Organization of Personal Relationships

People want stability and certainty in their personal relationships, as in other aspects of their lives. The state must provide adequate legal structures to support the relationships that citizens develop, structures that respect the values of equality, autonomy and choice. Marriage has long been the main vehicle by which two people publicly expressed their commitment to each other and sought to ensure certainty and stability in their own and their family's relationship. But marriage is no longer a sufficient model, given the variety of relationships that exist in Canada today. What legal frameworks can the state offer to respond to the need of all its citizens for certainty and stability in their personal relationships?

Four legal models can be used to regulate personal relationships: private law, ascription, registration and marriage. The **private law** model operates by default – when governments do not provide a legal framework, people are always at liberty to express their commitments through contracts. They can then turn to the courts when they feel that the other party has not fulfilled his or her contractual obligations. They may also rely on private law remedies, such as unjust enrichment or constructive trust. This mechanism is very burdensome. It can be costly, it favours the party with the greater resources or bargaining power and its after-the-fact remedies are uncertain.

Governments use **ascription** to prevent the risks of exploitation inherent in a contractual model by imposing (ascribing) a set of obligations on people in conjugal relationships that are presumed to correspond to the expectations of the majority of people involved in such relationships. While ascription may help to prevent exploitation, it is a blunt policy tool, treating all conjugal relationships alike. It infringes on autonomy, as people are not always aware they may opt out of certain provisions. While appropriate for conjugal relationships in some instances, it would be inappropriate for non-conjugal relationships.

Recently, there has been a move toward the creation of a new status, often called registered partnership. Its objective is to provide an alternative way for the state to recognize and support close personal relationships. When people register their relationships, a range of rights and responsibilities are then open to them. **Registrations** provide an orderly framework in which people can express their commitment to each other, receive public recognition and support, and voluntarily assume a range of legal rights and obligations. These regimes may also provide for an orderly and equitable resolution of the registrants' affairs if their relationship breaks down.

Registration schemes merit consideration because they provide a vehicle for recognizing a broader range of caring and supportive relationships, both conjugal and non-conjugal. They affirm the autonomy and choices of Canadians in their close personal relationships, offering the opportunity for public declarations of commitment that will be respected by government. Registration also does not compromise privacy within a relationship in the way that ascription often does.

Designing a Registration Scheme

1. Formal Attributes

There is no reason for governments to restrict a registration scheme to conjugal couples or only to same-sex couples. We also see no compelling reason to impose a residential requirement on registrations, just as there is no requirement that married couples live together. Registrations should be terminable by mutual agreement. Registered partners should also be able to register a unilateral dissolution of their registration. The state should ensure that the legal obligations and reasonable expectations of the registrants are respected when the relationship breaks down.

2. Legal Implications of Registrations

Registration should provide options to registrants: for example, models of predetermined rights and responsibilities reflecting a conjugal relationship or a variety of caregiving relationships.

The legal consequences of registration might be limited to the private rights and responsibilities within the relationship – both during and after the relationship. Registration would be about clarifying the mutual responsibilities each party is voluntarily assuming, both for the parties themselves and for potentially interested third parties.

3. Intergovernmental and International Implications

Although the federal government has constitutional jurisdiction over marriage and divorce, including support and custody issues, it is unlikely that this jurisdiction would allow it to enact a registration regime that regulates the private legal obligations between adults in close personal relationships or to pass legislation regulating entry into, or exit from, this new civil arrangement. The best scenario would be a coordinated initiative among the federal, provincial and territorial governments.

On the international level, Canada should participate in the efforts toward international recognition of registration systems. It should also attempt to design its international arrangements on the basis of the existence of a variety of relationships and move toward an international recognition of registrations.

Marriage

In assessing whether our marriage laws continue to meet the needs of our evolving society, a first fundamental question is whether we need marriage laws at all. Could registration replace marriage, for all legal purposes? Would this better serve the objectives of the state?

Registration Instead of Marriage

A registration scheme could be used to replace marriage as a legal institution. Religious marriage ceremonies would continue to exist, but they would no longer have legal consequences. Only a system of civil registration would bind two people to a range of legal rights and responsibilities, and any two people who wanted to obtain public recognition and support of their relationship could register. We conclude that, while further debate about the appropriate role of the state in marriage is worthwhile, removing marriage as a legal mechanism for expressing commitment in a personal relationship is unlikely to be an attractive option for the majority of Canadians currently.

Adequacy of Current Marriage Laws

An historical overview of marriage in the Western world shows that church and state have had varying degrees of control over this institution. In some countries, like France, the state has had exclusive jurisdiction over marriage for centuries, although of course people continue to participate in religious ceremonies. In Canada, civil marriage and religious marriage co-exist. Although it may be appropriate to revisit the role of religious authorities as state-delegates for the purpose of marriage celebrations, and consider adopting a regime that requires a civil ceremony for the marriage to have legal effect, it does lead to duplication for those who want a religious ceremony.

The state's interest in marriage is not connected to the promotion of a particular conception of appropriate gender roles, nor is it to reserve procreation and the raising of children to marriage. The state's objectives underlying contemporary regulation of marriage relate essentially to the facilitation of private ordering: providing an orderly framework in which people can express their commitment to each other, receive public recognition and support, and voluntarily assume a range of legal rights and obligations. As the Supreme Court of Canada recognized in 1999 (*M.* v. *H.*), the capacity to form conjugal relationships characterized by emotional and economic interdependence has nothing to do with sexual orientation. If governments are to continue to maintain an institution called marriage, they cannot do so in a discriminatory fashion. Accordingly, the Report recommends that Parliament and provincial/territorial legislatures move toward repealing legislative restrictions on marriages between persons of the same sex.

Conclusion

In this Report, we argue that governments have tended to rely too heavily on conjugal relationships in accomplishing important state objectives. Rather than advocating simply that the law cover a broader range of relationships, the Law

Commission is of the view that it is time for governments to re-evaluate the way in which they regulate personal adult relationships.

We are suggesting a new methodology for addressing the legal regulation of these relationships, consisting of four questions. Are the objectives of the legislation legitimate? If so, are relationships relevant to achieving them? If they are relevant, can individuals themselves choose which relationships should be subject to the law? Finally, if relationships are relevant and self-designation is not feasible, is there a better way for governments to include relationships?

Implementation of this methodology would greatly diminish government reliance on relationship status. However, the state would still have an important role to play with respect to personal relationships, providing the legal framework for the voluntary assumption of rights and obligations between the two parties. It should broaden the range of relationships that receive this kind of state recognition and support through the creation of a registration scheme and the legalization of same-sex marriage.

Acknowledgements

The Law Commission of Canada wishes to acknowledge the contribution of several people to this Report. It benefited enormously from the counsel and insight of members of its Study Panels, whose names appear below:

Wendy Adams, France Allard, Tom Anderson, Pat Armstrong, Katherine Arnup, Michael Bach, Martha Bailey, Sharon Bond, Susan Boyd, Gwen Brodsky, Michèle Caron, Andrée Côté, Michel Côté, Shelagh Day, Margaret Denike, Pamela Dickey Young, Margrit Eichler, John Fisher, Catherine Frazee, Robert Glossop, Dominique Goubau, Teresa Janz, Olga Kits, Kathleen Lahey, Marcel Lauzière, Nicole LaViolette, Hugues Lévesque, Diana Majury, Claudine Ouellet, Carol Rogerson, Carolyn Rowe, Diane Rowe, Alain Roy, Ros Salvador, Liliane Spector, Monica Townson, Frances Woolley and Claire Young.

The Law Commission also received much help in the form of background research from the following scholars and organizations:

Pat Armstrong, Katherine Arnup, Martha Bailey, the British Columbia Law Institute, Gwen Brodsky, Neil Brooks, Brenda Cossman, Martin Daly, Wendy Danson, Shelagh Day, Connie Dieter, EGALE Canada (John Fisher, Kathleen Lahey and Laurie Arron), Winifred Holland, Teresa Janz, Olga Kits, Kathleen Lahey, Nicole LaViolette, Brigitte Lefebvre, Allan Manson, The Roeher Institute (Michael Bach, Catherine Frazee, Orville Endicott and Phyllis Gordon), Alain Roy, Bruce Ryder, Monica Townson, Margo Wilson, Claire Young and Shauna Van Praagh.

Our special thanks as well to the participants in the Domestic Partnerships Conference at Queen's University organized by Professor Martha Bailey in 1999, and the International Family Law Conference (2001) held at Queen's University and organized by Professor Nicholas Bala. Both events were a great source of inspiration and ideas.

We would also like to thank all those who participated in our consultations and sent in their comments and insights, especially Mary Lou Dickey, who reviewed the final draft. Our thanks go out to Neil Brooks, Monica Townson, Nicole LaViolette and Francine Pelletier (moderator) for having participated in the Law Commission's webcast in January 2001.

Recognition must also go to Roderick A. MacDonald, former President of the Law Commission of Canada, who developed the initial vision for this project, and to Stephen Owen, Commissioner, who greatly contributed to this project prior to the end of his term with the Law Commission.

Within the Law Commission, Research Officer Susan Alter managed this project from its beginnings until her departure in the summer of 2001. She asked the right questions, administered the research, organized the consultations and worked on earlier drafts, and we gratefully acknowledge her enormous contribution. Susan Zimmerman, Director of Research, was instrumental in overseeing the enormous job of putting together a report of this magnitude. We also thank her for continuing to provide insight after her departure and for drafting the Executive Summary to this Report. We want to acknowledge the work of Research Officer Lorraine Pelot, who stepped in during the last few months of this project and helped to pull together and fine-tune the final portions of the Report. We must also thank Lucie Gagné, Annie Di Palma and Lise Traversy, who worked very hard on the consultations, webcast and production of this Report, along with Bruno Bonneville, Executive Director, and Suzanne Schreyer-Belair, Senior Administration Officer, whose work is invaluable to the Law Commission. Thank you to all the staff who contributed in various ways.

The work of full-time staff was capably supplemented by a number of part-time researchers. A valuable contribution was made by our student researchers Simon Archer, Patricia De Sario, Karen Gorby, Sofia Gutierrez, Shauna Labman, William MacLarkey and Robert Poirier.

The Law Commission owes an enormous debt of gratitude to Bruce Ryder, who held the pen on this Report, integrating the many pieces of research that others prepared for the Commission and weaving the various sections together. We also want to recognize the important contribution of Brenda Cossman, who, along with Bruce, drafted earlier versions of this Report.

Ultimately, the views expressed in this Report, along with any errors or omissions, are the responsibility of the Commissioners.

Introduction

Canadians enjoy a wide variety of close personal relationships that are important to them. Many marry or live with conjugal partners. Others have emotional and economically important relationships outside of marriage and conjugality. They may share a home with parents, with grandparents or with a caregiver. Sometimes it may be sisters. Other times, best friends.

Making choices in one's personal relationships is among the most cherished of values in Canadian society. Indeed, the right to freedom of choice in one's close relationships is one that we take for granted. As individuals, we each enter relationships for very personal reasons and expect that these choices will be respected. Canadians expect that governments will respect their autonomy and beliefs in the legal regulation of these personal relationships.

People value their close personal relationships for the quality of care and support they provide. Intimates usually provide the most meaningful forms of care and support, such as sharing resources to provide food, shelter and clothing, providing personal services and guidance, attending to emotional needs, volunteering information or advice, or using abilities or skills to offer assistance in solving problems. Many studies have shown that individuals' physical and mental well-being is often related to the quality of social support in their lives.[1] Of course, not all close personal relationships deliver care and comfort to adults; intimacy and interdependency give rise to vulnerability and thus to opportunities for abuse.

The state cannot create healthy relationships; it can only seek to foster the conditions in which close personal relationships that are reasonably equal, mutually committed, respectful and safe can flourish. Governments have long regulated close personal adult relationships in a number of ways. Some government regulation is related to benefits and obligations that flow between citizens and the government or employers and creditors. Other regulation is aimed at the rights and responsibilities that flow between people within the relationship. Governments are pursuing a number of objectives in regulating close personal adult relationships, such as recognizing economic interdependence, promoting the stability of relationships, protecting people's expectations, encouraging the provision of care and preventing exploitation and abuse. In doing so, governments have chosen to focus on particular types of relationships.

Through the legal regulation of personal adult relationships, the state has recognized and supported some relationships but failed to recognize others; as a result, people's choices are not being respected. The law at one time focused almost all of its attention on marital relationships to the exclusion of other personal adult relationships. Legislatures and Parliament have taken important steps to narrow the gap between legal assumptions and social realities, but while the law currently recognizes and supports personal relationships beyond marriage, it continues to be centred mainly on conjugal relationships.

By focusing mainly on conjugal relationships, governments have made statutes both under-inclusive and over-inclusive – that is, the statutes may not cover all the people intended, or they may apply to people they were not intended to cover. There are many instances where the law imposes rights and responsibilities on the basis of a particular kind of relationship, rather than examining the nature of that relationship. In other words, rights and responsibilities are imposed on the basis of the status rather than the function of a relationship.

The problem is not only one of failing to recognize important relationships. Oftentimes, the law simply assumes that relationships are relevant in achieving government objectives. For example, the law might simply assume that a married or common-law couple pool their resources. While this is no doubt often the case, it is certainly not always true. There are many instances where the law simply imposes rights and responsibilities on the basis of a relationship, rather than considering whether that relationship really is relevant to the law or program in question.

In keeping with its mandate to consider measures that will make the legal system more efficient, economical, accessible and just, the Law Commission of Canada examined the regulation of close personal adult relationships. The goal was to determine how well law and policy were responding to contemporary realities. From 1999 to 2001, numerous research papers were commissioned and many consultations were held with Canadians, ranging from expert study panels and consultations with community groups to an interactive webcast. The Law Commission received many stories and submissions during its consultations in which Canadians described the multiplicity of relationships in which they live and expressed the multiplicity of views that they hold about how these relationships should be governed. The Law Commission heard from hundreds of Canadians, many of whom reported that current laws and policies were not working.

In this Report, the Law Commission considers the ways in which the law should recognize and support close personal relationships between adults. This is not to say that other very close personal relationships, such as intergenerational relationships that involve the rearing of children, are not important. Clearly, they are. But they raise very different issues. The focus in this Report is on interdependent relationships between adults: those personal relationships that are distinguished by mutual care and concern, the expectation of some form of an enduring bond, sometimes a deep commitment, and a range of interdependencies – emotional and economic – that arise from these features. A focus on relationships defined by these functions rather than status is more consonant with the objectives pursued by governments. These economically and emotionally interdependent relationships are one of the very foundations of Canadian social life. They may or may not involve parenting responsibilities that certainly influence the range of interdependencies created. They may or may not involve sexual intimacy. They may or may not be characterized by deep economic interdependency. Governments need to ensure that the law respects the diverse choices that Canadians make.

Instead of simply arguing that some relationships that are currently excluded (such as non-conjugal relationships) should be included, the Law Commission also believes that it is time to rethink the way in which governments regulate relationships. Governments need to reconsider the more fundamental questions of when and why relationships should matter. This Report offers some guidance as to how governments can achieve their legitimate objectives while respecting the importance and diversity of personal relationships.

Chapter One begins with a consideration of the importance and diversity of close personal relationships that are found in Canadian society today. The chapter examines the diversity of close personal relationships, tracing the major demographic trends that have occurred in the nature of Canadian adults' close personal relationships, including the prevalence of non-marital cohabitation, adult children remaining at home and an aging population. This increasing diversity of close personal relationships poses significant challenges to the regulation of these relationships.

Chapter Two outlines the values that should animate the regulation of relationships: values such as equality and autonomy, as well as principles related to privacy, personal security, freedom of conscience and religion, coherence and efficiency.

Chapter Three turns to the question of redesigning the legal regulation of personal adult relationships. A new four-step methodology is presented as a tool for rethinking the way in which relationships have been regulated. Four questions are asked. First, are the objectives of the legislation or policy still legitimate? Second, are relationships relevant to the objective at hand? Third, assuming that relationships are relevant, could the law allow individuals to decide for themselves which of their close personal relationships should be subject to the law? Finally, assuming that relationships do matter, and self-selection of relationships will not work, is there a better way for the government to include relationships? Following the presentation of the methodology, it is applied to specific areas of the law to illustrate how this approach might lead to laws that are more responsive to the situations and needs of people in Canada.

Chapter Four addresses the nature of the state's role and interest in designing instruments for the legal organization of personal relationships. What should the state's role be in relation to committed relationships? The chapter reviews the role of private law and the ascription of "spousal" status on unmarried people in providing for the establishment of rights and responsibilities between individuals. It goes on to consider other mechanisms through which the state might recognize and support relationships of commitment, mechanisms such as registration schemes and marriage.

The diversity of relationships in Canadian society is a reality. It is something to be cherished and respected. For many Canadians, the relationships that they hold dear, their close personal relationships, as varied as they are, constitute an important source of comfort and what helps them continue to be productive members of society. In responding to this variety of relationships, governments have often moved to extend rights and benefits on the basis of conjugality. The Law Commission suggests that it is time to go beyond conjugality and to look at the reality of interdependencies that exist in other relationships as well.

---

[1] B.R. Sarason, I.G. Sarason and R.A. Gurung, "Close Personal Relationships and Health Outcomes: A Key to the Role of Social Support" in S. Duck ed., *Handbook of Personal Relationships: Section V. Clinical and Community Psychology* (New York: John Wiley & Sons, 2nd ed. 1997) at 551.

Chapter One

The Diversity of Personal Adult Relationships

Canadians have always formed a diverse range of adult personal relationships. Caring relationships are formed by married and common-law couples, relatives or friends sharing a household, and care recipients and caregivers, to name a few. Recognizing and supporting caring personal adult relationships is an important state objective. The diversity of personal adult relationships poses significant challenges to governments as they seek to align state policy with social facts. Before we discuss the ways in which the law has responded to the diversity of relationships, we will briefly describe what some of the available demographic data tells us about the nature of Canadians' personal relationships. In this chapter, we will also present some of the significant demographic shifts that have occurred over the last few decades.

A majority of Canadian households have long consisted of married couples or other conjugal couples living together with or without children. Alongside the nuclear family centred on the conjugal couple, a variety of other living arrangements have been enduring features of Canadian society. There have always been, for example, significant numbers of adult siblings living together, widows and widowers forming blended families with new partners, adult children living with their parents and multi-generational households. In the past, because of shorter life expectancy and the loss of life during wartime, it was not uncommon for children to lose a parent or for spouses to become widowed. Often widows or widowers would form new relationships, and the new partner would become a parent to any dependent children living in the household.[1]

Over the course of recent decades, particularly since the mid-1960s, a number of major, inter-related demographic shifts have occurred in the nature of Canadian adults' close personal relationships. As is the case in many other countries, domestic relationships in Canada appear to have become even more diverse in the past 30 years. However, it may be that our awareness of the diversity of personal adult relationships has simply increased in proportion to the range of statistical data available. For example, the Canadian census did not begin recording the number of opposite-sex couples living together in common-law unions until 1981. We now know that the number of common-law unions has increased dramatically in the ensuing years, but our knowledge regarding the number of such unions prior to 1981 is limited. Similarly, Statistics Canada collected data on the number of Canadians living in same-sex unions for the first time in the 2001 census; therefore, the statistical picture regarding such unions remains unclear. Many non-conjugal personal adult relationships are missing or largely invisible in the mainstream social science research. It is important to bear in mind, as we review the available demographic data below, that the picture we have of the diversity of personal adult relationships is a partial one, based on the predominant social attitudes and the assumptions of policy-makers in place at the time the data was collected.

We must bear in mind that many close adult relationships exist in the absence of a shared residence. Even without a common household, these relationships may also be characterized by shared economic, emotional, physical and/or intellectual interdependence. Census families and the broader concept of economic families both require that family members share a dwelling. As a result, we have limited information available about the nature and frequency of personal adult relationships that do not involve a shared residence.

We also want to note that the statistics provided below have not been broken down according to population groups based on factors such as national or ethnic origin, cultural and religious background, geographic location or age. A further breakdown would certainly depict the variety of ways in which different population groups organize their close adult relationships.

> "The assumptions of the last 30 years, taken for granted by Canadians as the cornerstones of the relationship among individuals, families, and governments, no longer hold sway. New stakes are being defined, and a new social contract is being crafted."
>
> Suzanne Peters, "Introduction" in *How Families Cope and Why Policymakers Need to Know* (Ottawa: Canadian Policy Research Networks, 1998) at v.

Conjugal Relationships

Almost all adult Canadians form a conjugal union at some point in their lives.[2] A clear majority of Canadians – over 60 percent – were married or cohabiting in a conjugal relationship at the time of the 1996 census.[3]

It remains the case that a strong majority of opposite-sex conjugal unions are marital relationships.[4] However, the marriage rate has declined steadily since 1971,[5] while the number of opposite-sex couples choosing to live in common-law relationships outside of marriage has increased steadily since they were first recorded in 1981.[6] Rates of opposite-sex cohabitation are highest among young never-married adults,[7] although growth rates in non-marital cohabitation are highest among older adults, many of whom were previously married.[8] Opposite-sex cohabitation – whether as an alternative to marriage, as a prelude to marriage, or as a sequel to marriage – is a growing phenomenon that now has widespread social acceptance.

There is as yet no census data or reliable studies on the number of lesbian and gay couples living together in Canada.[9] While same-sex couples were included in the census questionnaire for the first time in 2001, it will take some time before the data is compiled and available for analysis.[10] One federal government study estimated that there were approximately 270,000 persons living in same-sex relationships in 1994.[11] Until more comprehensive studies are completed, and the results of the 2001 census made public, we will lack reliable data on the number of same-sex couples. A number of smaller-scale studies of the lesbian and gay population in urban Canada suggest that gays and lesbians form enduring conjugal relationships in numbers comparable to the population as a whole.[12] Based on the available data, it appears that a significant minority of Canadian households consist of same-sex couples.

People today have more options in choosing whether to form a conjugal relationship and, if so, what type of conjugal relationship they wish to have. Once subject to punitive social and legal sanctions, both opposite-sex and same-sex common-law partners now enjoy much greater social acceptance and have many of the legal rights and obligations that attach to married spouses.

The ways in which individuals who form conjugal relationships are structuring their lives have also changed dramatically. The average age of marriage has increased.[13] There are significant numbers of step-families,[14] including blended families where children of different unions are raised in the same household.[15] An increasing number of adults are delaying having children until their late twenties or early thirties, or are deciding not to have children at all. Those who decide to become parents are having fewer children than previous generations.[16]

Women's participation in the paid labour force increased steadily from the 1950s to the 1990s. As a result, a declining minority of Canadian families rely on a sole male breadwinner for economic support. In 1996, the dual earnings of mothers and fathers supported 68 percent of married or opposite-sex common-law couples with children.[17] Even when young children are in the home, both parents are employed in a strong majority of families. Women's participation in the labour force has become essential to the living standards of families. Indeed, economic necessity has been an important driving force behind the emergence of more dual earner families than ever before.[18] While these changes have resulted in a decrease in women's financial dependence on men, women are still over-represented in the lowest paid occupations and in part-time and temporary work.[19] Moreover, women continue to perform the bulk of unpaid domestic and caregiving work even as their labour force participation increases. Men and women are both working longer hours and reporting significant stress in seeking to balance the competing demands posed by their jobs and their personal relationships.[20]

Non-Conjugal Households and Non-Conjugal Relationships

While 60 percent of adult Canadians live in a conjugal relationship, and the majority of Canadian households consist of conjugal couples living with or without children, a substantial minority of households involve adults living alone,[21] lone-parent families[22] or adults living together in non-conjugal relationships. And within households centred around conjugal relationships, often other adults are present, having non-conjugal ties to other members of the household. Non-conjugal relationships may be with unrelated friends or they may be with relatives other than spouses or minor children.

Non-Conjugal Relationships Between Relatives

Adult children are remaining at home longer and also leaving home and then moving back in increasing numbers. As a result, it is now common for adult children to live with their middle-aged parents.[23] It appears that adult children return home or stay at home mainly because of financial constraints imposed by difficulties in obtaining adequate employment or the need to complete their education; this allows them to benefit from the sharing of income and wealth within the household.[24]

Many Canadians who are not defined by Statistics Canada as belonging to a census or nuclear family nevertheless live with relatives in what have been called "economic families".[25] While a census family includes couples or parents with never-married children, an economic family is a broader concept that encompasses all relatives living in the same household, regardless of how they are related. For example, it would include an older woman living with her married children, or adult siblings sharing a home.

In 1996, 3 percent of the population in private households lived with relatives (other than a spouse or never-married children),[26] a proportion that remained stable compared with the previous two decades.[27] Domestic relationships between adult siblings form the largest component of economic families.[28] There is reason to believe that sibling relationships will increase in importance in the future. The high birthrate of the 1950s and the aging population mean that within the next 20 to 30 years, older adults will have substantially more siblings alive as compared with older adults today. This may mean that in the future more siblings will care for each other in old age.

Non-Conjugal Relationships Between Non-Relatives

Another 3.5 percent of the population lived with non-relatives in 1996.[29] Since same-sex couples were not counted in the census prior to 2001, by default they would have been included as households composed of non-relatives. Thus, same-sex conjugal relationships and non-conjugal relationships would together comprise unknown portions of this 3.5 percent of Canadians.

We know little about the characteristics of non-conjugal relationships between unrelated persons since it is a topic that has rarely been investigated. We do know that kinship relations between unrelated persons can be experienced as the equivalent of biological or legal ties. We also know that within gay and lesbian communities, individuals are more likely to form families of friends. If biological family members do not support an individual's sexual orientation or family decisions, then forming kinship relations with friends becomes a particularly important replacement or supplement to the family of origin.[30]

"Families of friends" also appear to be particularly important to older adults. One recent study of older people in Ontario found that 4 percent of non-widowed and 8 percent of widowed individuals include a friend in their description of family.[31] Friends are also particularly important in the lives of older women.[32]

Caregiving Relationships

People with disabilities have the same range of close personal relationships as other Canadians. They are spouses, friends, lovers, parents, children, aunts, uncles, cousins, grandchildren, grandparents and so on. Many people with disabilities are also in close personal relationships that are characterized at least in part by personal care or support that is related to their disabilities. Caregiving relationships involve the provision or exchange of a number of different kinds of care necessary to maintain or enhance the care recipients' independence. The research suggests that there is frequently interdependence or reciprocity – an exchange of personal and social supports – in the personal relationships of people with disabilities.[33] The kinds of care provided or exchanged include social and emotional support; assistance with the physical activities of daily living such as shopping, cleaning and cooking; and assistance with personal or medical aspects of daily living such as dressing, bathing and taking medications.[34] The literature distinguishes between formal care provided by paid professionals and informal care provided without pay by family and friends.

Over 90 percent of persons with disabilities live in their own homes. The vast majority must develop relationships of support with paid and non-paid caregivers for their basic survival and well-being.[35] In 1991, among the 1.8 million persons with disabilities residing in households and aged 15 or over who were in need of supports, almost 900,000 obtained those supports exclusively from family members.[36] Almost 100,000 persons with disabilities rely on friends only for personal supports, while another 53,000 rely on friends in combination with family and an agency.[37]

Persons with permanent disabilities are not the only Canadians whose relationships are characterized by the provision or exchange of personal care and supports. Everyone needs this kind of care at some point in their lives. The need for care, perhaps surprisingly, is not closely tied to age. Similar proportions of persons receive personal care across age groups.[38] Over half of persons over the age of 65 say that they get some help with household chores and personal tasks. Half also say that they provide care to others.[39]

The available data shows that women continue to provide the bulk of caregiving on an unpaid basis and spend more time than men in providing care.[40] For the most part, caregivers provide care willingly and as a reciprocal aspect of rewarding relationships. However, numerous studies have shown that supports to individuals with disabilities and their families are often insufficient.[41] The demands placed on informal caregiving have been increased by an aging population, reductions in public services and deinstutionalization. Many people are discharged from hospital while still requiring complex and skilled care. This situation puts stress on family members who are expected to compensate for gaps in formal care in their unpaid role as caregivers. The extent of their caregiving responsibilities can take a major toll on caregivers' economic security and physical, emotional and psychological health.[42] Inadequate social support for caregiving has a negative impact on caregivers and care-receivers, and on the quality of their relationships.[43]

> "Under conditions of declining public support, broader definitions of family may simply mean more people are conscripted into care rather than better caregiving or better relationships. Unless there are formal supports for unpaid caregiving, both the caregivers and their relationships are increasingly likely to fall apart. And such supports need to recognize the diversity in needs and the diversity in networks, networks that extend beyond kin to create the most satisfying care."
>
> Pat Armstrong and Olga Kits, *One Hundred Years of Caregiving* (Ottawa: Law Commission of Canada, 2001) at 33.

Conclusion

Canadians have always formed a diverse array of personal adult relationships. While about half of the adult population is married, significant numbers of Canadians are choosing to form same-sex unions or non-marital opposite-sex conjugal unions. In addition, there are significant numbers of blended families, lone-parent families, non-conjugal domestic relationships and families with adult children living at home. Families with a sole male breadwinner are becoming rare. Large numbers of older adults and persons with disabilities rely on family and friends for personal care and support.

Recognizing and supporting personal adult relationships that involve caring and interdependence is an important state objective. In the past, many policies were framed to apply only to married persons. Governments have taken important steps forward in recent years by extending rights and obligations to persons who are living with same-sex partners or with a person of the opposite-sex outside of marriage. But this extension of rights and obligations has maintained the legal focus on conjugal relationships. A more principled and comprehensive approach is needed to consider not just the situation of spouses and common-law partners, but also the needs of persons in non-conjugal relationships, including caregiver relationships. In seeking to recognize and support the full range of personal adult relationships, the state needs to be attentive to a number of basic principles and values. We will outline those values and describe their importance in the next chapter.

1   Margrit Eichler, *Family Shifts: Families, Policies, and Gender Equality* (Toronto: Oxford University Press, 1997) at 31.

2   C. Le Bourdais, G. Neill and P. Turcotte, "The Changing Face of Conjugal Relationships" (2000) 56 Canadian Social Trends 14-17, online: http://www.statcan.ca/english/indepth/11-008/feature/star2000056000s1a02.pdf.

3   See Statistics Canada, "Population 15 Years and Over by Marital Status, Showing Selected Age Groups and Sex, for Canada, Provinces and Territories", online: http://www.statcan.ca/english/census96/oct14/mar1.htm. The 1996 census data summarized by Statistics Canada is restricted to opposite-sex conjugal couples. The number of persons who reported that they were married or living in an opposite-sex common-law relationship amounted to 13,567,470 or 59 percent of a total population of 22,945,485 persons over the age of 15. If same-sex couples were counted, the total number of persons over 15 with a conjugal partner would exceed 60 percent.

4   According to the 1996 census data, 86.5 percent of opposite-sex conjugal unions are marriages. The remaining 13.5 percent, or approximately one out of every seven opposite-sex conjugal unions, is a common-law relationship. See *ibid.*; Statistics Canada, "Population 15 Years and Over Living in Common-law Unions", online: http://www.statcan.ca:80/english/census96/oct14/mar2.htm; Vanier Institute of the Family, *Profiling Canada's Families II* (Ottawa: Vanier Institute of the Family, 2000) at 36-38.

5   From 1971 to 1996, the marriage rate declined by more than 40 percent, from 8.9 to 5.2 marriages annually for every 1,000 persons: Statistics Canada, *1996 Census: Marital Status, Common-law Unions and Families* (Ottawa: Statistics Canada, 1997); Vanier Institute of the Family, *ibid.* at 41.

6   The 1981 census recorded 713,210 persons living in opposite-sex common-law relationships. This number rose to nearly a million in 1986 (973,880), 1.44 million in 1991 and 1.83 million in 1996. The increase from 1981 to 1996 was 158 percent. Zheng Wu, *Cohabitation: An Alternative Form of Family Living* (Toronto: Oxford University Press, 2000) at 43.

7   Wu, *ibid.*, at 44.

8   *Ibid.*, at 45.

9   Indeed, no large-scale demographic studies have been carried out in Canada on the size of the gay or lesbian population. Difficulties in estimating the numbers arise from the fluidity of sexual identity and from the fact that many people may not be willing to openly identify themselves as gay, lesbian or bisexual. Researchers have had to rely on estimates based on studies in other countries. For example, in the United States, Kinsey and his colleagues estimated that 13 percent of the male population could be classified as "homosexual" and that the proportion of women who are "homosexual" was roughly a half to a third lower than that of men. Alfred C. Kinsey, Wardell B. Pomeroy and Clyde E. Martin, *Sexual Behaviour in the Human Male* (Philadelphia: W.B. Saunders, 1948) at 651; Alfred C. Kinsey, Wardell B. Pomeroy, Clyde E. Martin and P.H. Gebhard, *Sexual Behaviour in the Human Female* (Philadelphia: W.B. Saunders, 1953) at 474-5. For a review of the literature, see Kathleen Lahey, *Are We 'Persons' Yet? Law and Sexuality in Canada* (Toronto: University of Toronto Press, 1999) at 177-82. Lahey suggests that the most reliable American study on the size of the gay and lesbian population in the United States is Edward O. Laumann, John H. Gagnon, Robert T. Michael and Stuart Michaels, *The Social Organization of Sexuality: Sexual Practices in the United States* (Chicago: University of Chicago Press, 1994) at 292-301. Laumann et al. estimated that the number of persons who self-identify as homosexual is 7 percent of men and 4.4 percent of women.

[10]   Even then, there will be a real risk that people's reluctance to reveal a minority sexual orientation or same-sex relationship status will lead to under-reporting of the true extent of same-sex cohabitation.

[11]   Affidavit of Albert Wakkary, based on a Statistics Canada survey of consumer finances, filed in *Rosenberg* v. *The Queen* (Ont. Gen. Div., Court File No. 79885/94), discussed in Lahey, *supra* note 9 at 186. Lahey notes that if we did rely on the survey data on the rate of relationship formation in urban Canadian gay and lesbian communities, together with Laumann's estimates of the proportion of the general population in the United States that self-identifies as gay or lesbian, then the resulting estimate of the number of persons cohabiting in a same-sex relationship would be over 600,000. Lahey, at 184.

[12]   A 1993 survey of gay men found that 36 percent reported being in an intimate relationship. Ted Myers, G. Godin, L. Calzavara, J. Lambert and D. Locker, *The Canadian Survey of Gay and Bisexual Men and HIV Infection: Men's Survey* (Ottawa: Canadian AIDS Society, 1993) at 28-30. A 1995 study found that 45.7 percent of Vancouver gays and lesbians were in relationships, and that 63.5 percent of these relationships involved cohabitation. Stephen Michael Samis, "'An Injury to One is an Injury to All': Heterosexism, Homophobia, and Anti-Gay/Lesbian Violence in Greater Vancouver" (M.A. Thesis, Simon Fraser University, 1995) at 69-70. A 1997 survey of lesbians and gays in Ontario found that 75 percent of the women and 58 percent of the men were in same-sex relationships. Coalition for Lesbian and Gay Rights in Ontario, *Systems Failure: A Report on the Experiences of Sexual Minorities in Ontario's Health-Care and Social Services System* (Toronto: CLGRO, 1997). Because of their small size, geographic limits and urban focus, these surveys cannot provide a reliable basis for national estimates of the number of same-sex couples.

[13]   In the past 30 years, the average age of brides at first marriage has increased from 22 to 28 years, and for grooms from 25 to almost 30 years. Vanier Institute of the Family, *supra* note 4 at 44-45.

[14]   Step-families are families that are formed when a widowed, separated or divorced person forms a new union, creating a family that includes the children of one or both of the partners. While in the past such families were most often formed following the death of a spouse, they are now most common following divorce. Vanier Institute of the Family, *supra* note 4 at 66. People who divorce are more likely to form another domestic relationship than remain single. Le Bourdais et al., *supra* note 2.

[15]   Le Bourdais et al., *supra* note 2.

[16]   Teresa Janz, *The Evolution and Diversity of Relationships in Canadian Families* (Ottawa: Law Commission of Canada, September 2000) at 27.

[17]   Vanier Institute of the Family, *supra* note 4 at 89.

[18]   It has been estimated that in 1991 the percentage of couples living below the poverty line in dual earner families would have been 17.9 percent instead of 4.6 percent if women did not work in the paid labour force. Statistics Canada, *Characteristics of Dual-Earner Families 1993* (Ottawa: Statistics Canada, 1995) at 8.

[19]   Pat Armstrong and Olga Kits, *One Hundred Years of Caregiving* (Ottawa: Law Commission of Canada, 2001) at 27-28.

[20]   Public Task Force on Balancing Work and Family, *Towards More Work-Family Balance in Saskatchewan* (Regina: Government of Saskatchewan, 1998); Linda Duxbury and Christopher Higgins, *Work-Life Balance in Saskatchewan: Realities and Challenges* (Regina: Government of Saskatchewan, 1998).

21 In 1996, 9.2 percent of the population lived alone. See Statistics Canada, "Population in private households, showing living arrangements, 1996 Census", online: http://www.statcan.ca/english/Pgdb/People/Families/famil52a.htm.

22 Vanier Institute of the Family, *supra* note 4 at 73; P. La Novara, "Changes in Family Living" (1993) 29 Canadian Social Trends 12; Colin Lindsay, *Lone-Parent Families in Canada* (Ottawa: Statistics Canada, 1992).

23 Findings from the 1991 census indicate that 50 percent of adults aged 20 to 34 were living with their parents. B.A. Mitchell, "The Refilled 'Nest': Debunking the Myth of Families in Crisis", in E.M. Gee and G.M. Gutman eds., *The Overselling of Population Aging: Apocalyptic Demography, Intergenerational Challenges and Social Policy* (Toronto: Oxford University Press, 2000) at 80-99.

24 Monica Boyd and Edward Pryor, "Young Adults Living in Their Parents' Homes" (1989) 13 Canadian Social Trends 17; David Cheal, "Poverty and Relative Income: Family Transactions and Social Policy", in *How Families Cope and Why Policymakers Need to Know* 1-26 (Ottawa: Canadian Research Policy Networks, 1998) at 14.

25 Nancy Z. Ghalam, "Living With Relatives" (1996) 42 Canadian Social Trends 20.

26 Statistics Canada, "Population in private households, showing living arrangements, 1996 Census," online: http://www.statcan.ca/english/Pgdb/People/Families/famil52a.htm. Adult relatives living with single parents or a conjugal couple numbered 482,090, and relatives living together in "non-family households" (i.e., without a single parent or an opposite-sex conjugal couple) numbered 360,555, for a total of 842,645 persons or 3 percent of the population of 28,390,685 living in private households.

27 *Ibid.*, at 20.

28 In her analysis of the 1991 census data, Ghalam, *supra* note 25 at 2, found that, of those aged 15 or over living with a relative, 30 percent shared a household with a sibling. Another 17 percent were living with a child's family, and 14 percent with a sibling's family. Eight percent were married or previously married individuals who had returned home to live with their mother and father, while 5 percent resided with one parent. Fourteen percent lived with other relatives, such as grandparents, aunts, uncles or cousins.

29 Statistics Canada, "Population in private households, showing living arrangements, 1996 Census," *supra* note 26. Persons living with non-relatives in a household with a single mother or a conjugal couple numbered 240,280, and non-relatives living together in "non-family households" (i.e., without a single parent or an opposite-sex conjugal couple) numbered 777,605, for a total of 1,017,885 persons or 3.5 percent of the population of 28,390,685 living in private households. For an analysis of the 1991 census data on non-relatives living together, see Pina La Novara, "Changes in Family Living" (1993) 29 Canadian Social Trends 12 at 13.

30 Teresa Janz, *supra* note 16 at 39.

31 A. Martin Matthews, "Change and Diversity in Aging Families and Intergenerational Relations" in N. Mandell and A. Duffy eds., *Canadian Families: Diversity, Conflict and Change* (Toronto: Harcourt Brace & Co., 2nd ed., 2000) at 323-360.

32 A study based on the 1996 General Social Survey found that about one-half of widowed women living on their own had a strong attachment to four or more friends. Irwin Bess, "Widows Living Alone" (1999) 53 Canadian Social Trends 2 at 3, online: http://www.statcan.ca/english/indepth/11-008/feature/stfeat.htm.

33 Roeher Institute, *Personal Relationships of Support Between Adults: The Case of Disability* (Ottawa: Law Commission of Canada, March 2001) at 4-5.

34 Armstrong and Kits, *supra* note 19 at 3-4.

35 The Roeher Institute, *supra* note 33 at 14.

36 *Ibid.*, at 13.

37 *Ibid.*, at 13.

38 N.C. Keating, J.E. Fast, J. Frederick et al., *Eldercare in Canada: Context, Content and Consequences* (Ottawa: Statistics Canada, 1999) at 17.

39 C. Lindsay, "Seniors: A Diverse Group Aging Well" (1999) (Spring) Canadian Social Trends 24-26.

40 For an overview of the literature, see Armstrong and Kits, *supra* note 19. The Roeher Institute has estimated, based on 1991 data, that about 650,000 persons with disabilities received help in the routine activities of everyday living from women in their family in 1991. An estimated 720,000 women provided this support. Roeher Institute, *supra* note 33 at 15. See also Roeher Institute, *Disability-Related Support Arrangements, Policy Options and Implications for Women's Equality* (Ottawa: Status of Women Canada, February 2001).

41 Caregiver burden and stress is a theme in the literature. See Armstrong and Kits, *supra* note 19 at 15-19.

42 Roeher Institute, *supra* note 33 at 20.

43 Janz, *supra* note 16 at 78-82.

Chapter Two

Fundamental Values and Principles

Two fundamental values ought to guide the development of government policies that have an impact on close personal adult relationships: equality and autonomy. These values have a constitutional dimension, and in the past two decades the interpretation of Charter rights and freedoms has played a significant role in articulating the ways in which they should guide the development of state policies. Although now constitutionally protected, these values have long been cherished by Canadians and reflected in government policies. They must guide governments' approach to regulating close personal adult relationships. There are also a number of other important principles and values that must be respected in order to enhance equality and autonomy in the area of close personal adult relationships; these include personal security, privacy, freedom of conscience and religion, coherence and efficiency. These are reviewed in the second part of this chapter.

Fundamental Values

Equality

Equality is a fundamental value of Canadians. It is also enshrined in international human rights documents, in section 15 of the *Charter of Rights and Freedoms*, and in Canadian human rights legislation. Multiple dimensions of our commitment to achieving equality are relevant to a consideration of the state's role in regulating personal adult relationships. First, governments must respect and promote equality between different kinds of relationships – this Report refers to this as "relational equality". Second, governments must also be attentive to the need to ensure equality within relationships. We are still seeking to overcome a long history of state regulation of personal relationships that has contributed to the subordination of women, persons with disabilities and other members of disadvantaged groups. State policies need to be framed to avoid replicating inequalities based on gender, race, disability, sexual orientation and other prohibited grounds of discrimination.

Relational Equality

As the review of demographic data in Chapter One revealed, Canadians enter a wide variety of close personal relationships out of choice or necessity. Governments are under pressure to better align the law with social realities by acknowledging and respecting the diversity of these close personal relationships.

In recent years, Canadian legislatures have debated and implemented statutes designed to give greater recognition to the principle of relational equality. Constitutional rulings by the courts have contributed to the acceleration of the pace of legislative change. In particular, two Supreme Court of Canada rulings have established the principle that governments should treat adult conjugal relationships with equal concern and respect, regardless of the personal characteristics, such as sexual orientation or marital status, of the two people involved. Rather than employing the formal status of relationships, or personal characteristics that are not related to legislative objectives, the law should respond to the factual attributes of relationships – their actual characteristics and the roles they perform.

In 1995, the Court held in *Miron* v. *Trudel*[1] that imposing legal disadvantages on unmarried opposite-sex cohabitants relative to their married counterparts violates the constitutional prohibition on marital status discrimination. At issue was whether the Ontario legislature was justified in requiring insurers to extend automobile accident benefits to husbands and wives of insured persons, but not to common-law spouses. In the principal majority judgement, McLachlin J. held that marital status was not a reasonable marker of the financially interdependent relationships relevant to the achievement of the legislative objective.[2] Equality rights required that the legislature find a better way of identifying relationships characterized by financial interdependence.

Four years later, in *M.* v. *H.*,[3] the Court ruled that imposing legal disadvantages on same-sex conjugal cohabitants relative to their unmarried opposite-sex counterparts violates the constitutional prohibition on discrimination on the basis of sexual orientation. At issue was whether the Ontario legislature was justified in excluding persons in same-sex relationships from the law imposing support rights and obligations on common-law spouses.[4] In the principal majority judgement, Iacobucci J. concluded that the objectives of the statute were to provide for the equitable resolution of economic disputes when intimate relationships between financially interdependent individuals break down, and to alleviate the burden on the public purse to provide for dependent spouses. Sexual orientation was not a reasonable marker of the relationships relevant to these statutory objectives. Indeed, the legislative objectives would be furthered by the inclusion of same-sex couples.[5]

When the rulings in *Miron* v. *Trudel* and *M.* v. *H.* are put together, the net result has been to put in place a constitutional requirement that governments respect a principle of relational equality, calling into question the validity of all differences in the legal status of married and unmarried (either same-sex or opposite-sex) cohabitants.[6] At the federal level, the passage of the *Modernization of Benefits and Obligations Act*[7] in 2000 has largely eliminated distinctions between married spouses and persons living in conjugal relationships outside of marriage.

With the exception of a few acts with respect to which reforms are pending,[8] unmarried cohabitants now have the same rights as married spouses in all federal legislation. According to the Act, a person cohabiting with another in a "conjugal relationship" for at least a year is now referred to as a "common-law partner". The new definition has been added alongside "spouses" (now a term reserved to husbands and wives) throughout the federal statute book. The new definition of common-law partner contains no reference to gender, thereby extending legal rights and responsibilities to same-sex couples. A number of provinces have also passed or introduced omnibus legislation that extends legal rights and responsibilities to two persons who cohabit in a conjugal (or marriage-like) relationship.[9]

All of this recent legislative activity has focused on narrowing the gap between the legal status of married spouses and persons living in conjugal relationships outside of marriage. The recent laws do not address the differences in the legal treatment of conjugal and non-conjugal cohabitants; indeed, such differences have been extended and entrenched in the law. This approach is inconsistent with the value of equality since conjugality, like marriage itself, is not an accurate marker of the qualitative attributes of personal adult relationships that are relevant to particular legislative objectives. As McLachlin J. pointed out in *Miron* v. *Trudel*, governments should turn their attention not to marital status or marriage equivalence, but to the relevant functional attributes of relationships:

> The record suggests that the legislators recognized that marital status was at best a problematic indicator of who should receive accident benefits upon injury in a motor vehicle accident. The debate centred on marital equivalence. To quote the amicus curiae, "[the legislators'] search was directed towards defining a "marriage-like" conjugal relationship, usually in terms of mutual commitment and permanence – a "near" marriage – instead of trying to define the underlying functional values, e.g. financial interdependence, relevant to the legislative subject matter of the Insurance Act". Having misconstrued the issue as one of marriage equivalence, the Legislature found itself unable to agree. But this provides no justification for failing, from 1980 to 1987, to deal directly with the problem of which family units were so financially interdependent and stable as to warrant provision of the benefits in question.
>
> If the issue had been viewed as a matter of defining who should receive benefits on a basis that is relevant to the goal or functional values underlying the legislation, rather than marriage equivalence, alternatives substantially less invasive of Charter rights might have been found.[10]

The recent legislative reforms at the federal and provincial level compound the problem identified in this passage – they also "misconstrue the issue as one of marriage equivalence". McLachlin J.'s comments remind us that the principle of relational equality requires more than equal treatment of conjugal couples.

Equality Within Relationships

Equality requires not only equality between relationships, but also equality within relationships. The legal regulation of personal adult relationships should attempt to promote equality within relationships and protect against potential inequality between individuals within these relationships. Close personal relationships between women and men have been and still are marked by unequal distributions of income, wealth and power. Women's primary responsibility for raising children and meeting the care needs of adults, and their unequal participation in the labour market, has often resulted in economic dependence upon the men with whom they share a close personal relationship. In the past, if those relationships broke down, women often found themselves without access to property or support. While family laws at both the federal and provincial levels have been reformed to better address women's economic dependency, the legacy of inequality remains, as does a sexual division of labour within the family. Women perform a greater share of unpaid domestic labour and remain the primary caregivers within families and, as a result, earn less in the work force. As our population ages, and with a reduction in the public provision of institutional and professional forms of care, the burden and complexity of women's informal or unpaid caregiving responsibilities is increasing.[11] Although women have made significant progress in the labour force since the 1950s, they are still disproportionately represented in the lowest-paid occupations. They are also over-represented in part-time and temporary work. The increases in women's non-standard work may in part be explained by their increasing caregiving activities.[12] Gender equality will be more

In May of 1999, my elderly mother was operated on…it was discovered that she had an unusual form of cancer…Because I was a palliative care nurse I offered to look after my mother in her home…I took time off from a contract job I had in [edit] in order to look after her. The unexpected happened. Mother, who was 91 at the time recovered, gained her health back and today, as she approaches her 93rd birthday is coping pretty well…I believe, firmly, that her recovery had everything to do with the care she was receiving from me. She is doing fine, however, my life has been shattered. I no longer have a job, I had to give up my residence in [edit] and my financial situation has become a mess!!!…I wish the government would look into the service that family members give to their elderly.

Law Commission of Canada Comments Board, website, June 2000 – January 2001, posted with permission.

difficult to achieve if women's economic dependency is encouraged by state policies that reinforced gendered patterns of participation in paid and unpaid work.

On the breakdown of relationships, some women still find themselves at a disadvantage. For example, women in common-law relationships still find themselves without recourse to most provincial and territorial family property regimes.[13] Some government laws and programs have the unfortunate consequence of encouraging women's dependence on men.[14] It is important that governments keep this legacy of inequality in close personal relationships in mind when redesigning policies and programs to recognize and support close personal relationships. The state's role should be neutral regarding the roles that people assume in their personal relationships. This means facilitating the formation of healthy relationships by creating conditions in which people are able to exercise choices free of coercion and by avoiding policies that encourage economic dependence.

Equality is not present in many support relationships involving adults with disabilities. Reciprocity between persons with disabilities and their caregivers may be undermined by economic inequality, diminished decision-making power, lack of status and recognition. This situation leaves adults with disabilities vulnerable to neglect and abuse.[15] Furthermore, the contributions of adults with disabilities in the caregiving relationship are not always recognized.[16] Because of the larger policy and social context, these relationships of support also diminish the equality of care providers vis-à-vis other adults in Canadian society. Many care providers find themselves with low wages, lack of benefits, lost income opportunity, extraordinary burden of care, limited personal control and reduced health status. Promoting equality in relationships of support should be a guiding principle of state regulation of relationships involving adults with disabilities.[17]

Autonomy

The freedom to choose whether and with whom to form close personal relationships is a fundamental value in free and democratic societies. In his classic article on what he called the "freedom of intimate association," Kenneth Karst argued that "it is the choice to form and maintain an intimate association that permits full realization of the associational values we cherish most," namely companionship, caring, commitment, intimacy and self-realization.[18] American constitutional doctrine has recognized that "freedom of personal choice in matters of family life" is a fundamental liberty interest.[19] Choice and personal autonomy are fundamental values in Canadian constitutional doctrine as well. As Iacobucci J. stated in *R. v. Salituro*,

> The idea of human dignity finds expression in almost every right and freedom guaranteed in the Charter. Individuals are afforded the right to choose their own religion and their own philosophy of life, the right to choose with whom

they will associate and how they will express themselves, the right to choose where they will live and what occupation they will pursue. These are all examples of the basic theory underlying the Charter, namely that the state will respect choices made by individuals and, to the greatest extent possible, will avoid subordinating these choices to any one conception of the good life.[20]

For adults with disabilities, the notion of self-determination requires more than simply having available choices. Rather, self-determination entails recognition that individuals are interdependent and must be supported in order to exercise choices that enable them to pursue their life vision. It's about transferring real power, control and status to a person so that they can make decisions that allow them to follow their own path.[21]

> Friends jump in regularly and help me get more frequent baths (bathe me)... I'm not satisfied with it. I'd rather have it as part of my paid routine. I don't feel it's fair to count on my friends. I'm not comfortable with it, but have no choice. It has affected my friendships. Some friends I have lost — they don't feel it's their role and they are right.
>
> The Roeher Institute, *Disability-Related Support Arrangements, Policy Options and Implications for Women's Equality* (Ottawa: Status of Women Canada, February 2001) at 62.

The value of autonomy requires that governments put in place the conditions in which people can freely choose their close personal relationships. The state must also avoid direct or indirect forms of coercive interference with adults' freedom to choose whether or not to form, or remain in, close personal relationships. While governments should do everything in their power to provide information and education and otherwise minimize the conditions that lead to the formation and continuation of abusive relationships, they should not create financial or other kinds of pressure to discourage relationships without reference to their qualitative attributes. Autonomy is compromised if the state provides one relationship status with more benefits and legal support than others, or conversely, if the state imposes more penalties on one type of relationship than it does on others. It follows then that an important corollary of the value of relational autonomy is a principle of state neutrality regarding the form or status that relationships take. The state ought to support any and all relationships that have the capacity to further relevant social goals, and to remain neutral with respect to individuals' choice of a particular form or status.

The value of relational autonomy and its corollary, the principle of state neutrality, does not mean that governments should never seek to influence relational choices or regulate personal relationships. Rather, autonomy requires that the nature of state intervention should be determined by the qualitative attributes of relationships. For example, the state has an obligation to ensure that autonomy is exercised in a manner that does not compromise the equal right to autonomy of others. The state must take steps to discourage the formation of exploitative or abusive relationships and to protect adults who are vulnerable to economic exploitation or physical and emotional abuse in their close personal relationships.

While we draw significantly on constitutional jurisprudence in discussing equality and autonomy, we do not mean to suggest that the importance of these two fundamental values should be limited to their constitutional dimensions. Governments should not just seek to develop laws and policies that will survive constitutional scrutiny in the courts. That is a necessary but too limited conception of their relevance. Constitutionality may mean "only that an unimpressive, minimal threshold has been met".[22] Equality and autonomy are important in their own right and transcend constitutional expression.

Other Principles and Values

While equality and autonomy are two important values that governments need to consider in framing policies designed to recognize and support personal adult relationships, a number of other principles and values play a prominent role in policy debates in this area. The regulation of personal relationships should seek to enhance personal security, privacy and religious freedom, and pursue the achievement of legitimate government objectives in a coherent and efficient manner.

Personal Security

Economic, psychological, emotional and physical security are preconditions to people's ability to make choices about whether to enter into and maintain personal relationships. A lack of these kinds of security means that people are not able to freely exercise relational choices. They may enter and remain in personal relationships out of economic necessity. People with needs for personal care and support may find themselves without the resources or support necessary to exercise any choice or control over the nature of their caregiving relationships.[23] The imbalance of power and dependencies that can result are not conducive to healthy personal relationships.

The combination of economic and emotional interdependence that arises in close personal relationships can produce distinct forms of vulnerability. Intimacy, privacy and interdependence are features that in combination afford unique opportunities for violence and exploitation to which the state must respond. Strong and effective sanctions need to be levied on all forms of violence in relationships, and legal means of protecting persons from continuing abuse need to be in place. The state can also advance physical, psychological and emotional security by ensuring that individuals have a measure of economic security that makes "exit" a real option: people need to know that they have choices other than destitution or entering into or remaining in an exploitative or violent relationship.

Moreover, the state ought to recognize and respond to the fact that people structure their lives around a set of reasonable expectations formed in personal adult relationships. It is common for people to rely on an expectation that they will continue to benefit in the future from the economic and emotional support provided by their personal relationships. In order to facilitate stability and certainty in relationships, the state has a role in providing legal mechanisms to help citizens fulfill their expectations and meet their needs should they suffer a sudden deprivation of emotional and economic support resulting from death, illness, injury or the breakdown of their relationships.

Privacy

Privacy includes the right to be free from unwarranted state intrusion or interference in one's intimate spaces,[24] including one's close personal relationships, as well as the right to control the dissemination of confidential information.[25] Privacy is, ultimately, "the control we have over information about ourselves".[26] Informational privacy is a necessary foundation of close personal relationships. It lies "at the heart of liberty in a modern state".[27]

While privacy is often conceptualized as an individual's "right to be left alone," a number of authors have pointed out that this view can obscure the importance of relational privacy, the shared privacy that arises in close personal relationships. As Mary Coombs has written,

> Much of what is important in human life takes place in a situation of shared privacy. The important events in our lives are shared with a chosen group of others; they do not occur in isolation, nor are they open to the entire world.[28]

Her conception of privacy is based on two assumptions:

> First, I assume that ordinary patterns of human behaviour embody shared privacies. That is, people are embedded in relationships and they act as if they expect those relationships to be respected by others. Second, I assume that shared privacy is invaluable. We need to be able to safely share with others to become fully human. We further need to be able to create enclaves from the world at large in which we can be with our chosen intimates.[29]

Healthy close personal relationships are founded on candour and trust. In these relationships we reveal thoughts and actions that we are not willing to reveal to others. Our personal relationships cannot flourish if we lack confidence that our intimate thoughts and acts will not be discovered by or revealed to others.

In Charles Fried's words, privacy is "necessarily related to ends and relations of the most fundamental sort: respect, love, friendship and trust". He suggests that:

To respect, love, trust, feel affection for others and to regard ourselves as the objects of love, trust, and affection is at the heart of our notions of ourselves as persons among persons, and privacy is the necessary atmosphere for these attitudes and actions, as oxygen is for combustion.

C. Fried, "Privacy" (1968) 77 *Yale L.J.* 475 at 477.

Trudy Govier's work on trust and confidentiality supports the view that informational privacy is crucial to the formation and maintenance of close personal relationships. She argues that trust is the glue of social life; "attitudes of trust and distrust affect the nature and quality of our social reality".[30] Indeed, she suggests that trust is a defining aspect of familial relationships, "our main locus of abiding affection and mutual support":[31]

> Good-enough families are founded, not on heterosexuality and stereotypical gender roles, not on male providers, not on biological reproduction, but on trust between people who live together in a home, trust each other, and are committed to building a life together. Adult partners who trust each other bring up children who trust them. Those children can then move into the greater world with basic security and confidence.[32]

There is always a degree of shared privacy in close personal relationships. Yet comfort with that shared privacy, and thus with the formation and maintenance of close personal relationships, cannot exist without trust and confidentiality. Trust and relational privacy thus cannot exist without each other.

At its most basic level, privacy requires that the state keep out of the "bedrooms of the nation". It also requires that the state avoid, wherever possible, the establishment of legal rules that cannot be administered effectively without intrusive examinations into, or forced disclosure of, the intimate details of personal adult relationships. In particular, absent violence or exploitation, sexual relationships between consenting adults should not be subjected to state investigation. Sexuality is one of the most intimate aspects of many personal relationships. The presence or absence of a consensual adult sexual relationship, or the nature of adults' consensual sexual acts, are matters that are not relevant to the promotion of legitimate state objectives. Sexual relationships may give rise to consequences, such as deepening emotional and economic bonds or the procreation of children that are relevant to the formation of state policies. But it is these consequences, not sexual activity itself, which ought to be taken into account in formulating state policies.

Like other rights and freedoms, privacy rights are not absolute. Privacy cannot be used to remove harmful acts from state scrutiny. Sexual assault within marriage, once shielded from criminal sanction by broad conceptions of marital privacy, is now a crime. Privacy rights must be balanced, and in some circumstances give way, to compelling objectives such as the state interest in prosecuting and preventing crime, including the commission of crimes involving violence and abuse.

Freedom of Conscience and Religion

The *Charter of Rights and Freedoms* has solidified the political character of Canada as a multicultural, pluralistic and secular society, in part by guaranteeing freedom of conscience and religion and by prohibiting religious discrimination.[33] The core of freedom of religion, as described by the Supreme Court of Canada, is the right to hold religious views, to declare them openly without fear of hindrance or reprisal and to manifest them by worship, practice, teaching and dissemination.[34] Freedom of religion requires that the state refrain from formulating laws that impose direct or indirect pressure on people to abandon their religious beliefs or practices.[35]

Religious freedom is not absolute; religious beliefs or practices will not be protected if they cause harm to others. Thus, parents' religious freedom does not prevail over the right to life or health of a child,[36] and religious beliefs cannot be expressed or acted upon if they have the effect of interfering with others' equal access to public services or benefits.[37] Similarly, the exercise of religious freedoms is bounded by the need to protect others' parallel rights to hold and manifest beliefs and opinions of their own. Thus,

> What may appear good and true to a majoritarian religious group, or to the state acting at their behest, may not, for religious reasons, be imposed upon citizens who take a contrary view.[38]

Governments in a secular state cannot pass laws for the purpose of aligning them with the views of any particular religious denomination. Rather, respect for freedom of religion requires that governments avoid laws or policies that seek to enforce the practices of a particular religion or indoctrinate citizens in particular religious beliefs. Thus, for example, the courts have held that public institutions cannot engage in religious indoctrination by compelling participation in prayers or religious instruction dominated by the perspective of a single denomination.[39]

Canadian understandings of freedom of religion have never mandated a strict separation of church and state. However, the degree of separation between church and state considered appropriate has evolved considerably over the course of our history. The use of the law to enforce Christian precepts or practices, once a common feature of Canadian political life, is no longer considered acceptable. Now, Canadian understandings of religious freedom and equality require that the state not take sides in religious matters. Government actions must not in their purpose or effects favour some religious traditions over others.

Evolving understandings of freedom of conscience and religion have had an important impact on state regulation of personal adult relationships. Consider, for example, changes over time in the legal regulation of the solemnization of marriage.[40] In the eighteenth century, legislation made a religious ceremony performed by ministers of the dominant denomination a precondition to a valid marriage. In the nineteenth century, colonial governments acknowledged the fact of religious pluralism, and reflected a growing commitment to religious freedom, by extending the authority to solemnize marriages to ministers of other denominations. However, a religious ceremony remained a prerequisite to a valid marriage. In most jurisdictions, a non-religious marriage ceremony remained a legal impossibility into the latter half of the twentieth century. Since marriage was the only close personal relationship between unrelated adults recognized by the state, religious compliance was a prerequisite to formalizing those relationships. Now, marriages in every province and territory may be solemnized either through a religious or a secular procedure. The history of marriage regulation in Canada has thus been characterized by a progressive uncoupling of religious and legal requirements, reflecting a growing emphasis on the separation of church and state in a secular and pluralistic political community.

Coherence

If the objectives of laws are not clear, or the design of laws does not line up with their stated objectives, then laws lack coherence. The policy objectives of laws must be clearly specified and communicated, and the legislative design must correspond to the achievement of those objectives. Coherence demands that statutes be drafted in a manner that closely connects the chosen legal forms with clearly articulated policy objectives.

For example, sometimes Parliament uses concepts like "marriage" or "spouse" to determine the scope of application of its laws. This will be coherent if the policy objective of a law is restricted to the support and regulation of marriage. The *Marriage (Prohibited Degrees) Act* and the *Divorce Act* have the objective of regulating entry into and exit from marriage. The restricted application of these laws to the marriage relationship is thus coherent.

More often, however, the policy objectives underlying legislation do not simply support or define marriage. Rather, Parliament's goal is to achieve some other outcome – like the support of children, the recognition of economic interdependence, the prevention of exploitation – that is connected to, but not exactly congruent with, the marriage relationship. When Parliament uses terms like "spouse" as a proxy for identifying the kinds of close personal relationships between adults to which such laws apply, problems of coherence arise.

Consider, for example, a law aimed at preventing exploitation or abuse that is limited in its application to spousal relationships. Such a law would lack coherence since exploitation of vulnerable people in relationships does not occur exclusively in marriages. The law is under-inclusive of the relevant range of relationships, since the risk of exploitation or abuse arises in a range of other close personal relationships.

To avoid problems of over-inclusiveness and under-inclusiveness in laws seeking to accomplish legitimate policy objectives, governments need to carefully assess all laws using relational terms to clarify objectives and reconsider whether using concepts like marriage and spouse is a coherent means of accomplishing those objectives.

Efficiency

Governments must ensure that their policies, laws and programs in relation to personal adult relationships are not only coherent, but also efficient. The efficiency of a law may be measured by its effectiveness in practice. If a program does not reach its intended beneficiaries, for example, it will not be efficient. In this sense, laws that are coherent are more likely to be efficient in achieving their goals.

Another component of efficiency that needs to be considered is cost. Policies should be able to be administered without undue costs, delays or uncertainties. Governments could set out detailed conditions of eligibility to specify the close personal relationships to which a law applies; theoretically, that would ensure a perfect fit between policy and outcome. However, this kind of perfect coherence may not be achievable in practice if the costs of administering such a specifically targeted law are prohibitive.

Conclusion

In the previous chapter, we discussed the diversity of personal adult relationships and the need for a more principled and comprehensive attempt by governments to recognize and support the full diversity of people's relationships. In this chapter, we have suggested that a comprehensive approach to the recognition and support of personal adult relationships should be guided, first and foremost, by the values of equality and autonomy. In addition, state policies should protect and advance personal security, privacy and religious freedom and they should seek to accomplish legitimate state objectives in a coherent and efficient manner. Proposed laws and the operation of existing laws should be carefully scrutinized to ensure that they uphold these values and principles. In the next chapter, we outline a new approach that governments can take to ensure that their laws and policies are consistent with the values we have outlined.

[1]   [1995] 2 S.C.R. 418.

[2]   *Ibid.*, at para.171.

[3]   [1999] 2 S.C.R. 3.

[4]   *Ibid.*, at para.106.

[5]   *Ibid.*, at para.116.

[6]   The Supreme Court will consider these issues again shortly when it hears the appeal of *Walsh* v. *Bona*, (2000) 186 D.L.R. (4th) 50 (N.S.C.A.), leave to appeal granted February 15, 2000, S.C.C. Bulletin, 2001, p. 284. The Nova Scotia Court of Appeal held that the exclusion of unmarried couples from statutory rights to division of family property on the breakdown of the relationship violates the equality rights in s.15 of the Charter.

[7]   S.C. 2000, c.12.

[8]   For example, the *Canada Evidence Act*, R.S.C. 1985, c.C-5, s.4 (spousal testimonial immunity rules); and Bill C-11, the *Immigration and Refugee Protection Act*, 1st Sess., 37th Parl., 2001 (passed the House of Commons June 13, 2001, online: http://www.parl.gc.ca/37/1/parlbus/chambus/house/bills/government/C-11/C-11_3/C-11_cover-E.html.; at the time of writing, awaiting 3rd reading in the Senate) (family class and family sponsorship provisions).

[9]   *Definition of Spouse Amendment Act, 1999*, S.B.C. 1999, c.29; *Definition of Spouse Amendment Act, 2000*, S.B.C. 2000, c.24; *An Act to amend certain statutes because of the Supreme Court of Canada decision in M. v. H.*, S.O. 1999, c.6; *Loi modifiant diverses dispositions législatives concernant les conjoints de fait*, S.Q. 1999, c.14; *Miscellaneous Statutes (Domestic Relations) Amendment Act, 2001*, S.S. 2001, c.50 and *Miscellaneous Statutes (Domestic Relations) Amendment Act, 2001 (No. 2)*, S.S. 2001, c.51; *An Act to Comply with the Supreme Court of Canada Decision in M. v. H.*, S.M. 2001, c.37; *Law Reform (2000) Act*, S.N.S. 2000, c.29.

[10] *Supra* note 1 at paras.169-70.

[11] Pat Armstrong and Olga Kits, *One Hundred Years of Caregiving* (Ottawa: Law Commission of Canada, April 2001) at 27.

[12] *Ibid.*, at 27-8.

[13] The Northwest Territories, Nunavut and Saskatchewan are the only jurisdictions to accord common-law opposite-sex spouses legislative rights to the division of family property on the breakdown of a relationship: *Family Law Act*, S.N.W.T. 1997, c.18, *Nunavut Act*, S.C. 1993, c.28, *The Homesteads Act, 1989*, S.S. 1989-90, c.H-5.1 as am. by S.S. 1992, c.27; S.S. 1993, c.C-26.1; S.S. 1994, c.27; and S.S. 2001, c.50 and 51. In Nova Scotia, two persons of either sex who are living together in a conjugal relationship can take on family property rights by registering as domestic partners: *Law Reform (2000) Act*, S.N.S. 2000, c.29, s.45, adding a new "Part II: Domestic Partners" to the *Vital Statistics Act*, R.S.N.S. 1989, c.494.

[14] Kathleen Lahey in *The Benefit/Penalty Unit in Income Tax Policy: Diversity and Reform* (Ottawa: Law Commission of Canada, September 2000) at 11-12 provides the following example from *Poulter* v. *M.N.R.*[1995] T.C.J. No. 228 (T.C.C.): "As soon as unmarried cohabitants were deemed in 1993 to be spouses for tax purposes if they cohabited for twelve months or more with a person of the opposex sex, Ms. Poulter was required to combine her income with that of her male co-resident in order to see if family income fell within the guidelines for the child tax credit. It did not, and she lost that tax benefit. Even though there was uncontroverted evidence that her co-resident did not contribute to her or her child's living expenses, that he played no role in relation to supporting or parenting her child, and that they did not live together with any expectation of

combining finances, the court rules that deeming her to be a 'spouse' for purposes of applying the eligibility criteria did not violate her constitutional equality rights. Rulings like *Poulter* leave low-income people with stark choices: become factually dependent on a co-resident or give up the relationship".

15   Roeher Institute, *Personal Relationships of Support Between Adults: The Case of Disability* (Ottawa: Law Commission of Canada, March 2001) at 57-58, 67, 116 and 120.

16   *Ibid.*, at 25-26.

17   *Ibid.*, at 116.

18   Kenneth Karst, "The Freedom of Intimate Association" (1980) 89 Yale L.J. 637.

19   *Zablocki* v. *Redhail*, 434 U.S. 374 (1978); *Santosky* v. *Kramer*, 455 U.S. 745, 753 (1982); *Loving* v. *Virginia*, 381 U.S. 1, 12 (1967).

20   *R.* v. *Salituro*, [1991] 3 S.C.R. 654 at 674.

21   Roeher Institute, *supra* note 15 at 109-111.

22   *Little Sisters Book and Art Emporium* v. *Canada (Minister of Justice)*, [2000] 2 S.C.R. 1120 at para.271 per Iacobucci J.

23   See the discussion of what self-determination means for people with disabilities in Roeher Institute, *Personal Relationships of Support Between Adults: The Case of Disability* (Ottawa: Law Commission of Canada, March 2001) at 108-11.

24   *R.* v. *Edwards*, [1996] 1 S.C.R. 128 at para.50 per Cory J.

25   *R.* v. *Mills*, [1999] 3 S.C.R. 668 at para.50 per Cory J.

26   Charles Fried, "Privacy" (1968) 77 Yale L.J. 475 at 477.

27   *R.* v. *Dyment*, [1988] 2 S.C.R. 417 at 427 per La Forest J.

28   Mary I. Coombs, "Shared Privacy and the Fourth Amendment, or the Rights of Relationships" (1987) 75 California L. Rev. at 1593.

29   *Ibid.*, at 1596.

30   Trudy Govier, *Social Trust and Human Communities* (Montreal: McGill-Queen's University Press, 1997) at 35.

31   Trudy Govier, *Dilemmas of Trust* (Montreal: McGill-Queen's University Press, 1998) at 58.

32   *Ibid.*, at 86.

33   "....the Charter has established the essentially secular nature of Canadian society and the central place of freedom of conscience in the operation of our institutions." *Rodriguez* v. *British Columbia (Attorney General)*, [1993] 3 S.C.R. 519 at 533 per Lamer C.J.

34   *R.* v. *Big M Drug Mart*, [1985] 1 S.C.R. 295.

35   *R.* v. *Edwards Books and Art Ltd.*, [1986] 2 S.C.R. 713.

36   *B. (R.)* v. *Children's Aid Society of Metropolitan Toronto*, [1995] 1 S.C.R. 315.

37   *Ross* v. *New Brunswick School District No. 15*, [1996] 1 S.C.R. 825; *Trinity Western University* v. *British Columbia College of Teachers*, 2001 SCC 31.

38 *Big M, supra* note 34 at 337.

39 *Freitag* v. *Penetanguishene (Town)*, (1999) 179 D.L.R. (4th) 150 (Ont. C.A.); *Canadian Civil Liberties Assn.* v. *Ontario (Minister of Education)*, (1990) 65 D.L.R. (4th) 1 (Ont. C.A.); *Russow* v. *British Columbia (Attorney-General)*, (1989) 62 D.L.R. (4th) 98 (B.C.S.C.); *Manitoba Assn. for Rights and Liberties Inc.* v. *Manitoba*, (1992) 94 D.L.R. (4th) 678 (Man. Q.B.); *Zylberberg* v. *Sudbury Board of Education (Director)*, (1988) 52 D.L.R. (4th) 577 (Ont. C.A.).

40 A useful review of the history of legislation in relation to the solemnization of marriage can be found in Katherine Arnup, *Close Personal Relationships Between Adults: 100 Years of Marriage in Canada* (Ottawa: Law Commission of Canada, 2001) at 8-14.

Chapter Three

Reconsidering the Relevance of Relationships

PART 1: METHODOLOGY

Governments have long relied on relationship status to legislate rights and responsibilities in a number of areas, such as income support, immigration, conflict of interest, caregiving and compensation for economic or emotional injuries. Terms dealing with close personal relationships between adults, such as husband and wife, spouse, common-law partner, relative or dependant appear thousands of times in federal statutes, regulations and policy manuals. However, laws and programs that rely on relational status often miss their mark. Sometimes these laws are over-inclusive, and other times they are under-inclusive. In this chapter, we reconsider the ways in which governments have taken relationships into account in legislation. We try to take a step back from the current law and reconsider whether governments can accomplish their legitimate objectives without unnecessary regulation of personal relationships. Instead of simply arguing that some relationships that are currently excluded (such as non-conjugal relationships) should be included, we are of the view that it is time to fundamentally rethink the way in which governments have relied on relational status in allocating rights and responsibilities. Is it possible to redesign the way in which rights and responsibilities are allocated in a manner that reduces the problems of over- and under-inclusion? In other words, can we imagine a legislative regime that accomplishes its goals more effectively by relying less on whether people are living in particular kinds of relationships?

In this chapter, we first set out a new methodology for rethinking the way in which relationships have been used as a vehicle for achieving a variety of policy objectives. We pose four questions that need to be brought to bear on any existing or proposed law that employs relational terms to accomplish its objectives. First, are the objectives of the law still legitimate? If the objectives of a law are no longer appropriate, the response may be to repeal or fundamentally revise a law rather than to adjust its use of relational terms. Second, if a law is pursuing a legitimate objective, are relationships relevant to the objective at hand? If relationships are not important, then the legislation should be redesigned to allocate the rights and responsibilities on an individual basis. Third, assuming that relationships are relevant, could the law allow individuals to decide which of their close personal relationships should be subject to the law? Fourth, if relationships do matter, and self-definition of relevant relationships is not a feasible policy option, is there a better way for the government to include relationships? In the first section, we elaborate on these four questions. In the sections that follow, we then pose these questions in relation to specific areas of the law to illustrate how this methodology leads to a different role for relationships in federal laws.

Reconsidering the Relevance of Relationships

Four questions need to be brought to bear on any law that currently includes personal adult relationships:

Question 1: Does the law pursue a legitimate policy objective?
- If not, the law ought to be repealed or fundamentally reconsidered.

Question 2: If the law's objectives are sound, do relationships matter? Are the relationships that are included important or relevant to the law's objectives?
- If not, revise the law to consider the individual and to remove the unnecessary relational reference.

Question 3: If relationships do matter, could the law allow individuals to choose which of their own close personal relationships they want to be subject to the law?
- If so, revise the law to permit self-definition of relevant relationships.

Question 4: If relationships do matter, and public policy requires that the law delineate the relevant relationships to which it applies, can the law be revised to more accurately capture the relevant range of relationships?
- If so, revise the law to include the appropriate mix of functional definitions and formal kinds of relationship status.

A New Methodology: Four Questions

1. First Question: Are the objectives of the law legitimate?

Before turning to a consideration of whether laws that currently employ relational terms ought to be revised, it is necessary to identify clearly the objectives that these laws are pursuing. Many laws that currently employ relational terms were first enacted many years ago, prior to some of the major shifts in family demographics and fundamental values that were identified in chapters one and two.

Consider, for example, the special evidentiary rules that make a spouse incompetent to testify if his or her spouse is the subject of a criminal prosecution. This rule can be traced back to a time when the legal fiction of marital unity prevailed: husband and wife were one; the wife's legal personality was submerged in that of her husband. Since accused persons were not competent to testify, it followed that their spouses, being the same legal person, must be incompetent also. Since we have long abandoned the notion of marital unity, this rule of evidence must find its justification in some other objective or be repealed. The question that needs to be asked of such laws is whether they are pursuing objectives that are compelling in light of contemporary social realities and fundamental values. If not, then they ought to be repealed or revised. If they are pursuing legitimate objectives in contemporary terms, then we can move on to a consideration of whether relationships ought to matter in their formulation.

Recommendation 1

Governments should review all of their laws and policies that employ relational criteria to ensure that they are pursuing objectives that respond to contemporary social realities in a manner consistent with fundamental values.

2. Second Question: Do relationships matter?

Once we have concluded that a law is pursuing a legitimate objective, the second question that needs to be asked is whether relationships are actually important in a particular legislative context. Should relationships matter, or alternatively, should the right or responsibility in question be allocated on an individual basis? Is it possible and desirable to individualize the burden or benefit? If relationships do not actually matter, then the government can entirely avoid the problems of relying on relational status. In the sections that follow, we explore some of the contexts in which relationships may not in fact be relevant to state objectives or may provide an inefficient means of pursuing state objectives. In such contexts, it is inappropriate for the law to take one's relational status into account. We will explore several important areas of the law – laws designed to prevent fraudulent transactions, rules of evidence in criminal trials, and income support schemes – where state objectives could be better accomplished if laws were purged of their reliance on relational status.

Removing relationships from legislative contexts where they are not relevant will promote the values of equality, autonomy and privacy and bring greater coherence to the pursuit of legislative objectives. By eliminating unjustifiable differences in the law's treatment of persons, we will give expression to the value of equality. Legal equality is advanced if differential treatment is founded on differences that are relevant to the objectives of a law. Autonomy is furthered if the state's stance is one of neutrality regarding individuals' choices whether to enter into personal relationships. State neutrality, and thus personal autonomy, is therefore promoted if the state does not impose unjustifiable burdens or benefits on particular kinds of relationships. And, since the administration of laws that incorporate relational definitions frequently involves an examination into people's intimate lives, removing unnecessary reliance on relational definitions will result in greater protection of personal privacy. Finally, where relationships are not relevant to state objectives, changing the design of the legislation promotes coherence.

In this chapter, we will consider a range of laws in which it might be possible and desirable to remove relational definitions altogether. We will look at a number of examples where the answer to this second question is that relationships do not in fact matter in a particular legislative context, and we will suggest ways in which the benefit or obligation could be individualized.

Recommendation 2

> Governments should review all of their laws and policies that employ relational terms to determine whether relationships are relevant to, or an effective means of accomplishing, each law's objectives. If not, legislation should be revised to remove the unnecessary relational references.

3. Third Question: If relationships do matter, can individuals be permitted to designate the relevant relationships themselves?

If the answer to the second question is that relationships do matter to the particular legislative objectives, then the third question that needs to be asked is whether it is possible for individuals to decide for themselves which relationships ought to be included. Instead of having the government decide in advance which relationships are included, is it possible to redesign the law or program so that individuals could designate the relationships that are most important to them and ought to be included?

Like the second approach of individualization, this third approach of allowing individuals to designate or select their chosen beneficiaries under a particular law has the advantage of reducing government reliance on relationship status as defined by the government.

Self-designation has a number of advantages over leaving it to government to determine what counts as a relevant relational status. First, it is based on the choice of the individuals involved and affirms the value of autonomy in personal relationships. Secondly, it may reduce the invasions of privacy that accompany the use of relational status under the current law. There is less need for extensive surveillance of the intimate details of relationships. Thirdly, it is an approach that allows for the recognition of the relationships that are of primary importance to the sponsor – which will sometimes include close personal relationships beyond marriage, conjugal or blood ties. The approach is therefore consistent with the value of equality. It is an approach, then, that advances many of the fundamental values that should guide law and policy.

Throughout the chapter, we will explore some of the contexts in which it may be appropriate for individuals to decide for themselves which relationships ought to be included. We will consider whether laws that do need to take relationships into account might be amended to do so on the basis of self-designation. We examine how some laws might be reformed to allow individuals to self-select those relationships that ought to be included, rather than using spousal or familial status as the basis for inclusion. We will suggest that that the sponsorship and family reunification provisions of immigration law, and survivor's benefits in pension laws, are two areas that could operate more fairly and effectively if an element of individual choice was added to the legal definitions of potential beneficiaries.

Recommendation 3

> Governments should review all of their laws and policies to consider whether legislative objectives could be better accomplished if individuals were entitled to choose which of their close personal relationships they want to be subject to particular laws or policies. If so, legislation should be revised to permit self-designation of included relationships.

4. Fourth Question: If relationships matter, and self-designation is not feasible or appropriate, is there a better way to include relationships?

Sometimes it will not be possible to individualize rights and responsibilities, nor to allocate them on the basis of self-designation. In these contexts, governments must then address a fourth question: how should governments include personal adult relationships? Is there is a better way for governments to target the relevant relationships? More specifically, is it possible to design a better test for including relationships that avoids some of the problems with the current focus on spouses and the ascription of common-law partnership status?

While there are various ways in which individuals could be allowed to opt into relational rights (such as marriage and registration, which are discussed in the next chapter), relationship status may still need to be ascribed in some contexts in order to effectively accomplish state objectives, such as the prevention of exploitation. Individuals in close personal relationships who are not married or registered, nor designated through a self-selection mechanism, may have many of the characteristics of economic and emotional interdependency that ought to give rise to rights and responsibilities. To fail to include these individuals may undermine the state's interests in recognizing and supporting the full range of committed, mutually supportive personal adult relationships.

There are at least two options available to Parliament to improve the way in which partnership status is ascribed. The first would be to improve the definition of common-law partner and continue to use it uniformly across the full range of federal laws. The second would be to develop a range of relational definitions that would be more carefully tailored to the objectives of particular statutes. While there are relative advantages and disadvantages to each of these options, both share an emphasis on developing functional definitions that better capture the diverse range of relationships in which Canadians live.

(a) A new, uniform functional definition for ascribing partnership

Personal adult relationships range from fleeting connections to committed, lifelong partnerships. The law seeks to draw distinctions between diverse personal adult relationships by identifying those relationships most relevant to state objectives. As far as unmarried cohabitants are concerned, much of this work in federal legislation is currently done by the term "common-law partners," defined as persons who have lived together in a conjugal relationship for at least one year. The notion of conjugality that is central to this definition has a number of disadvantages. It lacks clarity, it is under-inclusive of the range of personal adult relationships that deserve recognition and it is at least potentially unduly intrusive of individual privacy. In the first option, Parliament could attempt to design a new definition for common-law partnership that avoids some of these problems and better captures the particular dimensions of personal adult relationships that ought to give rise to legal rights and responsibilities.

Any new definition would need to focus on the functional attributes of a relationship. However, it may be possible to devise a definition that focuses on the most significant functional attributes of relationships, that is, on the functional attributes of relationships that give rise to the need for legal recognition and protection. The existence of sexual relations within a relationship, for example, is not relevant to legitimate state objectives. The current definition of common-law partners, by incorporating the notion of conjugality, makes the existence of a sexual relationship a factor that needs to be considered in the administration of state policies. Privacy would be better protected, and state objectives better accomplished, if relational definitions were reformulated to make the existence of a sexual component to a relationship an irrelevant consideration. A new definition could focus on the two functional attributes that appear to be particularly significant across a number of contexts: emotional intimacy and economic interdependency. A third attribute that might also be relevant is a shared residence.

This could provide the basis for a rethinking of how relationships are recognized and included within a broad range of laws. Rather than focusing on the particular features of a relationship that makes it spousal or conjugal, the law could put in place a new functional test that focuses on emotional and economic interdependency, and impose a range of rights and responsibilities on relationships with these attributes, regardless of their formal status. It would, in other words, no longer be a question of first deciding whether people were living in spousal or conjugal relationships, and then imposing rights and responsibilities on them. Rather, it would be a question of whether people were living in a relationship of economic and emotional interdependency.

The advantage of such an approach is that it would focus more effectively on the functional attributes of relationships that are normally relevant to state policies. If such a definition were incorporated uniformly across the range of federal laws, the legal regime applicable to cohabitants would be less complex and more easily understood than if a range of different definitions were included in different laws. The disadvantage of a test focused on economic and emotional interdependence is that by extending rights and obligations to an uncertain group of non-conjugal cohabitants, it may have the effect of disrupting the reasonable expectation of persons living together in relationships that lack the degree of commitment and longevity that is a more common characteristic of conjugal relationships. The disadvantage of employing a uniform test across all federal laws is that the attributes of relationships that are relevant to state policies shift depending on the nature of the policy at issue. These concerns suggest that a better approach is to develop a range of relational definitions that focus more precisely on the factual characteristics of relationships that are relevant to the state objective at issue.

(b) Tailoring definitions to particular statutes

A second and, in our view, preferable option would be to consider the possibility of devising a range of functional definitions for including personal adult relationships in certain laws and programs. Instead of assigning rights and responsibilities on the basis of relationship status or a single, uniform definition of common-law partners, it may be possible to rewrite laws in a more carefully tailored way to take into account the functional attributes of particular relationships. The current approach incorporates a uniform definition of spouse and common-law partner in all federal legislation. As we have suggested, a uniform approach could be defended on the grounds that it promotes greater certainty regarding cohabitants' legal rights and obligations. On the other hand, it gives rise to disadvantages from the point of view of equality and coherence. A uniform definition will not always be well tailored to particular legislative objectives. A better approach would be to adopt different definitions that precisely identify the functional attributes of relationships that are relevant to the different objectives of particular laws.

Since laws have different objectives, it follows that the definition of the relevant relationships should differ as we move from one law to another. For example, economic dependence or interdependence is the most important relational attribute for the purposes of a law that seeks to respond to the economic consequences of the breakdown of a relationship. Emotional intimacy is the most important relational attribute to be considered by a law that seeks to protect the value of trust and candour in intimate relationships. Relational definitions that do not focus on the relevant factual attributes of relationships will miss their mark, excluding some relationships that ought to be included, and including some relationships that ought to be excluded. Thus, carefully tailoring relational definitions to the objectives of particular laws will eliminate inequalities and enable laws to accomplish their objectives more effectively. In the sections that follow, we will explore whether there are better functional definitions that could more accurately identify the range of personal adult relationships relevant to particular legislative objectives.

Recommendation 4

> Governments should review all of their laws and policies to determine whether they could more accurately capture the range of relationships relevant to their particular legislative objectives. If so, laws should be revised to more precisely target relationships by reference to the factual or functional attributes relevant to those particular legislative objectives.

Let us briefly recap the approach we have outlined. The first question is whether a law is pursuing legitimate objectives that respond to social realities in a manner consistent with fundamental values. If not, the law should be repealed or revised. The second question is whether relationships even matter in a particular policy context. If the existence of relationships is not relevant to a legislative objective, then the law should not take them into account. If relationships do matter, a preferred option is to allow individuals to identify the relationships most important to them. If that option is not workable, then consideration needs to be given to revising legal definitions to more accurately capture relationships that have characteristics relevant to the state objectives at issue.

Recommendation 5

> Governments should apply this four-step methodology in the development and implementation of all future laws and programs. Before they initiate any new laws or programs that employ relational criteria, governments should ensure that they are pursuing legitimate objectives and they should consider whether relationships are relevant to, or an effective means of accomplishing, those legislative objectives. If so, governments should consider whether individuals should be permitted to designate the relationships most important to them. If this is not a

feasible option, governments should precisely target relationships by reference to the factual or functional attributes relevant to particular legislative objectives.

We will now illustrate the operation of this approach by bringing it to bear on a number of areas of federal jurisdiction where relationships currently figure prominently in the law: the family compensation provisions of the *Marine Liability Act*; the provisions dealing with leave from employment in the *Canada Labour Code*; the family sponsorship provisions of the *Immigration Act*; the spousal evidence rules in the *Canada Evidence Act*; the regulation of economic transactions between related persons in the *Employment Insurance Act*, the *Bankruptcy and Insolvency Act* and the *Bank Act*; the *Income Tax Act;* benefits provided to older persons pursuant to the *Old Age Security Act*; and the survivor's pensions available under the *Canada Pension Plan* (and laws dealing with veterans' and employees' pensions). The ensuing discussion is not intended to provide an exhaustive analysis of all areas of federal jurisdiction in which close personal relationships play a role in the formulation of laws and policies. We have selected a representative sampling of some important areas to illustrate the need for a more comprehensive and systematic approach to law reform, and to illustrate how our four-step methodology can help point the way towards a more principled and coherent approach to the achievement of federal legislative objectives.

PART 2: APPLICATION

I. The *Marine Liability Act*: Compensating for Negligently Caused Harm to Relationships

When someone is injured or killed as a result of another's wrongdoing, it is not just the immediate victim who suffers a loss. Persons with whom the victim had relationships also suffer harm. The private law in Canada, whether in the common law or the civil law tradition, has recognized that a wrongdoer's liability may properly extend to relational losses.[1] In common law jurisdictions, statutes have been passed to overcome the common law's traditional failure to recognize relational victims.[2] Beginning with the passage of *Lord Campbell's Act*[3] in England in 1846, "wrongful death" legislation has identified the kinds of relationships that can qualify for compensation for pecuniary loss. The initial list of qualifying relationships included wives, husbands, parents, grandparents, children and grandchildren of a deceased victim.

The list of qualifying relationships has expanded in some contemporary legislation to include siblings and common-law partners. The scope of recovery has expanded in some jurisdictions as well: relational claims, once limited to wrongful death actions, now can be brought in cases of wrongful injury, and non-pecuniary loss, such as loss of emotional support, can now be recovered. One feature of the approach in common law jurisdictions that has remained constant, however, is the reliance on relationship status to determine eligible claimants. If a claimant had a relationship with the victim that falls within the statutory list, then he or she may bring an action to recover his or her relational losses. The common law bar to relational claims remains in place for claims brought by persons in relationships with the deceased that do not fall within the applicable statutory list.

The approach taken by the civil law in Quebec, by contrast, is much more flexible. The right to recover relational losses is not limited by relationship status. A chief distinguishing characteristic of extra-contractual liability in the civil law tradition is its openness to all claims of wrongful injury. Every person has a duty to abide by legal rules so as not to cause injury to another.[4] Liability for wrongfully caused harm to another is not restricted to immediate victims of that harm. Relationships are not identified prior to the inquiry into the nature of the loss suffered. Anyone can bring a claim and attempt to establish that the defendant's wrongdoing caused the loss of economic or emotional support flowing from the claimant's relationship with the victim.[5] Thus, for example, in *Regent Taxi & Transport Co.* v. *Congrégation des Petits Frères*,[6] the Supreme Court held that a religious community could recover the expenses it incurred when one of its members was injured while travelling in the defendant's bus.

The civil law approach does not allow recovery by anyone affected by another's wrongful death or injury. The quality of the relationship is investigated in order to evaluate the claim of injury.[7] In contrast to the situation in common law jurisdictions, the question is not whether a particular status of relationship counts, but rather whether the quality of the injury complained of, grounded in the facts of the particular relationship, amounts to a recognizable loss.[8] Causation serves as the most important mechanism for limiting liability in the civil law approach: losses must be shown to be the direct and immediate result of the wrongdoing.[9]

While the private law of obligations is a matter that falls generally within provincial jurisdiction, Parliament does have jurisdiction to deal with the civil consequences of accidents occurring in federally regulated activities. Two federal statutes provide for a right to sue for wrongful death or injury. In both cases, the legislation adopts the categorical approach to relational loss taken by common law jurisdictions rather than the more functional, flexible approach taken by the civil law. The *Carrier by Air Act* imposes liability on airlines to each member of a passenger's family who suffered damage because of a passenger's death.[10] Family members are defined to include spouses, common-law partners, parents, grandparents, siblings, children and grandchildren. As for liability for maritime accidents, Parliament recently passed the *Marine Liability Act*[11] to replace the civil liability provisions of the *Canada Shipping Act*,[12] which had been condemned by the Supreme Court for their "anachronistic and historically contingent" understanding of relational harm.[13]

By passing the *Marine Liability Act*, Parliament has in many respects brought compensation for relational losses incurred in maritime accidents into line with contemporary values and realities. The list of "dependants" who may bring a claim has been expanded to include siblings and common-law partners (in addition to spouses, parents, grandparents, children and grandchildren).[14] The types of loss that can be recovered have been expanded to include the loss of guidance, care and companionship.[15] Relational losses can be claimed in situations of wrongful injury as well as wrongful death.[16]

But, despite these improvements, the continued use of a list of qualifying relationships in the *Maritime Liability Act* is a feature that cannot be justified in our four-step methodology. It is clear that the Act is pursuing a legitimate objective – providing a mechanism for individuals to seek compensation for wrongfully caused relational harm. It is also clear that relationships are relevant to this objective. Turning to our third question, rather than the state setting out a list of qualifying relationships, this is a context in which individuals should be permitted to determine for themselves which relationships they consider to be most meaningful. The civil law approach, in other words, is more consistent with our methodology. By allowing individuals to initiate civil actions for relational harm, without any *a priori* restrictions on what kind of relationship counts, the civil law approach in essence allows for self-selection. Individuals determine which relationships matter to them, and they are given the opportunity to demonstrate a relational loss in court. We are not suggesting, of course, that claimants should be able to determine whether or not they should recover damages in any given case; we are simply suggesting that no barriers based on relationship status should be put in the way of individuals' ability to prove a relational loss in court. In our view, there is no reason to restrict the right to sue by reference to the kind of relationship at issue. At trial, the question of compensation should focus on the quality of the relationship, not its status.

It is important to emphasize that the removal from the *Marine Liability Act* of the relational preconditions to bringing an action would not automatically entitle anyone to anything other than the right to sue. This means that an individual claimant would be given no more than the right to try to prove an emotional or economic loss in a court proceeding. It is not an automatic entitlement to compensation. If no loss is proven, then no damages will be awarded. There is, then, not a significant disadvantage to broadening the group of potential claimants to include currently excluded relationships. The entitlement to compensation is based on proving relational loss, rather than on the status of a relationship. In our view, this is a preferable approach that should be adopted in federal laws.

Recommendation 6

> Parliament should amend laws like the *Marine Liability Act* that confer a right to sue for negligently caused harm to relationships, to permit recovery by any individual who can prove that the defendant's fault caused a recognized kind of relational loss.

II.   The *Canada Labour Code*: Relationships and Leave from Employment

Employment standards legislation in all Canadian jurisdictions establishes basic rights for workers that prevail over inconsistent provisions of individual employment contracts or collective agreements. Relationships are of no concern to many of the topics, such as minimum wages or maximum hours, addressed by employment standards legislation. Relationships are taken into account in some provisions determining when employees have a right to take leave from employment. We will discuss two kinds of leave provisions that need to take relationships into account: bereavement leave and caregiver leave.

Bereavement Leave

At the federal level, as is the case in a number of provinces, legislation entitles employees to a defined leave of absence upon the death of a relative falling within a recognized category of relationship. The purpose of these bereavement leave provisions is to ensure that employers respect employees' need to mourn the loss of those close to them or to support others who are mourning. The *Canada Labour Code* entitles employees in federally regulated workplaces to take bereavement leave for the three days following the death of an "immediate family member".[17] The regulations define immediate family member as including spouses, common-law partners, parents (including in-laws), grandparents, children, grandchildren, siblings and any relative of the employee with whom the employee permanently resided.[18]

The bereavement leave provision is pursuing an important government objective, and relationships are obviously relevant to that objective. But this is a context in which self-selection of the relationships that are most important to an employee is preferable to the current approach that relies on a list of qualifying relationships. While the list of qualifying relationships has expanded over the years to recognize the diversity of family relationships, any list will inevitably be under-inclusive. It is futile to attempt to define all of the relationships important to employees by reference to their status. As Jody Freeman has argued:

> …a definition of family in the context of employment benefits ought not to be limited to those whom the state, or an employer recognizes as a family member but expanded to include people the employee cares about, respects, depends upon, or with whom he or she shares a special relationship…[19]

It does not cost the government any money and the cost to employers would be minimal or non-existent; if people are distressed, their work performance is likely to suffer, so allowing bereavement leave makes sense for both the employee and the employer.

M. Eichler, *Family Shifts – Families, Policies, and Gender Equality* (Toronto: Oxford University Press, 1997) at 163.

The only argument against self-identification of the relevant relationships by employees is that it would be vulnerable to abuse – it would be difficult for employers to monitor the *bona fides* of an employee's assertion that he or she needs time to mourn the loss of particular person. This risk exists even when bereavement leave is limited to a list of relatives, but the risk would be augmented if employees were free to determine which relationships ought to count. This concern could be easily addressed in a number of ways. The legislation could place a cap on the number of days that an employee could take for bereavement leave. Another possibility would be to permit employees to provide a list to employers of those persons with whom they have close personal relationships. By adopting one of these approaches, or some other solution, it would be possible to protect employers from being exposed to undue costs.

Recommendation 7

> Parliament should amend the *Canada Labour Code* to permit employees to designate the relationships most meaningful to them for the purposes of bereavement leave or place a cap on the number of days that an employee can take for bereavement leave.

Caregiver Leave

A number of provinces enable employees to take unpaid leave without employment consequences to care for family members. Quebec was the first Canadian jurisdiction to legislate unpaid family leave, providing for a five-day leave to attend to obligations relating to the "care, health or education" of a minor child in cases where the employee's presence is required due to unforeseen circumstances.[20] A number of reports have recommended that other provinces follow Quebec's lead.[21] Parents, especially single parents, badly need the flexibility such a leave can provide. Furthermore, persons in caregiving or enabling relationships with persons with disabilities are also in need of more support so that they can attend to their relationships without sacrificing their positions in the paid labour force.[22] Providing employees with the right to take unpaid caregiving leave will not remove the financial and emotional pressures on caregiving relationships, but it is a modest step in the right direction.

Legislation in a number of provinces provides for limited unpaid leaves for family caregivers. In British Columbia, employees have the right to take up to five days of unpaid leave each year to meet responsibilities related to the care, health or education of a child or the care or health of any other member of the employee's immediate family.[23] The legislation contains a list of qualifying family relationships, including spouses, children, parents, grandchildren, grandparents and "any person who lives with an employee as a member of the employee's family".[24] Similarly, in Ontario, employees of large employers are entitled to take up to 10 days of unpaid "emergency leave" each year to attend to an illness, injury, medical emergency or urgent matter concerning a family member.[25] The qualifying family relationships listed by the legislation are spouses, same-sex partners, parents, children, grandparents, grandchildren, siblings and "a relative of the employee who is dependent on the employee for care or assistance".[26] Saskatchewan legislation provides the lengthiest entitlement to unpaid leave: up to 12 weeks in the case of a dependent immediate family member who is seriously ill or injured.[27] The definition of "immediate family" is limited to spouses, parents, grandparents, children and siblings.[28] New Brunswick legislation is distinguished by its recognition that caregiving leave is required in relationships that involve connections other than blood or marriage: "close family relationship" is defined as including "a relationship between persons who…demonstrate an intention to extend to one another the mutual affection and support normally associated" with ties of blood or marriage.[29]

These caregiver leave provisions are small steps that advance the important and neglected government objective of supporting caregiving relationships. Identifying the relevant relationships is obviously a task that such laws must confront. As is the case with bereavement leave and other family employment benefits, this is a context in which the law should permit employees to determine for themselves which relationships ought to matter. At the moment, federal legislation does not extend to employees in federally regulated workplaces the right to take caregiving leave. In the 2001 Speech from the Throne, the government committed to moving forward on this issue:

> The Government of Canada will take immediate action with its partners to improve the support available to parents and caregivers in time of family crisis. No Canadian should have to choose between keeping their job and providing palliative care to a child. The Government will take steps to enable parents to provide care for a gravely ill child without fear of sudden income or job loss.[30]

If Parliament does amend the *Canada Labour Code* to introduce family caregiving leave, it should not limit the right to take caregiving leave to parent-child relationships. This would fail to support the large numbers of other family members providing essential care to related persons.[31] Indeed, it would be a mistake for legislation to rely on any closed list of qualifying family relationships.[32] Such an approach fails to support the significant numbers of non-kin caregiving relationships. Instead, legislation should enable employees to decide for themselves which relationships require them to take caregiving leave. To control the risk of abuse, the legislation could consider placing a cap on the number of days that an employee could take for caregiving leave, or it could consider permitting employees to provide a list to employers of those persons with whom they have relationships that may give rise to the need to provide care.

Recommendation 8

> Parliament should amend the *Canada Labour Code* to provide employees with the right to take caregiving leave and to permit employees to designate the relationships most meaningful to them for the purposes of caregiving leave. To control the risk of abuse, the legislation could place a cap on the number of days that an employee could take for caregiving leave, or it could permit employees to provide a list to employers of those persons with whom they have relationships that may give rise to the need to provide care.

III. The *Immigration Act*: Family Sponsorship

The primary objective of the *Immigration Act*[33] is to control the flow of immigrants and refugees into the country. Within this overall objective, the Act contains a commitment to the reunification of families. In its immigration policy, the Canadian government has consistently recognized the importance of families "to Canadians and the socio-economic stability of a nation"[34] and that families "have been the backbone of our communities".[35]

"While family structures continue to evolve, the family remains the foundation for Canada's social cohesion. Family reunification has long been a key objective of Canada's immigration policy and legislation. It permits both recent immigrants and long-established Canadians to be reunited with close family members from abroad, enriches the emotional lives of those involved, assists them in achieving self-reliance, and supports the building of communities".[36]

The provisions of the Act and regulations dealing with dependants and family sponsorship are designed to reflect the importance the government attaches to the maintenance of close personal relationships. The Act and regulations allow an individual who has been granted an immigration visa to bring his or her "accompanying dependants" to Canada.[37] An "accompanying dependant" includes a spouse and any unmarried son or daughter under the age of 19. The Act and regulations also allow Canadian citizens and permanent residents to sponsor a member of his or her "family class" for immigration to Canada.[38] "Family class" is defined as including a sponsor's spouse, dependent child, parent, grandparent and fiancée as well as a sibling, niece, nephew or grandchild who is an unmarried orphan under the age of 19, any child under the age of 19 that the sponsor intends to adopt and one more distant relative if the sponsor does not have any close family members in Canada.[39] Spouse is defined as a person "of the opposite sex to whom that person is joined in marriage".[40] While the "accompanying dependants" and sponsorship provisions are both crucial to the support of personal relationships, and both are in need of similar kinds of reforms, we will restrict the discussion below to reform of the sponsorship rules.

The sponsorship provisions of the *Immigration Act* allow individuals to sponsor a range of family members for immigration to Canada. However, family is defined in a formal and rigid manner. All of the provisions require that the sponsor be related to the individual by blood, marriage or adoption. Some close blood relationships – like those between siblings – are excluded. The law still does not officially recognize common-law partnership. However, many same-sex couples and unmarried opposite-sex couples have been able to sponsor their partners, relying on the humanitarian and compassionate provisions of the Act.[41] This process is at the discretion of the Minister and is open to inconsistent and arbitrary application. The situation will be rectified soon, as the government has included common-law partners in the definition of family class in the new *Immigration and Refugee Protection Act* which, at the time of writing, is awaiting final approval in the Senate.[42] The full range of relationships to be included in the family class will not be known until the regulations accompanying the new legislation are revealed. Persons who likely will not fall within a revised list of qualifying family relationships – best friends, for instance – will still have to cope with the uncertainty of humanitarian and compassionate consideration.

The objective of the family class sponsorship provisions is to recognize and protect the integrity of close personal relationships by facilitating the reunion of family members. Recognizing and promoting the integrity of ongoing interdependent relationships is an important government objective that, by definition, must take relationships into account. The question is how the law should go about identifying the relevant relationships. Rather than relying on a closed list of the kinds of family relationships that qualify for sponsorship, is this a context in which self-designation would work? If feasible, it would be preferable not to artificially restrict individuals' ability to decide for themselves which relationships are most important to them.

Some immigration experts have suggested that the sponsorship provisions of the *Immigration Act* should be amended to allow for a broader definition of family class that would increase the choices available to an individual sponsor. For example, in *Not Just Numbers: A Canadian Framework for Future Immigration*, the

Immigration Legislative Review Advisory Group was critical of how the *Immigration Act* defines the relationships that can serve as the basis for sponsorship.[43] The Advisory Group was of the view that "individuals best understand where their emotional priorities lie, and consequently what constitutes their family".[44] The Report recommended that the family class be divided into three categories or tiers. The first would include spouses and dependent children. The second would include fiancé(e)s, parents and grandparents. The third would be much broader, and would allow the sponsor "to decide who is most important to them, and who is part of what they consider family in the broadest sense. It could even include a best friend".[45] Sponsors within this tier would only have to prove that the individual they are sponsoring is "known and emotionally important to them".[46] The crucial aspect of this third tier would be that the sponsor is prepared to assume "a long term enforceable sponsorship commitment".[47]

The argument against permitting individuals to sponsor persons of their choice, regardless of the existence of a relationship of blood or marriage, is that family sponsorship could become an easy means of circumventing the provisions of the law and "jumping the queue" of immigration applicants. The number of sponsored immigrants could increase significantly if Canadians were entitled to sponsor persons with whom they are not connected by blood, marriage or adoption. These concerns could be addressed by placing limits on the right to sponsor. The number of persons an individual could sponsor over the course of a lifetime could be capped, as suggested by the Advisory Group. Moreover, the ability to choose whom one wishes to sponsor ought not to be open-ended.

The law might adopt the requirement suggested by the Advisory Group that the sponsored person be "known and emotionally important" to the sponsor. A more restricted approach could be to limit the new category of sponsorship to persons who have had a close personal relationship characterized by emotional or economic interdependence for at least one year. Such a requirement would be consistent with the objective of protecting the integrity of interdependent relationships. It would also help avoid potential abuse of the sponsoring system (such as individuals being offered a financial incentive to sponsor strangers).

...the criteria used to identify the beneficiaries of close adult personal relationships other than the traditional concepts of marriage and spouse should fall along a continuum of qualities and characteristics of any kind of healthy, connected relationship. This would foremostly involve self-declaration. To curb abuses, however, there would have to be descriptive criteria as well, such as duration and nature of the relationship.

Law Commission of Canada Comments Board, website, June 2000 – January 2001, posted with permission.

Sponsorship always involves self-selection. By initiating the process, individuals decide whom they would like to support in coming to Canada. At the moment, sponsorship is unduly constrained by under-inclusive definitions that limit qualifying relationships to persons related by blood, marriage or adoption. Rather than having the government set limits on the kinds of relationship status that can be most important to them, Canadians should be allowed to identify their most meaningful relationships themselves. It is important to emphasize that the choice to sponsor is not made lightly. Immigration sponsorship involves a serious financial commitment. Sponsors must assume financial responsibility for the persons they sponsor. A system that allowed for self-selection beyond ties of blood and marriage would significantly advance the value of choice or autonomy, at the same time as it would respect the diversity and equality of close personal relationships.

Recommendation 9

> Parliament should amend the sponsorship provisions of the *Immigration and Refugee Protection Act* and regulations to permit individuals to sponsor persons with whom they have a close personal relationship, even if that relationship does not involve ties of blood, marriage, common-law partnership or adoption.

IV.   The *Canada Evidence Act*: Limits on Spousal Testimony in Criminal Trials

The Need for Reform

The current law of evidence treats a potential witness who is a spouse of the accused differently than other witnesses in a number of important respects. First, a spouse of the accused is not a competent witness for the Crown. The incompetence rule means that a court cannot permit a willing spouse to testify for the Crown. Second, a spouse of the accused is not a compellable witness for the Crown. The non-compellability rule means that a spouse cannot be forced to testify for the Crown against his or her will. These spousal incompetence and non-compellability rules are subject to a number of common law and statutory exceptions.[48] Third, if a spouse testifies for the defence,[49] or for the prosecution pursuant to one of the exceptions, he or she is entitled to invoke the marital communications privilege.[50] A witness spouse has a legal right to refuse to answer questions about communications with his or her spouse during the marriage.

Many courts and commentators have noted that the Canadian law dealing with spousal testimony is unprincipled.[51] The original rationales for the common law rules of incompetence and non-compellability have long been discredited. They are now defended on the grounds that they are necessary to preserve marital harmony. Piecemeal reform has limited the scope of the common law rules and attempted to balance the marital harmony rationale with the pursuit of truth in criminal prosecutions. However, the current law balances these objectives in a manner that is incoherent and incomplete.

There are two basic problems with the current regime. First, it can lead to the exclusion from the trial process of relevant and probative evidence in circumstances where the state's interest in discovering the truth outweighs the relational interests at stake. Second, in circumstances where the relational interests at stake do outweigh the state's interest in discovering the truth, the law protects only marital relationships. Clearly there are other close personal relationships that are worthy of legal protection. As a result, a consensus exists that the law in this area needs to be reformed. The courts have been able to make some incremental changes, but have indicated that only Parliament can undertake the needed comprehensive reforms.[52] Two general directions of reform need to be pursued. First, the law needs to develop a more principled approach to determining when the relevant testimony of a spouse should be available to the Crown. And the protection afforded by the law to witnesses needs to be extended to encompass other socially valuable relationships.

We will begin our discussion by describing the evolution of the statutory and common law rules that deal with the issues of competence, compellability and privilege, and the rationales that have been offered for them. We will then turn to a discussion of the reform options.

Common Law Background

At common law, a spouse was not competent to give evidence for or against his or her spouse in a criminal trial. The origin of the rule can be traced back to the sixteenth century. There were two common law justifications for the rule. First, anyone with an interest in litigation was not competent to testify because of perceived bias. An accused person, therefore, could not testify at his or her trial. And since a husband and a wife were deemed to have the same interest, an accused person's spouse was also barred from testifying. Second, because the doctrine of marital unity held that a husband and wife are one person in law, a wife's incompetency followed from that of her husband.[53] Theses rationales for the rule of spousal incompetence have long been abandoned.[54] The rule prohibiting interested parties from testifying has been abrogated[55] and the marital unity doctrine replaced by a conception of marriage as a partnership between juridical equals.

The contemporary justifications of the common law rule that a spouse is not a competent witness for the Crown are, first, that it is necessary to preserve the integrity and harmony of ongoing marital relationships, and, second, that it is too harsh to demand that spouses give evidence that will bring punishment upon those they love or entail social and economic hardships.[56] As a result, it is the status of the relationship at the time of the trial that determines whether a witness is competent and compellable. At common law, a legally married spouse cannot give evidence, even if the events in question occurred before the marriage.[57] Spousal incompetence is terminated upon divorce[58] or the irreconcilable separation of the spouses,[59] since in those circumstances there is no marital harmony left to protect.

The common law recognizes an important exception to the rule of spousal incompetence. A witness spouse is competent for the prosecution in cases where the subject matter of the charge is injury or threat of injury to the witness' person, life or health.[60] In *R. v. McGinty*,[61] McLachlin J.A. (as she then was) held that spouses are also compellable witnesses for the Crown in such circumstances – that is, they are obliged to testify even if that would not have been their choice. She noted that offences against the personal security of the spouse were usually committed in private with no witnesses present. Accordingly, the evidence of the spouse is essential. Moreover, she reasoned that competence without compellability risked exposing the witness to further intimidation or violence aimed at preventing his or her testimony, and thus would be "more likely to be productive of family discord, than to prevent it".[62] It is better to give the spouse no choice but to testify. The common law exception prevents the marital harmony rationale from being used as a shield to protect an accused from being effectively prosecuted for spousal abuse.

However, the common law does not permit spouses to testify if their evidence is vital to the prosecution of other serious crimes. Parliament has attempted to address this concern by altering the common law in the *Canada Evidence Act*.

Statutory Alteration of the Common Law

The *Canada Evidence Act* alters the common law regarding spousal evidence in criminal trials in two ways that are significant to our analysis. First, it preserves the common law rule that spouses are not competent witnesses for the prosecution,[63] but limits the scope of the rule by introducing a number of new exceptions. Section 4(2) provides that a spouse of the accused is a competent and compellable witness for the prosecution with respect to the listed offences, most of which are sexual offences against children and youth or offences involving domestic relations. Section 4(4) adds a further list of offences in respect of which a spouse is a competent and compellable witness for the prosecution if the victim is under 14 years of age. The section gives the Crown access to the testimony of a spouse in prosecutions regarding virtually all crimes of violence against a child.

The offences listed in sections 4(2) and 4(4) do not include all of the most serious offences in our criminal law. Murder, for example, is included only if the victim was under 14. A spouse of an accused person is not competent to testify for the Crown in a prosecution for murder if the victim was over 14. The listed offences are ones that tend to be committed in the private or domestic sphere. The rationale that appears to explain the list is that the included offences are ones in relation to which a witness spouse is most likely to have relevant information about the commission of the crime.

The second significant aspect of the *Canada Evidence Act* for our purposes is that it contains a marital communications privilege that did not exist at common law. Because the basic position at common law was spousal incompetence, there was no need to consider whether any privilege ought to apply to marital communications. This development occurred by statute in the nineteenth century after legislation made spouses competent witnesses, at least to some extent, in criminal trials.[64] The current situation is that a spouse who testifies as a competent witness for the defence or a co-accused, or as a competent and compellable witness for the Crown (pursuant to one of the common law or statutory exceptions),[65] can refuse to divulge communications made to him or her by his or her spouse during the marriage.[66] The privilege belongs to the witness, not to the accused person.[67] Thus, it is the listener, and not the person who made an incriminating marital communication, who has control over whether it can be divulged. The Supreme Court has also held that telephone conversations between spouses intercepted by wiretap are subject to the privilege and thus cannot be admitted in evidence.[68]

The justification for the marital communications privilege is that, even when a spouse chooses or is compelled to testify, it is necessary to promote candour and trust in marital relationships by protecting confidential communications from unwanted disclosure. Spouses ought to be entitled to treat their marriages as safe havens where they can unburden themselves through intimate conversation without fear of incriminating themselves.[69] Hence, section 4(3) of the Act treats as privileged all communications made to a witness spouse by the accused "during the marriage". The law must balance this relational objective against the search for truth. The balance currently drawn by the law comes down strongly in favour of promoting candour and trust in marital relationships: the marital communications privilege is a class privilege that always prevails over the search for truth. There are no exceptions that require witnesses to disclose marital communications.

Reconsidering the Rules

Spousal Incompetence

According to our four-step methodology, the first question is whether there is a valid objective being pursued by a rule that prevents a spouse from testifying even if he or she wants to do so. The idea of incompetence is repugnant to ideals of equal respect and dignity. It demeans the individual who may be forced to remain silent regardless of a desire to give evidence. Testimonial competence is a mark of personhood. The law should not deny competence to spouses in the absence of a compelling justification.

The objective of the rule of spousal incompetence cannot be the prevention of hardship to the witness. The rule visits hardship upon a spouse by denying him or her the choice to testify. The objective must be the protection and promotion of the integrity of the marital relationship, which the law presumes to be placed at risk whenever a spouse testifies for the Crown.

The pursuit of the marital harmony objective through an incompetence rule is not consistent with the values of equality and autonomy. Other witnesses, including children, are not presumptively denied the choice to testify. If a spouse chooses to give evidence, that choice ought to rank higher than any presumptive claim that incompetence preserves the harmony of his or her marriage. The witness spouse can determine better than the law whether it is worth taking the relational risks that testifying entails. Overriding his or her choice on the grounds that his or her marriage might be compromised is "inconsistent with respect for the freedom of all individuals".[70]

Since the objective underlying the spousal incompetence rule is not consistent with the values of equality and autonomy, there is widespread agreement that it should be repealed, as it has been in many other jurisdictions.[71]

...serious criticisms have been levelled against these two surviving justifications of the traditional rule. It has been called arbitrary for excluding other familial relationships, and antiquated, because it is based on outmoded notions of marriage. Perhaps most importantly, rendering a person incapable of testifying solely on the basis of marital status does strip an individual of key aspects of his or her autonomy.

Lamer, C.J.C. and Iacobucci, J. in *R. v. Hawkins*, [1996] 3 S.C.R. 1043.

Recommendation 10

Parliament should amend the *Canada Evidence Act* to repeal the common law rule that a spouse of the accused is not a competent witness for the Crown.

Spousal Non-Compellability

Under what circumstances the spouse of an accused person who is an unwilling witness should be compellable to provide evidence for the Crown is a more difficult issue. If a spouse would prefer not to testify for the Crown, the principle that the state is entitled to every person's evidence clashes with the value of individual choice. Moreover, forcing spouses to testify against one another presents a threat to the integrity of ongoing intimate relationships and could impose significant hardship on witnesses. But to say that important relational interests are at stake is not to say that they should prevail over the search for the truth. The objective of the current combination of common law and statutory law is to balance the objectives of preserving relational harmony and ascertaining the truth. This is a valid legislative objective to which relationships are obviously relevant.

The problem is that the current law regarding spousal compellability pursues this objective in an unprincipled fashion. Whether a spouse can be compelled to testify for the Crown depends upon whether the offence falls within the common law exception or one of the exceptions created by the crude and apparently arbitrary categorization of offences in section 4 of the *Canada Evidence Act*. For example, a witness can be compelled to testify if his or her spouse is charged with assaulting or murdering a person under the age of 14, but can refuse to testify if his or her spouse is charged with assaulting or murdering a person over the age of 14. The law does not consider factors such as the seriousness of the charge, the likely importance of a spouse's testimony in a given case, or the state of the marriage. As a result there are serious cases in which a spouse cannot be compelled to testify.

Furthermore, the rule of spousal non-compellability is restricted to married persons. Other persons in close personal relationships with an accused, such as common-law partners or non-conjugal cohabitants, can always be forced to testify for the Crown despite the potentially serious consequences for their relationships with the accused. Given that Parliament has recognized the equality of marital and common-law relationships by passing amendments to most other federal statutes,[72] the continued limitation of the non-compellability rule to married spouses stands out as anachronistic. Beyond the need to consider the situation of common-law partners, non-conjugal relationships may also be characterized by the kinds of emotional and economic interdependency that the spousal non-compellability rule is intended to protect. For example, being forced to testify against one's adult child can also be traumatic for a witness.

For these two reasons, the case for reform of the spousal non-compellability rule is strong. One option would be to treat spouses like other witnesses and make them compellable in all cases. In other words, this option concludes that relationships ought not to matter because the judgement made by subsections 4(2) and 4(4) of the *Canada Evidence Act* – that the pursuit of truth outweighs the protection of relational harmony – should not be limited to the listed offences, but is equally convincing in any criminal trial. The main advantage of abolishing the rule of spousal non-compellability is that judges and juries would have the benefit of relevant spousal testimony and therefore the pre-eminent goal of a criminal trial – ascertaining the truth – would be advanced. A further advantage is that a witness spouse might be less exposed to intimidation or violence at the hands of the accused (or associates of an accused) since he or she would have no choice but to testify.

The disadvantage of making spouses compellable for the prosecution is that witnesses will be forced to testify even in circumstances where they believe that the integrity of their relationships with accused persons will suffer. Forcing people to participate in the prosecution and potential incarceration of their loved ones can impose substantial hardship on them. These concerns are tempered somewhat by the likelihood that the Crown will not lightly make the choice to compel testimony by unwilling spouses, since the risk of obtaining unhelpful or even perjured testimony from such hostile witnesses is high.

Nevertheless, abolishing the non-compellability rule is not consistent with the objective of balancing the protection of relationships with the search for truth. It presumes that the relational objective is always outweighed by the truth-seeking function of the criminal trial. Such an absolutist approach is inconsistent with the balance the law attempts to achieve in other areas of criminal evidence. Other privileges and exclusionary rules sometimes operate to interfere with the pursuit of the truth. While the law places great weight on the admissibility of all relevant evidence, this interest does not always prevail over competing state policies.

A better approach would be to design a rule that achieves a balance between protecting relationships and ascertaining the truth by removing the discriminatory and arbitrary features of the current law. Judges could be granted a discretionary power to excuse a witness from testifying if the relational interests at stake outweigh the public interest in having access to his or her testimony. This approach could be extended to all witnesses who are in a close personal relationship with an accused.

Marital Communications Privilege

A consideration of the case for reform of the marital communications privilege leads to similar conclusions. The objective of the privilege is to encourage and preserve confidences between spouses. Promoting candour and trust in close personal relationships is an important relational objective. Candour and trust are essential aspects of emotionally supportive personal relationships. Forcing witnesses to violate that trust jeopardizes what may be their most important sources of affection and emotional support, and sends a signal to others that the privacy of communications with loved ones will not be respected by the state.

The law, however, needs to be reformed to better balance the pursuit of this objective against the state interest in admitting all relevant evidence in criminal trials. The current law is unsatisfactory in a number of ways.

First, the absolute nature of the privilege means that the law makes no attempt to balance the relational objective with the fact-finding function of a criminal trial. The privilege always trumps the pursuit of truth. The divulgence of communications cannot be compelled even if they may be the only means of revealing the truth about the commission of a serious crime. The value of promoting trust and candour in close personal relationships does not always outweigh the state interest in admitting all relevant evidence in criminal trials. The absolute nature of the marital communications privilege is anomalous. Other class privileges recognized by our law, like solicitor-client privilege, are subject to exceptions.[73] Whether privilege attaches to confidential communications in other socially valuable relationships, like the relationships between doctors and patients, is determined by balancing the competing interests on a case-by-case basis.[74]

Second, the objective of promoting trust and candour in close personal relationships would be better achieved if it were made clear that protection should attach, not to the witness in an ongoing relationship, but to any communications made with an expectation of confidentiality in a relationship that was close at the time the communication was made. Therefore, the legal protection accorded private communications should survive the end of a relationship, and control over the divulgence of a communication should rest with the speaker not the listener.

Third, the relational objective underlying the privilege does not justify its limitation to marital communications. This is an area where the relational definition employed by the law needs to be more carefully tailored to the legislative objective. Parliament needs to extend protection to communications made in a broader range of emotionally interdependent relationships. It has been suggested that the test should be whether the witness is connected to the accused by "family or similar ties"[75] or whether the witness has an "intimate relationship"[76] with the accused, or a "close personal relationship of primary importance in the individuals' lives" at the time that the communication was made. One is mindful of allowing an individual on trial to claim that their communications are privileged with almost anyone with whom they had an incriminating discussion. Nevertheless, this would allow the privilege to extend beyond a conjugal relationship to include, for example, a best friend. It would prevent an accused from claiming that communications with multiple friends are privileged.

The Australian Balancing Approach

Statutory reforms in Australia have introduced a balancing approach to the issues of compellability and privilege that provides a sensible direction for reform in the Canadian context. This approach was first adopted in the state of Victoria.[77] After being endorsed by the Australian Law Reform Commission,[78] it was later adopted in Commonwealth legislation, the *Evidence Act 1995*.[79] The 1995 Act starts with an assumption that every person is a competent and compellable witness.[80] However, if called as a witness for the prosecution, a spouse, "de facto spouse," parent or child of the accused can object to giving any evidence or to divulging a communication between the witness and the defendant (i.e., the accused).[81] If an objection is raised, a court can excuse a witness from giving evidence, or from divulging a communication, if it finds that:

(a) there is a likelihood that harm would or might be caused (whether directly or indirectly) to the person, or to the relationship between the person and the defendant, if the person gives the evidence; and

(b) the nature and extent of that harm outweighs the desirability of having the evidence given.[82]

In balancing the relational interest with the state's interest in admitting the evidence, the Act provides that judges must take the following factors into account:

(a) the nature and gravity of the offence for which the defendant is being prosecuted;

(b) the substance and importance of any evidence that the person might give and the weight that is likely to be attached to it;

(c) whether any other evidence concerning the matters to which the evidence of the person would relate is reasonably available to the prosecutor;

(d) the nature of the relationship between the defendant and the person;

(e) whether, in giving the evidence, the person would have to disclose matter that was received by the person in confidence from the defendant.[83]

This approach puts in place a principled framework for reconciling the competing interests at stake. Rather than confining compellability to the common law exception and the list of offences in the *Canada Evidence Act*, and rather than always treating marital communications as privileged, it achieves a much more sensitive and flexible balancing of interests. Where warranted, it protects relationships and confidences and avoids hardships to witnesses. Yet it recognizes that a witness's objection to testifying cannot always prevail over the importance of permitting the justice system to secure relevant evidence. It has proved to be a workable and satisfying solution in Australia for some time.[84]

The balancing approach embodied in the Australian legislation has been criticized on the grounds that it adds complexity and uncertainty to criminal prosecutions.[85] The Crown would not know ahead of time whether it will be able to rely on the testimony of a person with a close personal relationship with the accused. This is a significant disadvantage of the balancing approach. It is, however, a disadvantage that the law considers worth enduring for the benefits of more nuanced decision making on a wide range of evidentiary matters, including a case-by-case assessment of many other claims of privilege. In any event, the balancing approach is not likely to make a huge difference in practice to the strength of the case the Crown is able to present in court. As Allan Manson has argued,

The prospect of relying on the evidence of someone closely linked with the accused will always present some uncertainty given the dynamics of personal relationships. The prosecutor will have a problem whether the witness is compellable and recants or balks, or is exempted from testifying.[86]

In either case, Manson points out, recent jurisprudence expanding the admissibility of previous out-of-court statements may assist the Crown in getting the evidence of a person close to the accused before the court.[87]

With three modifications, we believe that the Australian balancing approach provides a sound model for law reform in Canada. First, it is the speaker of a confidential communication (either the accused or the witness) that should be entitled to raise an objection to its disclosure in testimony. Second, as discussed above, in addition to spouses, common-law partners, children and parents, the right to object to giving evidence (or to the disclosure of communications) should be extended to any witness who has a close personal relationship with the accused. Finally, the right to object should be available when a witness is testifying for the prosecution or for a co-accused.

Recommendation 11

Parliament should replace the spousal non-compellability rules with an amendment to the *Canada Evidence Act* that enables judges to excuse a witness from having to testify if he or she objects to testifying, has an ongoing close personal relationship with the accused, and the judge finds that the harm that would be caused to the witness or to the relationship by having to testify outweighs the desirability of admitting the testimony.

Recommendation 12

Parliament should replace the marital communications privilege with an amendment to the *Canada Evidence Act* that enables judges to prevent the divulgence of a confidential communication if the witness had a close personal relationship with the accused at the time the communication was made, and the need to protect and promote candour and trust in close personal relationships outweighs the desirability of admitting the testimony.

V. The *Employment Insurance Act*: Preventing Fraud

Many laws that regulate close personal relationships are directed towards preventing potential fraud and conflicts of interest. These laws aim to prevent parties from entering into economic transactions for the sole or primary purpose of avoiding penalties (like tax liabilities) or claiming benefits (like employment insurance). Or, if they have entered into such transactions, the law aims to prevent the parties from keeping what are seen as unfairly obtained benefits. We do not doubt that these laws are pursuing important government objectives. What is less clear is the answer to our second question: are relationships relevant to the attainment of government objectives in this context? Currently, relationships do figure prominently in laws designed to prevent fraud and conflicts of interest. The assumption underlying these laws is that personal relationships must be subject to special scrutiny because they provide the opportunity, or the shared interest, that creates a heightened risk that persons in those relationships will engage in collusive fraud.

The question then is whether relationships are relevant to the state interests in this context and, if so, how should they be taken into account. Is the fact that a transaction occurred between persons in a close personal relationship in itself a sufficient indication that the transaction was fraudulent or tainted by suspect motivations? Some laws operate in this manner: they put in place irrebuttable presumptions that transactions between closely related persons are not valid.

For example, a provision of the *Bankruptcy and Insolvency Act*[88] provides that parents, children, siblings or aunts and uncles of a bankrupt cannot take advantage of the preference the Act gives to claims for wages due.[89] Since wages due employees normally have a high priority in the scheme of distribution,[90] this provision must be based on the premise that employment by a relative is not real employment. The provision, in this case, does more than cast a pall of suspicion. It puts in place a bar to a specified relative making a claim for wages before any of the preferred creditors. Even if the relative of the bankrupt could demonstrate the *bona fides* of the employment relationship, his or her claim would rank last in priority.

Irrebuttable presumptions treat transactions between relatives as automatically illegitimate. They put in place absolute bars to certain benefits or entitlements. The difficulty with this approach is that it is over-inclusive. Commercial transactions entered into by related parties are not necessarily fraudulent, illegitimate or otherwise tainted by *mala fides*. For this reason, the law should avoid the use of irrebuttable presumptions when regulating commercial transactions between relatives. The law should give persons who have entered into a commercial transaction with a related person the opportunity to demonstrate the *bona fides* of the transaction.

Recommendation 13

> Parliament should amend laws seeking to prevent fraudulent transactions to remove irrebuttable presumptions based on relationship status.

Other laws put in place rebuttable presumptions: they assume that transactions between related persons are suspect and need to be subject to heightened scrutiny to determine whether they were entered into for fraudulent purposes. Persons who transacted with relatives are given an opportunity to demonstrate that legitimate purposes motivated the transaction. In theory, rebuttable presumptions should operate more fairly. In practice, they may lead to excessive scrutiny of family transactions, and inadequate attention may be given to transactions between non-relatives who may also have something to gain from concocting fictitious commercial transactions.

Whether they are rebuttable or irrebuttable, relational presumptions may distract attention from the real issue: whether a transaction was entered into on self-serving preferential terms or for fraudulent purposes. The use of relational presumptions may also have negative consequences for the privacy and autonomy of family members. Thus it can be argued that relationships are not relevant to many laws designed to prevent fraud or avoid conflicts of interest. The legitimate state objective of preventing fraud and avoiding conflicts of interest may be better accomplished by simply targeting fraudulent transactions and requiring disclosure of conflicts without relying on relational presumptions.

Recommendation 14

> Parliament should amend laws seeking to prevent fraudulent transactions to remove rebuttable presumptions based on relationship status. The objectives of these laws would be better accomplished if they prohibited fraudulent transactions and required disclosure of conflicts of interest without relying on relational presumptions.

In the discussion below, we will use provisions of the *Employment Insurance Act* that define insurable employment to illustrate the implications of our approach.

Defining Insurable Employment

The *Employment Insurance Act*[91] provides a measure of income security to unemployed workers. To qualify for benefits, a claimant whose employment has ended must have worked the required number of hours in insurable employment. The Act provides that employment is not insurable if the employer and employee were not dealing with each other at arm's length.[92] The objective of this provision is to prevent people from fraudulently claiming unemployment benefits by manufacturing fictitious or artificial employment relationships. The Act further provides that persons related by blood, marriage, common-law partnership or adoption are deemed not to deal with each other at arm's length.[93] On the other hand, whether employment relationships between unrelated persons are at arm's length, and thus insurable, is to be determined on a factual analysis of each case.[94]

As they stood, these provisions put in place an unjust irrebuttable presumption. Their application would have deprived all employees who work for a related person of their entitlement to unemployment benefits upon termination of their employment. This was, in fact, the law prior to 1990. Family employment was not insurable under the Act. Family employment was used as a proxy for fictitious employment. Meanwhile, whether employment relationships between non-relatives was real and therefore insurable was a question of fact to be determined in each case.

Recognizing the harshness of an irrebuttable presumption that employment between relatives is not real employment, Parliament amended the Act in 1990.[95] The amendment gives the Minister a discretionary power to treat employment by a relative as insurable employment if the claimant can demonstrate, "having regard to all of the circumstances of employment," that the contract of employment was "substantially similar" to an arm's length contract.[96] The 1990 amendment thus abandoned the view that family employment is always manufactured with an eye to taking advantage of unemployment benefits. Whether family employment qualifies as insurable employment depends on an examination of all of the relevant facts ("having regard to all the circumstance of the employment").

Parliament improved the legislation when it replaced the irrebuttable presumption that family employment is not "real" employment with a rebuttable presumption to that effect. After the 1990 amendment, the ultimate question is the same whether the employment at issue was between related or unrelated persons: in both cases, it is quite properly the factual elements of the employment relationship that determine whether the employment was real and thus insurable.

Despite this improvement in the legislation, it nevertheless continues to operate harshly in practice. Unemployed claimants who were employed by relatives have the onus of convincing the Minister that their employment was *bona fide*. If they fail initially, they can attempt to persuade the Tax Court that the Minister exercised his or her power in an arbitrary or capricious manner. Claimants rarely succeed in meeting this high evidentiary burden.[97] The operation of the legislation, despite the 1990 amendment, continues to involve what appears to be excessive scrutiny of family employment relationships and the denial of unemployment insurance benefits to many persons laid off by related employers. In a number of cases, the Minister has sought to justify the decision to deny benefits by proving the existence of a conjugal relationship between an employer and employee, while the employee has strenuously resisted the Minister's characterization of the nature of the relationship.[98] This is an unnecessary spectacle that is demeaning to unemployed claimants and a distraction from the real issue at stake: whether the employment relationship was *bona fide*.

We conclude that relationships are not relevant to the accomplishment of the state objective of preventing fraudulent unemployment insurance claims. The administration of relational presumptions entails significant invasions of privacy. By forcing people to sacrifice a measure of economic security if they engage in transactions with related persons, relational presumptions may have the unanticipated consequence of deterring the formation or continuation of personal adult relationships. The use of relational presumptions to deny access to important economic benefits has the potential to impose significant hardship on worthy claimants.

The law would better accomplish the objective of preventing fraud if it focused on the features of the employment contract at issue, rather than the nature of the personal relationship between the parties. The 1990 amendment took an important, but incomplete, step in this direction. The premise of the reform needs to be followed through to its logical conclusion. In the context of unemployment insurance benefits, the relevant question in all employment contexts should be the same: whether the employment contract was manufactured for the purpose of claiming benefits. The existence of a personal relationship between an employer and employee may be a factor but ought not be the most significant one in the administration of the scheme.

Recommendation 15

The *Employment Insurance Act* should be amended so that employment by a relative is not treated as presumptively uninsurable. All employment contracts manufactured for the purpose of claiming benefits, whether the parties are in a close personal relationship or not, should be excluded from the definition of insurable employment.

VI.   The *Bankruptcy and Insolvency Act*: Protecting Creditors' Interests

A number of provisions of the *Bankruptcy and Insolvency Act*[99] take relationships into account when determining or protecting the rights of creditors.[100] We will consider two of these provisions. The first, dealing with "reviewable transactions," empowers courts to determine whether a bankrupt received fair market value when disposing of property in non-arm's length transactions during the year prior to the initial bankruptcy event. Because the courts should be capable of examining the facts surrounding any transaction that raises suspicions that property or assets were disposed of at less than market value, we argue that relationships ought not to be relevant in this context. The second provision we examine deals with "fraudulent preferences". Transactions made with a view to preferring a creditor in the three-month period prior to the initial bankruptcy event are treated as fraudulent and void. This period is extended to twelve months if the transaction in question involved a creditor who is related to the bankrupt person. We argue that relationships are not relevant to defining the period in which preferential transactions should be sanctioned. Instead the test should be whether the person who receives the preferential transfer knew of the bankrupt's insolvency at the time of the transfer.

Reviewable Transactions

Transactions that a bankrupt entered into in the year prior to the initial bankruptcy event are treated by the Act as reviewable in court if they were not at arm's length. If a judge finds that the amount received by a bankrupt was "conspicuously less" than the fair market value of the bankrupt's property or assets, then the court may make an order that the difference in the amount received be made available to creditors.[101] This power of judicial assessment applies only to "reviewable transactions," defined by the Act as transactions between persons who were not dealing with each other at arm's length.[102] Transactions between persons who are related by blood, marriage, common-law partnership or adoption are deemed not to have been at arm's length.[103] On the other hand, whether unrelated persons dealt with each other at arm's length is a question of fact in each case.[104] The result is that all transactions between related persons are reviewable by a court, and transactions between unrelated persons are reviewable if they were not at arm's length.

The objective of the "reviewable transactions" provisions of the *Bankruptcy and Insolvency Act* is to prevent an individual facing impending bankruptcy from dissipating assets or resources to the detriment of the creditors. If the owner disposes of assets to family or associates for a return conspicuously below fair market value, thus diminishing the assets available to meet the claims of creditors, the trustee in bankruptcy can seek a remedy in court to vindicate the creditors' interests. Seeking to protect creditors in this way is certainly a valid legislative objective.

But are relationships relevant to the attainment of this objective? The argument that they are relevant rests on the proposition that close personal relationships provide incentives and opportunities to engage in collusive transactions that unfairly ignore the interests of other creditors or protect assets from their claims on the bankrupt.

While close personal relationships do provide potential motives and opportunities for collusion in transactions that may harm creditors, the current emphasis on close relationships is needlessly complex and unfairly overbroad. Personal relationships are not relevant to the objective of protecting creditors.[105] Where the transaction has the effect of diminishing the amount of property that would otherwise be available to the creditors, the focus should be on whether the debtor was insolvent at the time of the transaction.

> The arbitrariness inherent in the concept of "related persons" and "non-arm's length" transactions is displayed in the case law dealing with sections 3 and 4 of the BIA. "Related persons" are conclusively presumed, regardless of the actual facts, to be not dealing at arm's length. Even if husband and wife are not on friendly terms, they are still deemed to be not dealing at arm's length. A child born out of marriage, a daughter-in-law and a son-in-law are not "related persons". Uncles, aunts, nephews and cousins are not persons "related to" a debtor. A widow is not related by marriage to her father-in-law.
>
> R.C.C. Cuming, "Transactions at Undervalue and Preferences under the Bankruptcy and Insolvency Act: Rethinking Outdated Approaches", (31st Annual Workshop on Commercial and Consumer Law, Faculty of Law, University of Toronto, 19-20 October 2001) at footnote 34 [unpublished].

Recommendation 16

Parliament should amend the *Bankruptcy and Insolvency Act* so that all transactions entered into by a bankrupt may be set aside if the transaction was entered into at a time when the bankrupt was insolvent, and the effect of the transaction was to diminish the assets that would otherwise vest in the bankrupt's estate.

Fraudulent Preferences

The provisions of the Act dealing with fraudulent preferences are also designed to protect the interests of creditors in the period leading up to bankruptcy. Transactions made by an insolvent person with a view to giving a preference to one creditor over others in the three-month period prior to the initial bankruptcy event are treated as fraudulent and void against the trustee.[106] The three-month period of legal regulation is extended to twelve months in the case of creditors who are related to the bankrupt: transactions made with a view to giving a related creditor a preference over other creditors in the twelve-month period prior to the initial bankruptcy event are deemed to be fraudulent and void against the trustee.[107] The extended period appears to be based on the assumption that debtors are more likely to "plan a bankruptcy" with the related person and make the payment or transfer outside the three-month time period.[108]

Protecting the interests of creditors from such planned bankruptcies is a valid legislative objective. However, the problem of planned bankruptcies is not exclusive to dealings with a related person. What is important to the legislative objective is that the preference was given to a creditor who was aware of the debtor's insolvency at the time of the preference and who, therefore, knew or should have known that he or she was receiving an unfair preference. The existence of a relationship or not is irrelevant.[109] In other words, section 96 is too narrow in one respect and too broad in another. It is too narrow in that it does not cover planned bankruptcy where the recipient of the payment is not a relative. It is too broad in that if the recipient is a relative, then it simply assumes that the relative knew of the bankrupt's financial difficulties, whether or not that was in fact the case.

We conclude that the objective of protecting creditors would be better achieved by eliminating the emphasis on the relationship between the bankrupt and the recipient. The legislation should be amended so that the one-year period for attacking a transaction as a preference would apply whenever the recipient knew of the bankrupt's insolvency at the time the preferential transaction was entered into.

Recommendation 17

Parliament should amend the *Bankruptcy and Insolvency Act* so that the extended one-year period for setting aside preferences would not depend on relationships but would apply whenever a creditor knew of the bankrupt's insolvency at the time of the preference.

VII. The *Bank Act*: Avoiding Conflicts of Interest

Laws that regulate financial institutions try to prevent conflicts of interest by prohibiting transactions with related persons unless special measures have been taken to minimize any risk or appearance of preferential treatment. For example, the *Bank Act* says that banks cannot enter into transactions with relatives of bank directors or senior officers unless special procedures are followed.[110] The objective of this sort of provision is to prevent the parties from benefiting, or appearing to benefit, from the presumed shared economic interests they have with relatives. This is a legitimate government objective, directed at maintaining the integrity of financial institutions and the fair treatment of their customers. Are relationships relevant to this objective? It seems a fair assumption that individuals with close personal relationships with bank officials have incentives and opportunities to take economic advantage of their relationships. Therefore, it can be argued that relationships do matter. The existence of a close personal relationship gives rise to the potential for the conflict.

Since these laws seek not only to prohibit actual conflicts, but also to preserve the appearance of fair and impartial treatment of all customers, relationships should be taken into account. Rules against dealings between relatives further the objective of promoting public confidence in financial institutions. Any potential hardship to related parties (such as the denial of access to financial services) can be avoided by not putting in place an absolute bar to transactions between relatives. Instead, laws regulating financial institutions should put in place rebuttable presumptions against transactions between relatives. So long as the law permits dealings between relatives if special procedures have been observed to ensure the integrity of transactions, as the *Bank Act* does, then the use of relational definitions in this context is justifiable.

While the *Bank Act* provision prohibiting transactions with relatives of bank officers or directors is pursuing a legitimate objective to which relationships are relevant, the relational definitions it employs are not accomplishing this objective very well. The definition of related parties includes spouses, common-law partners and minor children of the directors, senior officers or significant shareholders.[111] Persons who have other close personal relationships with bank officials are not covered by the conflict rules. The current provisions are clearly under-inclusive. A much broader range of close personal relationships could give rise to the kinds of conflict or risk of preferential treatment with which the legislation is concerned.

This is an area in which the law could do a better job of identifying the relevant relationships by relying on a combination of self-identification and better legislative definitions. Individuals seeking to deal with a bank should be required to disclose the existence of a close personal relationship with an officer, director or significant shareholder of a bank. In this way, the law could make use of individuals' ability to identify which close personal relationships in their lives could give rise to a conflict or the appearance of a conflict, and thus would trigger special review procedures. These changes would correct the overly narrow definition of related parties in the current legislation, which places banks under special obligations only when they are dealing with related businesses or the spouses, common-law partners or minor children of bank officials or owners.

Recommendation 18

> Parliament should amend the *Bank Act*, and other legislation regulating financial institutions, so that the special rules regulating transactions with related parties apply to any prospective customer with a close personal relationship with a director, officer or significant shareholder of the institution.

VIII. The *Income Tax Act*[112]

A. *Purposes of the Laws of Income Tax*

The *Income Tax Act* has become one of the federal government's most significant policy instruments. Traditionally, the tax on personal income was used primarily as an instrument for raising revenues fairly to finance the broad range of collective goods and services provided by government. Throughout most of its history — in Canada the first income tax laws were enacted in 1917 — it has also been used to redistribute income and wealth and to assist in stabilizing the economy. In more recent years, however, the income tax system has been used extensively as an instrument for delivering government subsidies and transfer payments to individuals. Over the past 30 years, many of the federal government's most significant social policy initiatives have been enacted as "tax expenditures". Therefore, the income tax legislation provides an excellent prism through which to examine the role of government in regulating close personal adult relationships. Since the distinction between technical tax provisions and tax expenditures is so fundamental to any analysis of the income tax, we begin by briefly explaining these concepts.

Technical Tax Provisions

The first step in applying our methodology is to inquire into the legitimacy of the objectives of any law that employs relational terms. Determining the objectives of laws contained in the *Income Tax Act* is complicated by the fact that tax laws might be serving one of two quite different broad purposes. On the one hand, they might be furthering the objective of ensuring that income tax laws impose the cost of government services fairly across individuals resident in Canada. The short-hand way of referring to this broad objective of the tax laws is to say that taxes ought to be imposed on individuals on the basis of their ability to pay. Therefore, for example, the purpose of a provision allowing individuals to deduct an amount from their gross income might be to arrive at a net income figure that reflects their ability to pay. If this is the purpose of the provision, the provision is part of the technical tax system. In the context of this paper, the question is when, if ever, for income tax purposes, should the personal relationships of individuals be taken into account in determining their ability to pay. In evaluating technical tax provisions, tax policy analysts not only assess whether the provisions are necessary to assist in arriving at an individual taxpayer's ability to pay, but they also evaluate them using the standard criteria of equity, neutrality and simplicity. Technical tax provisions should ensure that individuals in similar circumstances are taxed in the same way (equity); that the tax laws do not unnecessarily influence the behaviour of individuals (neutrality); and that they are relatively easy to administer and comply with (simplicity).

Tax Expenditures

On the other hand, particular provisions in the *Income Tax Act* might be furthering social policy goals rather than the objectives of the technical tax system. These provisions, which are normally designed as tax deductions or credits, apply to taxpayers who engage in particular kinds of activities the government wishes to encourage or to taxpayers who are deserving of some form of income support.

These tax provisions are similar to direct government spending measures and are frequently referred to as "tax expenditures". Instead of requiring individuals to apply directly to the government for a subsidy, when the government enacts a tax expenditure it delivers the subsidy through the tax system by allowing individuals to reduce their taxes payable by claiming an amount as a deduction or tax credit. If a tax provision can be classified as a tax expenditure, then it should not be analyzed as a technical tax provision, but instead it should be analysed in the same way as a direct government spending measure. Does it serve a legitimate government objective? Is it well-designed to achieve its objective? Could the objective be better served through the use of some other government policy instrument? In the context of this paper, the relevant question in analysing tax expenditures is when, if ever, should the personal relationships of individuals be taken into account in determining their eligibility for tax expenditures.

It is not always easy to determine whether a particular tax provision was enacted, and therefore should be analyzed, as a technical tax measure or as a tax expenditure. Therefore, in our discussion of the objectives of particular tax provisions, and in deciding whether an individual's personal relationships are significant in pursuing these objectives, we assess the provisions both as tax measures and as tax expenditures.

Although the income tax is imposed on the income of individuals, recently some groups have suggested that the tax should be imposed on the family as a unit. Among other reasons, they argue that, because there are so many provisions that consider whether an individual has a conjugal relationship, the income tax system is really a hybrid individual/family unit system and that instead of attempting to individualize the system, the government should simply make the family the basic unit of taxation.[113] As a prelude to arguing that many of the provisions in the income tax that now turn on an individual's personal relationships should be repealed or amended, we restate the case as to why the individual should remain the basic unit of tax.

B.   The Basic Taxpaying Unit

General

Although the *Income Tax Act* contains countless provisions in which an individual's taxable income might be affected by their personal relationships, the basic unit of Canada's personal income tax is the individual. All individuals resident in Canada who owe income tax must file a tax return and pay tax on their income. Consistent with the general direction of the other recommendations in this report – to account for the increasing diversity of personal relationships, to encourage the formation of personal relationships and to ensure the protection of values such as gender equality and personal autonomy – we recommend that, generally, in computing an individual's taxable income under the technical tax system, and in determining whether an individual is eligible for a particular tax expenditure, personal relationships should be less significant than they are at present in the law.

In recent years, some groups have suggested that tax policy should be moving in precisely the opposite direction to that which we are recommending. In particular, they have contended that because the tax system is based on the individual, it discriminates against families with only one earner. Therefore, they have suggested that the basic unit should be the family and not the individual. Because the question of whether the tax system should be based upon the individual or the family is so central to the subject matter of this report, we briefly discuss it here. Also, the justifications for individual taxation provide a baseline that can be used in assessing whether particular provisions of the tax system should turn on the taxpayer's personal relationships. Moreover, the case for family-unit taxation, which we reject, illustrates more generally many of the problems of basing laws on an individual's personal relationships.

> The current Canadian income tax system does not disadvantage one-earner families with children in favour of two-earner families with children. In fact, one-earner families have more consumable income left after taxes and work-related expenditures than do two-earner families with the same money income. On top of that, the non-taxation of household production is an important, though rarely considered, tax advantage of one-earner families.
>
> Michael Krashinsky and Gordon Cleveland, *Tax Fairness for One-Earner and Two-Earner Families: An Examination of the Issues* (Ottawa: Canadian Policy Research Networks, 1999).

A tax system based upon the individual requires individuals to file a tax return each year and report their income. A tax system based upon the family as the taxpaying unit would require the members of a conjugal family unit – or some other definition of the family – to file a return jointly. Basically, a conjugal couple's income tax liability would be calculated as if the members were two individuals each earning one-half of their combined incomes. The difference for individuals of shifting from an individual-based to a conjugal couple-based tax system is seen most easily by comparing two couples earning the same amount of income, one couple with only one member working outside the home and the other couple with both members working outside the home. If one spouse is working outside the home and earning $100,000, and the other is working inside the home, under the present Canadian income tax system the spouse working outside the home would pay income tax of approximately $33,000. If both spouses are working outside the home and each earning $50,000 (for a total family income of $100,000), they will each pay tax of approximately $13,000, for a total family tax liability of $26,000. Thus, the one-earner family will pay $7,000 more tax than the two-earner family, even though the combined incomes of the members of both families are the same. As a second example, in 2001 one spouse working outside the home in Ontario and earning $50,000 would pay tax of $11,192. An individual earning $25,000 in Ontario would pay $3,904. Thus, the one-earner family will pay $3,384 more in tax than the two-earner family earning the same amount. This result is the inevitable consequence of the fact that the income tax rate structure is progressive, and therefore higher reported incomes are taxed at higher marginal tax rates, and that the basic taxpaying unit is the individual and not the family. However, it is this result that has led some groups to suggest that basing the tax system on the individual is unfair because it discriminates against one-earner families.

Background

By way of background, since the introduction of the personal income tax in 1917, Canada has always had an individual-based income tax system. In contrast, the personal income taxes in many European countries, which enacted their income tax statutes in the nineteenth century, were historically family-based. The explanation for the use by these countries of the family as the basic unit of tax is straightforward. At the time they introduced their income taxes, married women had few property rights and generally did not have the legal capacity to dispose of their own income. Therefore, requiring married women to aggregate their income for tax purposes with that of their husbands was a logical extension of family property laws. Over the past 40 years, fuelled by the conclusion that some forms of family taxation discriminate against women, most of these European countries have moved to individual-based systems.[114]

Like Canada, the United States originally adopted an individual-based income tax, since women had full property rights when it enacted its first modern income tax act in 1913. However, in 1948 the United States converted to a family-based tax system.[115] Largely because of the political difficulties of reforming an entrenched tax system, family-based taxation remains in the United States even though it has undergone constant tinkering and is the source of ongoing dispute, and in spite of the almost unanimous view of tax analysts that it is inappropriate and creates perverse incentives and administrative problems.[116]

The case for individual taxation rests upon the claims that a tax system based on the individual is a more appropriate policy instrument for achieving the government's objectives than one based on the family, that it is less likely to influence the relationships that individuals form, and that it is more likely to further values such as gender equality and individual autonomy.

Before briefly reviewing each of these claims, an important conceptual point should be clarified. The case for family-unit taxation is often put in terms of comparing two conjugal couples with the same income and arguing that these couples should pay the same amount of tax regardless of the relative share of the total family income earned by each member. But this is a misleading way to conceptualize the issue. Families or personal relationships cannot, of course, pay tax. Ultimately, only individuals can pay tax. Thus, for policy purposes the question is not whether two families whose members in aggregate earn the same amount of income should pay the same amount of tax, but rather whether the income earned by other members of the family should be considered when deciding how much income should be attributed to a member of a family for tax purposes.

Nevertheless, even accepting that it is the well-being of individuals that is the ultimate goal of legal policy, a case can still be made for family-unit taxation. The argument rests upon the combination of a normative and an empirical claim. The normative claim is that in a just tax system individuals should pay tax on the income they benefit from. The empirical claim is that members of a family benefit equally from the income that each earns. Consequently, in a just tax system, the income of the members of a family should be totalled and split equally between them. For example, the members of a family in which one member earns $100,000 and the other works in the home should be treated for tax purposes as if the income of each was $50,000. That is, they should be treated in the same way as the members of a family in which each member in fact earned $50,000.

Empirical Case for Individual Taxation

The factual judgement that the case for family-unit taxation rests upon is that members of a family typically share equally all of their income. There is extensive empirical literature on the extent to which families pool their income.[117] Not surprisingly, although these studies find that there is equal pooling in some families, in fact, the pattern of sharing varies considerably across families. With reduced stability in relationships and changing family forms, it has become increasingly difficult to generalize about the sharing and control of resources between individuals in close personal relationships. Any attempt to define family for the purposes of family-unit taxation, in order to identify sharing relationships, would be doomed to be both under-inclusive and over-inclusive. If, for example, family-unit taxation was based on the conjugal couple, it would treat conjugal couples as pooling their incomes even though some would not, and it would treat non-conjugal cohabitants as not pooling their incomes even though some would.

Normative Case for Individual Taxation

Even if we could overcome the difficulty of identifying personal relationships in which significant sharing of income occurs, we would still need to confront the normative issue raised by the individual or family-unit taxation debate. The normative basis underlying the case for individual-unit taxation is that individuals should be taxed on income they control or earn; the normative basis underlying the case for family-unit taxation is that individuals should be taxed on income that they benefit from in terms of personal consumption. It is clear that the present Canadian income tax, in all of its major design features, rests upon the assumption that individuals should pay tax on income they control and not on income from which they simply benefit. For example, under the present law individuals are not able to deduct the value of gifts they make to others, nor do the recipients of gifts have to include the value of the gifts they receive in their income. If the tax system were premised on the benefit theory of income, donors would deduct the value of gifts (and bequests) and donees would be required to include that value in their income. Moreover, under a tax system based on the benefit theory of income, presumably the aggregate income of all members of a household should be split among the members in some proportion. Children, parents and other members of extended families, as well as spouses and common-law partners, benefit from the income earned by the income-earning members of a family. Consequently, the consistent implementation of the normative claim that underlies the case for family-unit taxation would result in a very different tax system than Canada has at present.

Individual-unit taxation rests upon two widely held moral judgements. First, that it is fair to tax two individuals who earn (or control) the same amount of income the same since they both face the same options and choices. They have complete control over the disposition of their earned income: they can share it with whomever they wish, enter into whatever type of personal relationship they wish, or consume it in whatever way they wish. The personal decisions they make should not affect the tax they pay. Individual-unit taxation thus rests upon a fundamental ethical judgement about the autonomy of individuals and a respect for the personal decisions they make. Among other things, a tax system based upon the individual unit treats all living arrangements and personal relationships neutrally – it does not seek to favour some arrangements or relationships over others.

Second, individual-unit taxation rests upon the moral judgement that it is fair to tax individuals on income they earn since one important purpose of the income tax is to achieve a more socially acceptable distribution of income and wealth than that which results solely from market forces. The fact that the present income tax rate structure is progressive is an indication that the government intends the tax system to be used to redistribute income. The moral case for redistributing the economic and social power of income is much stronger than the moral case for redistributing the market value of the personal goods and services an individual consumes.

Effect of Family-Unit Taxation on the Role of Individuals in Personal Relationships

There is another reason for retaining the individual as the basic unit of taxation. Laws relating to personal relationships should not only ensure that members of that relationship are treated fairly in relation to other individuals, but they should also not affect the nature of the relationship or the personal choices of members of that relationship. Using the individual as the basic tax unit results in the tax system being neutral as to the types of relationships individuals form and the roles they assume within them. Family-unit taxation, by contrast, is likely to influence the decisions made by members of the family; most significantly, it might encourage the member of the family with the least attachment to the paid labour force to work inside the home and become economically dependent upon the other member. The member of the family with the least attachment to the paid labour force is frequently referred to as the secondary earner. In deciding whether to work outside the home, secondary earners are more sensitive than primary earners to marginal after-tax wage rates. Secondary earners often have less attachment to the paid labour force because they cannot earn as much as primary earners in the paid work force or because they have specialized skills to bring to work at household production.

The bias that family-unit taxation introduces into the tax system in favour of unpaid work in the home arises primarily because of the "stacking" effect under family-unit taxation. Under the present individual-based income tax, when secondary earners in a family enter the paid work force at least $7,400 of their earnings are completely sheltered from tax by the basic personal income tax credit. The next approximately $23,300 of earnings is taxed at the lowest marginal tax rate. However, under family-unit taxation, all of the secondary earner's income would be taxed at the rate applicable to one-half of the primary-earner's income since the aggregate income of the members is split equally for tax purposes. Thus even the first dollar the secondary earner earns might be taxed at the highest marginal tax rate. This higher rate of tax might have the effect of discouraging the secondary earner from entering the paid work force even though that is his or her preferred choice.

Attempting to ensure that, to the greatest extent possible, the tax system does not bias the members of a family to work in the home is particularly important because, even with individual-unit taxation, generally the tax system discriminates against the members of a two-earner family. This discrimination occurs for a number of reasons. First, the value of household production, which can be substantial, is not taxed. Under the control theory of income, it is clear that the value of the work of the family member who works at household production should not be taxed; however, in designing the tax system the behaviour effect of not taxing the value of this labour should not be ignored. It results in pressure on the secondary earner to contribute to the family economy by engaging in household production instead of paid work. Second, when both members of the family work outside the home they incur all sorts of costs associated with earning the extra income that are not deductible – including expenses for additional clothing, transportation, household services and meal preparation. Because of these and other aspects of the tax system,[118] one-earner families with children often have more consumable income after taxes and work-related expenditures than two-earner families with the same income do even under a system of individual taxation.

The bias of family-unit taxation against paid employment by the secondary earner in the family is particularly serious since in the majority of families the secondary earner is a woman. Women still generally earn less than men in the paid work force as a result of gender stereotyping and are often more skilled at household production. Thus the bias hinders the achievement of gender equity.

Administrative Considerations

In addition to being more equitable and neutral with regard to different types of relationships and the role played by partners in a relationship, individual-unit taxation is much simpler to administer than family-unit taxation and provides greater protection for the privacy and autonomy of the partners. Any form of family-unit taxation would require an acceptable definition of a "family unit". Since the objective of family-unit taxation presumably would be to tax individuals on income they had benefited from, this would require a definition that embraced as many sharing relationships as possible. This would impose an enormously complicated and intrusive, if not impossible, task on the tax administration. Like all relationship-neutral laws, individual-unit taxation greatly reduces administrative costs and the complexity of legal provision and provides individuals with genuinely free choice in creating their own intimate relationships.

In summary, our tax system is and should continue to be premised on the individual as the basic unit of taxation. Family-based taxation is not consistent with the control theory underlying Canada's income tax, nor is it consistent with the empirical evidence demonstrating the unpredictable degree of income sharing in families. Individual taxation is consistent with the control theory and has the advantages of administrative simplicity and neutrality regarding personal relationships.

Recommendation 19

> The individual, rather than the conjugal couple or some other definition of the family unit, should remain the basis for the calculation of Canada's personal income tax.

We will now turn our attention to an analysis of specific provisions of the Act.

C. Specific Tax Provisions That Rely Upon Relational Status

The *Income Tax Act* contains a bewildering variety of provisions that refer to the personal relationships of the individual taxpayer. For example, there are over 200 provisions in the *Act* and the regulations to the *Act* that contain references to the phrase (or variations of it) "spouse and common-law partner". The Act contains over 500 references to the concept of "related person," which includes, basically, all persons related by blood or adoption to the taxpayer and their spouses and common-law partners.[119] These provisions are so diverse that it is difficult to generalize about the reasons why relational status is used in many of them.[120] We have chosen a number of provisions that raise representative issues for analysis.

Dependent Relative Tax Credits

Credits are available to taxpayers with relatives (other than spouses or partners) who are dependent by reason of age or disability. A taxpayer who cannot claim the spousal and common-law partner tax credit, reviewed in the next section, and who lives with and supports a "wholly dependent" child, parent, grandparent or "infirm" relative, can claim the "equivalent to married" or "wholly dependent person" credit.[121] A taxpayer who lives with an elderly or "infirm" dependent adult relative can claim the "caregiver credit".[122] A taxpayer can claim the "infirm dependants' credit" for each adult relative dependent on him or her by reason of "infirmity".[123]

Like the spouse and common-law partner tax credit, these credits may be pursuing technical tax objectives and tax expenditure objectives. The technical tax justification is that taxpayers with dependent spouses or relatives are assumed to have a reduced ability to pay tax if a portion of their income is spent on the support of dependants. The tax expenditure objective is to provide income support to families supporting and caring for relatives unable to support themselves.

Friends and family members frequently provide support to children, older adults or persons with disabilities out of a sense of moral obligation. Therefore, persons who support others who are unable to support themselves can be argued to have a reduced ability to pay; this is the technical tax justification. As for the tax expenditure objective, the state ought to recognize the social value, and alleviate the burden, of providing economic and social support to persons who are unable to support themselves by reason of age, illness or disability.[124] It could be said that the credit pursues a legitimate objective and that relationships are relevant to this objective.

Turning to our third question, rather than setting out a list of qualifying dependent relatives, could the *Income Tax Act* be revised to enable taxpayers to identify the dependency relationships that have given rise to a reduced ability to pay? Self-selection is built into the system to some degree since taxpayers have to claim the credits. But relying solely on self-selection of qualifying dependency relationships may not be feasible since the potential for abuse is too great.

Since dependency relationships do matter, and public policy requires that the law set out which dependency relationships entitle taxpayers to claim the credit, our last question asks whether the *Income Tax Act* could be revised to more accurately capture the relevant range of dependency relationships. We believe it could. There is no justification for limiting entitlement to these credits to persons with dependants who are relatives, or to dependants with whom a taxpayer lives. Taxpayers who support dependants – whether related or not, whether living in the same household or not, whether wholly or partially dependent – should be entitled to claim the tax credits because the provision of support itself reduces the resources they have available to meet their tax obligations. The credit should be available to taxpayers who have provided financial support or unpaid caregiving to a person who is dependent by reason of age, disability or illness. The caregiver credit should be delivered to the person who has actually provided the care. Consideration should be given to making the dependant's credits refundable. At the moment, since they are non-refundable credits, they are of no assistance to persons who have provided financial support or unpaid caregiving to dependants but who lack sufficient taxable income to benefit from the credits. Refundable tax credits would better accomplish the objective of providing income support to persons who have made substantial financial sacrifices by providing unpaid care to dependants.[125] Even better would be to deliver income support to caregivers in the form of direct grants delivered outside the tax system – direct grants are more efficient than tax credits in reaching persons in need. Some persons with very low incomes do not complete tax returns and thus may unwittingly miss out on refundable tax credits to which they are entitled.

Recommendation 20

Parliament should extend the tax credits for dependent relatives so that they can be claimed by any taxpayer who has provided financial or caregiving support to a person who is dependent by reason of age, disability or illness, without reference to relationship status. Consideration should be given to extending income assistance to caregivers by making the dependants' credits refundable or by delivering direct grants outside of the tax system.

Consideration should also be given to providing tax credits directly to individuals with disabilities to allow them to exercise choice in obtaining the assistance that they need. Adults with disabilities tend to be poor, on fixed incomes (estimates are that about 30 percent of adults on social assistance have disabilities) and without secure attachment to the labour force.[126] Under the current law, the tax credits for dependent relatives do not flow directly to the benefit of persons with disabilities who are in need: persons who are living with or supporting a dependent relative can claim the credits. Those in need of care should have a say in who cares for them and should not have to rely on family members who may be able to take advantage of the tax credit for caregiving. Income support, by way of direct grants or refundable tax credits, should be provided to persons with disabilities who need assistance to allow them more control over key decisions in their lives and more choice in the caregiving that they need.

Recommendation 21

Parliament should consider providing income support, by way of direct grants or refundable tax credits, to persons with disabilities to enable them to hire or purchase the supports they require.

Spouse and Common-Law Partner Tax Credit

One of the most anomalous tax provisions that depends upon a relational status is the tax credit that was formerly referred to as the "married status" credit but that now may be more accurately referred to as the "spouse and common-law partner" credit.[127] Taxpayers who support a spouse or common-law partner are entitled, in addition to their personal tax credit of $1,186 (in 2000), to a tax credit of $1,007.[128] The value of this credit is reduced by 16 percent of the spouse or common-law partner's income for the year in excess of $629. Thus the credit is reduced to zero if the spouse or common-law partner's income exceeds $6,923. The cost of this tax credit to the federal government is substantial – almost $1.4 billion annually.[129]

In its basic design the spouse and common-law partner credit offends against the principle that government should be neutral with respect to the roles assumed within personal relationships. The credit appears to be designed to promote economic dependency in conjugal relationships. Indeed, historically, it has been used explicitly for this purpose. For example, in 1942 the credit's dependency requirement and the income limit on the dependent spouse were repealed so that husbands could claim the credit even though their wives were working in the paid labour force. This amendment was intended to encourage women to contribute to the war effort by taking up work in factories. After the war, the dependency requirement and the income limit were reinstated. The obvious purpose of reinstating these requirements was to encourage married women to return to unpaid labour in the home and make more paid jobs in factories available for soldiers returning from the war. [130]

> Taking account of taxpayers' conjugal relationships in determining their tax liability reduces the effectiveness of the tax system in achieving an appropriate distribution of society's resources, misperceives the nature of tax law, leads to serious horizontal inequities, hinders the achievement of gender equity, complicates the tax system, intrudes into the privacy of intimate relationships, and furthers male dominance in the private realm.
>
> Neil Brooks, "The Irrelevance of Conjugal Relationships In Assessing Tax Liability" in Richard Krever and John Head, eds., *Tax Units and the Tax Rates Scale* (Melbourne: Australian Tax Research Foundation, 1996) at 36.

This tax provision does not satisfy the first criteria of our four-step methodology – it is a law that employs relational terms but does not serve a legitimate government objective – and should, therefore, be repealed. The spouse and common-law partner credit is sometimes justified as a technical tax measure and sometimes justified as a social policy measure. As a technical tax provision, it is justified on the grounds that an individual who undertakes to support another has less ability to pay and, therefore, should be entitled to a tax reduction. As a social policy measure, it is justified on the grounds that the dependent spouse or common-law partner likely is providing care-giving services and, therefore, the members of the relationship should be entitled to some form of income support. We do not find either of these justifications conclusive, for the reasons that follow.

Technical Tax Policy Justification

In assessing the equity of the credit, it might also be noted that it is claimed disproportionately by relatively well-off individuals. This should not be surprising. Generally, middle- and high-income individuals are more able to afford to support an economically dependent spouse. An argument can be made that individuals who enter into relationships in which they choose to support other individuals capable of supporting themselves do not have reduced ability to pay, as this term is understood in tax policy analysis.[131] Individuals enter into personal relationships with others capable of supporting themselves, presumably because they think such relationships will increase their well-being. Therefore, the resulting costs of those relationships should not be assumed to affect their ability to pay. Moreover, in relationships in which one partner works full-time at household production, that partner presumably provides substantial personal benefits to the partner working in the paid labour force. The credit appears to be based upon the assumption that the work of the partner in the home is unproductive or provides no personal benefits to the other partner. In fact, in many cases the valuable household services performed by the partner in the home will likely exceed the cost of supporting him or her. Far from reducing the ability to pay of the partner working in the paid working force, supporting a partner who works in the home will often increase the working partner's ability to pay because it will substantially reduce the services they will have to purchase in the marketplace.

> In most cases the wife who works at home as a housekeeper, far from being a
> dependant, performs essential services worth at least as much to her as to her
> husband as the cost of food, shelter and clothing that he provides for her.
>
> Royal Commission on the Status of Women in Canada
> (Ottawa: Information Canada, 1970) at 293-94.

As a tax measure, the credit can also be criticized for not being neutral because it may affect the choices made by those who enter into personal relationships. The credit provides an incentive for one spouse or common-law partner to remain economically dependent on the other. Under the general rules of the *Income Tax Act*, an individual can earn up to $7,400 and pay no tax since the tax owing on this amount will be completely offset by the personal tax credit. However, if a spouse working in the paid labour force is claiming the spouse credit, every dollar the dependent spouse earns over $629 will be taxed, in effect, because the working spouse's tax credit will be diminished. Although the effect of the loss of this credit on the work choices of the dependent spouse may not be significant, it might act as a disincentive for a dependent spouse to enter the paid labour force, especially for part-time work. Again, as reviewed earlier, laws and government policy should seek to minimize the effects on the decisions made, or the roles assumed, by those who enter into personal relationships.

Tax Expenditure Justification

The spousal credit is sometimes justified, not as a measure designed to increase the equity or neutrality of the tax system, but on the grounds that it provides income support to those families in which one spouse is looking after children in the home or acting as a caregiver for elderly parents. Providing support and recognition of the social value of these kinds of unpaid caregiving work is an important government objective. However, if this is its justification, the credit is over-inclusive. Over one-half of the spouses who receive the credit are not supporting children.[132] It is impossible to determine in how many of these cases the dependent spouse is providing care to individuals other than children. Importantly, if it is intended as an allowance for caregivers, it is being given to the wrong person. The spouse in the labour force receives the credit. If it is intended to be a care-giving allowance it should be given directly to either the caregiver or to those in need of care so that they can reimburse their caregivers directly.

Tax provisions of this kind have been repealed in most countries. Most recently, in the United Kingdom a tax allowance analogous to the spouse and common-law partner credit was increasingly limited over the past decade and in 2000 was abolished altogether except for those married couples over the age of 65 at the time the repeal was announced. The revenue from the abolition of the allowance was used to fund a new children's tax credit.[133]

Dependency provisions should be eliminated. These provisions undermine the important contribution that women working in the home make to the economy. Equally important, they raise the costs of entering the work force, thereby distorting their choices and undermining their autonomy.

Maureen Maloney, "What Is the Appropriate Tax Unit for the 1990s and Beyond?" in *Issues in the Taxation of Individuals*, Allan Maslove, ed. (Toronto: University of Toronto Press, 1994) at 146.

Because its primary objective appears to be to promote dependency in personal relationships, the spouse and common-law partner credit should be repealed. To further the important government objective that is served so imperfectly by the credit, the saved revenue could be used in a program that directly targets caregivers and children. There are many ways this could be done. For example, the Canadian Child Tax Benefit could be enriched and converted to a direct income supplement for families delivered outside the tax system.[134] The Canada Pension Plan "child-rearing drop out" provisions, which currently permit the years devoted to care of a child under the age of seven to be ignored in calculating pension entitlements based on average annual earnings, could be extended to allow years devoted to other caregiving responsibilities, such as caring for the elderly or those with disabilities, to be "dropped out" as well.[135]

Recommendation 22

Parliament should replace the *Income Tax Act*'s spouse and common-law partner tax credit with enhanced or new programs that more carefully target caregivers and children for direct income support.

Goods and Services Tax Credit

<u>General</u>

The Goods and Services Tax (GST) is a 7 percent flat-rate consumption tax levied by the federal government. This tax consumes a larger percentage of the income of low-income individuals than high-income individuals, since low-income individuals necessarily must consume all their income while high-income individuals are able to save a portion of their income. Because of this fact, the federal government enacted a refundable sales tax credit to provide a compensating income transfer to low-income individuals.[136] The basic credit amount is $205; however, if individuals have earned income they might be entitled to an additional credit of $107.[137] Thus, ignoring the additional credit for children, the total credit available to an individual is $312. To target this credit primarily at low-income individuals, the credit is phased out by five percent of the individual's "adjusted income" over the threshold amount of $26,284.[138] When an individual's adjusted income is $41,884 he or she will lose all entitlement to the credit.

This tax credit serves a legitimate government objective: to reduce the effect of a regressive tax on low-income individuals. Our concern is with two design features of the credit that take into account individuals' personal relationships to determine their ability to claim the credit. One way in which an individual's personal relationships might affect eligibility for the credit is that an individual cohabiting with a spouse or common-law partner is entitled only to the basic credit of $205. A cohabiting individual is not entitled to the $107 additional credit. Thus, two individuals living apart might be entitled to total GST tax credits of $624 ($312 each), but if they marry or become common-law partners, the maximum amount of their entitlement will be only $410. The GST credit is reduced for cohabiting spouses and common-law partners since it is assumed that by living together in such a relationship the individuals will realize economies in household production and consumption that will result in a higher standard of living for each.

The second way in which an individual's entitlement to the GST credit might be affected if he or she is cohabiting with a spouse or common-law partner is that an individual's "adjusted income" – which, if it exceeds the threshold amount of $26,284, results in the GST credit being phased out – is the combined income of the individual and his or her spouse or common-law partner. Thus, to take the extreme example, if two individuals each with incomes of $25,000 become common-law partners, they will lose GST credits worth $624.

Although the amount of the GST credit is modest compared to other government programs, it raises two fundamental issues about government regulation of, and support for, personal relationships that arise in a number of different policy contexts. First, when, if ever, should governments attempt to account for the economies in household production and consumption that might be realized by individuals living with others with whom they have close personal relationships? Second, if a government program is targeted at low-income individuals, when, if ever, should the program be designed so that the income of persons with whom an individual has a close relationship is considered in determining that individual's entitlement to the benefits provided by the program?

> I am a woman of 59 and my husband is 75. We do not live together. We live approximately 100 km from each other. At our ages we do not want to go through the stress and expense of a divorce. I received a notice from Revenue Canada that I was not eligible for the GST rebate, which I already knew, because of my salary. What upset me is the reason why I was not eligible and neither was my husband. The reason stated when I called, was that we were married, therefore the combined salary and pension did not permit us to collect the GST rebate. I proceeded to explain that we do not live together, as a matter of fact, we do not live in the same city. I was told to get a divorce.
>
> *Law Commission of Canada Comments Board, website,*
> *June 2000 – January 2001, posted with permission.*

We are of the view that, given the purpose of the GST credit, an individual's personal relationships should not be relevant in determining his or her entitlement to the credit. The credit should be redesigned so that it operates purely on an individual basis. The amount of the tax credit individuals receive should not be reduced when they marry or cohabit in a conjugal relationship. Moreover, the credit should be phased out solely on the basis of the income of an individual and not on the combined income of that individual and his or her spouse or common-law partner. Our analysis leads to the same conclusions regarding other federal income-tested benefits, such as the child tax benefit, the medical expense credit and the guaranteed income supplement.

<u>Taking Account of Economies in Household Production and Consumption</u>

In addition to the GST credit, under a number of government programs, such as the guaranteed income supplement, the amount to which an individual is entitled is automatically reduced if he or she cohabits with another in a conjugal relationship. This reduction is not a result of the application of income testing; it is based on an assumption that the combined needs of two individuals are reduced if they marry or form a conjugal relationship. The GST credit received by each member of a cohabiting couple is reduced to about 65 percent of the amount that would be received by them as individuals. A rule that reduces a transfer payment when two individuals marry or live together in a conjugal relationship can only be defended on the assumption that adults living conjugally generally achieve a measurable reduction in the cost of living not achieved in other living arrangements. However, there are a number of reasons for doubting whether reducing benefits when individuals marry or cohabit in a conjugal relationship can increase the equity of the program.

First, the validity of the factual assumption that there are consumption economies when two individuals cohabit in a conjugal relationship is at best questionable. To be sure, there are a number of potential sources of cost savings when individuals in a personal relationship cohabit: they might be able to realize savings by sharing living accommodations and durable consumer assets such as dishwashers and televisions, by buying goods in volume at a discount, by combining household chores and by developing specialized skills and thus performing household chores more efficiently. Even the listing of these potential sources of cost savings reveals that attempting to determine standards of living by reference to the relationships of individuals is fraught with uncertainties. For example, some individuals who enter into personal relationships might have been living with others, such as parents or roommates, before the relationship. For these individuals, cohabiting with another individual in a conjugal relationship might result in a loss of consumption economies. For other individuals, cohabiting with someone in a conjugal relationship might involve moving out of a single-bedroom apartment and into a two-bedroom apartment or even a house. For these individuals, consumption economies are likely to be small or nonexistent.

Even if individuals who cohabit with others need fewer resources than people living alone to reach the same level of economic welfare, why should the economies that might be realized when two individuals live together be treated any differently than the economies that an individual might realize by buying goods in bulk, sharing consumer durables or car pooling, for example? Individuals are free to form together to do their shopping, share ownership of consumer durables and generally to join with others in multi-faceted ways to take advantage of economies of scale in the household production and consumption process. It is not necessary to enter into a conjugal relationship in order to reduce living costs. The tax and transfer system should not penalize individuals who are able to achieve economies in the production or consumption of personal goods and services.

Finally, even if consumption economies exist when individuals live together and share resources, and even if one takes the view that they should be taken into account in government transfers, conjugal cohabitation has become an increasingly poor proxy for the identification of such economies. The current rules, which reduce the level of benefits for spouses and conjugal cohabitants but not for others sharing accommodation, have been characterized as imposing an unfair "tax on marriage" or "tax on conjugal cohabitation".[139] Close to 40 percent of adults do not have a conjugal relationship,[140] but most share accommodation with others.[141] The current design of the GST credit (and other federal income security programs) entitles non-conjugal co-residents to retain the advantages of any economies they achieve through shared living arrangements. Taking back these advantages from married persons and common-law partners, but not others, amounts to discrimination on the basis of marital status.

This inequity could be eliminated if we could identify all relationships in shared households in which the individuals are realizing consumption and production economies. However, it is hard to imagine how such a rule could be equitably enforced. In the past, it was acceptable for the state to focus its definition of interdependent adult relationships on households headed by married couples. Marriage provided an administratively convenient bright-line test for determining when adults were living together in interdependent relationships. But now it is no longer acceptable for the state to ignore the fact that adults share households for a variety of reasons in a variety of relationships. It has become increasingly common for conjugal couples to cohabit outside of marriage; for young adults to live at home with their parents for extended periods of time; for older persons or adults with disabilities to live together in mutually supportive relationships; for parents and other members of extended families to share accommodation with their adult children; for students and young adults to form roommate groups; and for older individuals to live in institutional arrangements that allow for economies in the production and consumption of household goods and services.

The state has had to leave behind its reliance on a bright-line marriage test. Now unmarried couples, provided they have a conjugal relationship, are presumed to have realized household economies after a year of cohabitation. However, conjugality is a poor means of isolating relationships that are likely to give rise to household economies. Living arrangements have simply become too diverse to permit accurate generalizations about the savings generated in any particular form of relationship.

Is it possible to devise a rule that moves beyond the use of conjugality (or any other relational attribute) as a proxy for household economies? What if, for example, every individual who shares living space and expenses with another adult received reduced benefits compared to persons living alone? In theory, such a rule could do a better job of identifying relationships that give rise to household economies than the current rule based on conjugality. However, the enforcement of such a rule would have to be either highly arbitrary or would have to vest an unacceptably high degree of discretion in administrative officials. It is not obvious what should count as a separate dwelling or what amounts to sharing. It is impossible to imagine a rule that would be reasonably objective and at the same time would not produce a significant number of very incongruous results.

For all these reasons, the technical tax system wisely ignores personal bargains and economies in determining an individual's ability to pay, and the income support system should do the same in determining an individual's standard of living. For some individuals, a rule that reduces benefits on the expectation that economies will be realized when they cohabit with another might have the effect of discouraging the formation of relationships. More generally, for the same reason the law should be neutral with respect to the relationships individuals form, how individuals choose to live should be regarded as their own business. Certainly, the tax and transfer system should not encourage or expect, for example, that one individual in a relationship should specialize in domestic work and the other paid work in order to realize economies in the production of household goods and services, particularly since prevailing social norms continue to suggest that women should do most of the work in the home. The inequities that arise when the state presumes that economies arise in some kinds of relationships but not others, and the administrative difficulties of identifying all sharing relationships between co-residents, support the conclusion that relationships should not be used as a proxy for reduced needs in the design of income security programs.

Recommendation 23

Income security programs should not assume that consumption and production economies always arise in conjugal relationships and never in other relationships. Parliament should amend the *Income Tax Act* so that the amount of the Goods and Services Tax credit to which individuals are entitled is not reduced if they are married or cohabiting in a conjugal relationship.

Phasing Out the GST Credit Based on Family Income

The GST credit is an income-tested benefit. For individuals who are neither married nor living with a common-law partner, entitlement to and the amount of the credit is determined by individual income alone. If an individual has a spouse or common-law partner, entitlement to and the amount of the credit are determined by the combined income of the individual and his or her spouse or common-law partner. The credit is reduced by 5 percent of the amount by which their combined income exceeds the income threshold of $26,284. Indeed, when an individual enters into a marriage or common-law partnership, the partners do not continue to receive the credit separately as individuals; instead, one of the partners must claim the combined credit to which both are entitled.

Phase-outs are common in transfer programs that the government wishes to deliver only to low-income individuals. The most significant, of course, are the phase-outs contained in the various social assistance programs administered by provincial governments. The largest direct federal government program that is phased out or income-tested is the Guaranteed Income Supplement (GIS) available to older persons pursuant to the *Old Age Security Act*. The *Income Tax Act* contains three income-tested programs: the GST credit, the child tax benefit and the refundable medical expense credit for taxpayers eligible for the mental and physical impairment credit. An important issue that arises in the design of these income-tested programs is when, if ever, the income of a person with whom an individual has a close personal relationship should be considered in determining whether that individual is entitled to benefits and, if so, in what amount. Should entitlement to benefits be determined by individual income alone? Or should it be based on some notion of family or household income?

At the moment, federal programs give contradictory answers to this crucial design issue. Old age security benefits available to all Canadians over the age of 65 are currently taxed back from high-income individuals. Calculation of the "clawback" is made on the basis of individual income alone. The income of family members is not considered.[142] However, the guaranteed income supplement and the three income-tested programs in the *Income Tax Act* (the GST credit, the child tax benefit and the refundable medical expense supplement) are all phased out based upon the combined income of the eligible individual and his or her spouse or common-law partner.[143]

To achieve its purposes of allocating the cost of taxes fairly and redistributing income earned in the marketplace, the liability for income tax is based upon the individual's control of the source of income rather than on the consumption of income. Therefore, it must necessarily be based upon the individual. By contrast, these transfer payments are, by and large, intended to provide income support for people in need. Therefore, in judging their need it makes sense to look at the income that they benefit from, or the resources that are available for their personal consumption, instead of just the income they earn or control. That is to say, it is not inconsistent for a control-based tax system to be based on individuals, while a needs-based income support program would combine the income of individuals who live together in interdependent relationships. Moreover, basing transfer payments on the combined income of a conjugal couple does not imply full sharing of their resources. It only implies that a low-income earning spouse or common-law partner is not likely to be in need if his or her spouse or common-law partner has adequate income and if they are sharing basic living expenses such as accommodation, food and clothing expenses.

However, there are a number of persuasive reasons why the GST credit and other federal income security programs should rely on individual rather than family income to determine entitlement to benefits. First, the use of the combined income of conjugal couples in determining eligibility for income-tested benefits creates troubling disincentives. For two individuals with a close personal relationship it can act as a substantial cost to cohabiting. As noted above, if two individuals each earning $25,000 marry or cohabit in a conjugal relationship for a year, they will lose GST credits worth $624. In addition to appearing unfair, this might discourage the development of their relationship, particularly when considered along with the loss of other income-tested benefits such as the child tax benefit or the guaranteed income supplement. Even if the negative effects on family formation are modest, penalties on low-income individuals for entering into and maintaining a relationship should be reduced wherever possible.

In addition to avoiding the disincentive to family formation created by family income tests, an individual income test promotes autonomy and gender equality. Reducing women's economic dependence on their family relationships has been a key component of the strides towards greater gender equality that our society has achieved. By providing economic security to individuals within families, the state is supporting and promoting the formation and maintenance of positive family relationships. If individuals are not reliant on family members for basic income security, the likelihood is increased that family relationships will be based on choice rather than economic necessity. A family income test, on the other hand, compels economic dependence. Government policy would be more respectful of autonomy and gender equality if it neither assumed nor encouraged economic interdependence in personal relationships.

> The Canadian tax system at present privileges some family responsibilities and ignores others. For example, eligibility for child tax benefit is supposedly based on 'family income' But this 'family income' ignores much that may be relevant, for example, income brought into the family by grandparents or older children, …and child support received. It assumes couples share all their income when many do not, because of obligations to children from previous marriages, because work requires couples to live apart for periods of time, or simply because of personal choice. Avoiding tests based on family income removes this incoherence.
>
> Frances Woolley, "For a Radical Redesign of our Tax Treatment of the Family"
> *Policy Options*, (September 1998) 7 at 9.

Another reason for preferring individual income tests is that defining family for the purposes of a family income test raises intractable problems. Marriage once served as a bright-line test for identifying family relationships of concern to the state. Currently, the GST credit and other federal income support programs take into account the combined income of spouses and common-law partners. The income of non-conjugal co-residents is ignored. The use of conjugality as a proxy for sharing relationships is problematic. The line between conjugal and non-conjugal relationships is not a bright one; it is, rather, an increasingly blurry and contested distinction. Moreover, conjugality as a proxy for sharing is obviously both over-inclusive and under-inclusive. It is over-inclusive because there is often less than full sharing in conjugal relationships. It is under-inclusive because adults live together in a wide variety of non-conjugal relationships that involve sharing. Why should an assumption of mutual benefit from each other's income be limited to conjugal couples? The current form of the family income test creates inequities between individuals depending on whether their ties to a household are based on conjugal or non-conjugal relationships.

Consider the situation of a wealthy individual whose parents or adult children live with him. They are entitled to claim the GST credit or other federal income-tested benefits on the basis of their individual income alone. Only the individual's wife (or common-law partner) is disentitled on the grounds that she benefits from his income. By imposing financial disadvantages on conjugal living that are not imposed on persons sharing households as a result of non-conjugal ties, the current family income test discriminates on the basis of marital status.[144]

In theory, the inequities created by the reliance on conjugality could be avoided if eligibility for the GST credit was determined by combining the income of all persons living in a common household where the benefits of income are shared. But as we argued above in the discussion of the economies flowing from shared living, the identification of all such households would be too complex, costly and intrusive to administer.

The main argument in support of using a family income test to determine entitlement to the GST credit (and other income-tested benefits) is that it is most consistent with the objective of targeting benefits according to need. Since persons living together in close relationships normally do benefit from each other's income, it follows that benefits are more closely targeted according to need if entitlement is based on family income. An individual income test produces inequities by ignoring differences in individuals' actual standards of living that result from their differing family situations. The scenario of the "wealthy banker's wife" is often used to illustrate these points. She is a homemaker and he is a bank executive with a high income. Homemakers in this situation may have no income of their own and may have limited access to and control over their spouses' income and assets. Nevertheless, they will likely enjoy a home, food, clothes, vacations and other benefits made possible by the breadwinners' income.[145] Therefore, the situation of the wealthy banker's wife is not comparable to that of low-income persons living on their own with no family support. Yet an individual income test would treat her as if she were destitute.[146]

Another reason why governments might find family income tests attractive is that they reduce the costs of income security programs. Indeed, the broader the definition of family used for the purposes of calculating family-based income entitlements, the more the state is relieved of the costs of providing basic income support to individuals. It is likely that fiscal concerns are a significant part of the explanation for the current popularity of targeting benefits on the basis of the income of conjugal couples. A shift to individual income testing will entail additional program costs unless income cut-offs are lowered or benefit levels reduced. For this reason, governments will not be interested in adopting individual income testing in the absence of compelling justifications. We believe that the arguments we have outlined above do set out compelling reasons for consistently favouring individual income testing. Family income testing creates troubling disincentives, compromises women's equality and autonomy in their personal relationships, and gives rise to intractable problems of family definition. Parliament should explore the cost implications of implementing individual income testing on a consistent basis, and amend its laws as soon as resources permit.[147]

The respective weaknesses of family and individual income testing in effectively targeting need could be overcome, in theory, if eligibility was based not on relational presumptions, but on a full accounting of an individual's financial means and needs, including his or her contributions received from a variety of sources. This kind of means testing is employed in the administration of provincial social assistance schemes. However promising means testing may be in theory, targeting benefits to actual rather than presumed needs, it leads to extremely complex and intrusive systems of implementation. It would require the reporting and investigation of a whole host of matters that are not part of the administration of income taxation. A major advantage of income testing, on the other hand, is that it is relatively easy to administer and much less intrusive than means testing:

> Income-tested programs have their own unique advantages. They are seen to be objective, administratively simple and non-stigmatizing. Eligibility can be established easily through the income tax form. There are no decisions made on the basis of detailed assessment of personal circumstances. There is little or no contact between recipients and government officials. Once eligibility is established, payment can be triggered automatically by computer. Benefits can be delivered on a consistent and equitable basis throughout the country.[148]

For this reason, income testing rather than means testing should remain the basis on which entitlement is determined in federal income security programs. The question is whether to rely on individual income or some definition of family income. While both imperfectly accomplish the objective of targeting benefits according to need, we have argued that there are a number of persuasive reasons for preferring individual income testing. Individual income testing promotes the values of gender equality and autonomy. It avoids the disincentive to the formation and maintenance of family relationships that can result from family income testing. It also avoids the intractable definitional problems that plague family income testing, currently manifest in the uncertain and unprincipled distinction between conjugal and non-conjugal relationships. Finally, individual income testing is by far the simplest and least intrusive approach to administer.[149]

Recommendation 24

Income security programs should not assume that the benefits of individual income are always shared with others in conjugal relationships, and that sharing never occurs in other relationships. Parliament should amend the *Income Tax Act* so that the amount of the Goods and Services Tax credit (and other income-tested benefits) to which individuals are entitled is determined by reference to individual income without reference to the income of spouses, common-law partners or other cohabitants.

Transfers of Property Between Individuals in a Close Personal Relationship

Normally, for tax purposes, when capital property is transferred from one individual to another, either by way of a gift or bequest, the individual transferring the property is deemed to have disposed of the property for proceeds equal to its fair market value. Consequently, if the fair market value of the property at the time of transfer exceeds the amount the transferor paid for it, the transferor will have to include 50 percent of the resulting capital gain in income for tax purposes. A significant exception is made to this rule for property transferred between spouses or common-law partners (or former spouses or former common-law partners of the taxpayer in settlement of rights arising from their marriage or common-law partnership). The *Income Tax Act* provides a "rollover" for these transfers. Whether the transfer is made by way of gift[150] or bequest,[151] basically, unless the transferor elects not to have the rollover rule apply, the transferor spouse or common-law partner is deemed to have disposed of the property for proceeds equal to the cost of the property, and the transferee spouse or common-law partner is deemed to have acquired the property for this amount. Consequently, any capital gain accrued on the property will be "rolled over" to the transferee spouse or common-law partner and only be included in income for tax purposes when the transferee spouse or common-law partner disposes of the property.

What is the justification for permitting capital properties to be transferred between spouses or common-law partners on a tax-free basis, thereby deferring any tax liability? Like many of the special provisions in the *Income Tax Act*, this provision for spouses and common-law partners has been justified on both technical tax policy and tax expenditure grounds.

Technical Tax Justifications

A series of largely administrative considerations explain the "rollover". First, two individuals who are living together in a close personal relationship are often indifferent as to who acquires the legal title to property. They both consider that they have equal beneficial title to all property acquired by one or the other. Consequently, legal transfers between the partners often do not result in a change in the beneficial ownership of the property. Second, in many relationships it would often be difficult, if not impossible, to determine whose funds were used to acquire particular items of property. Providing a rollover for transfers between these two individuals recognizes this degree of economic mutuality and eliminates what would be a serious tracing problem. Third, often transactions between individuals in a close personal relationship take place informally, with neither party realizing there might be tax consequences. By not making such transfers taxable events, the tax administration does not have to embark on the impossible task of tracing all such transactions to ensure that any tax owing was paid.[152] Fourth, if tax was due when transfers of property took place between spouses and common-law partners, the property would have to be valued and the cash raised to pay the tax. The problem is that transactions between spouses and common-law partners do not take place in the open market, and this fact presents a liquidity problem. There may be no funds with which to pay the taxes owing as a result of the disposition of the property.[153]

Tax Expenditure Justifications

The rollover also serves the social policy objective of encouraging, or at least not discouraging, the redistribution of property within personal relationships.[154] Other social policy objectives served by the rule include facilitating property settlements upon a division of family property on the breakdown of a marital or common-law partnership and simplifying estate planning.

One potential concern with this rollover of tax liability upon the dissolution of a relationship is that it could disadvantage the spouse or common-law partner who acquires property subject to the rollover and who does not account for the large potential tax liability that accompanies the property. But generally there is no reason for believing that assets with a low cost basis will not usually be shared equally between the partners or that the tax consequences of the division of property will not be fully considered. Moreover, although it is possible a property division that fails to take account of future taxes may unfairly disadvantage one partner, an alternative to the rollover is not obvious. A rule that required the cost of all the property divided between the partners to be allocated among the properties would be impossible to administer.

The rollover is available not only to outright transfers of property between partners, but also to transfers to a trust in which the transferee partner has a beneficial interest provided certain conditions are met. These conditions include that the property vest indefeasibly in the trust, that the transferee spouse or common-law partner is entitled to receive all of the income of the trust, and that no person except the transferee spouse or common-law partner may, before the death of this surviving partner, receive or otherwise obtain the use of any income or capital from the trust.[155]

<u>Extending the Rollover to Non-Conjugal Cohabitants</u>

In our view, the technical tax justifications for the capital property "rollover" provisions reflect the realities of the relationships that exist between most spouses and common-law partners. Taxing the transfers of capital property within conjugal relationships would be too costly and intrusive to administer. The rollover provision justifiably reduces the intrusiveness of the tax system in the lives of those with close personal relationships. Similarly, the tax expenditure goal of encouraging the redistribution of property within conjugal relationships is a valid state objective, although it suggests that the rollover should apply only to outright transfers of property. Given that it is pursuing valid technical tax objectives and a valid tax expenditure objective, the rollover should be retained.

Relationships are obviously relevant to these objectives. The entangled kinds of economic interdependencies that characterize close personal relationships are the very *raison d'être* of the rollover rules. The question is whether marriage and conjugality are the best ways of identifying the close personal relationships to which the rollover provisions should apply. Self-selection of the appropriate range of relationships is obviously not a feasible option. However, turning to our fourth question, can the law be revised to more accurately capture the relevant range of relationships? We believe that it could. The current limitation of the rollover provisions to spouses and common-law partners is over-inclusive (since not all of their relationships will be characterized by high degrees of economic interdependence). More importantly, it is seriously under-inclusive. The technical tax justifications for the rollover rules should apply to any relationship between persons living together in economically interdependent relationships.[156]

Recommendation 25

>   Parliament should amend the *Income Tax Act* so that the provisions that allow capital property to be transferred tax-free between spouses and common-law partners apply to all persons who are living together in economically interdependent relationships.

IX.   The *Old Age Security Act*: Relationships and Old Age Pensions

The *Old Age Security Act*[157] provides a basic pension entitlement to all residents of Canada over the age of 65. Entitlement to the basic old age pension is determined on an individual basis. Relationships are not considered. The universal nature of the entitlement has now been altered by provisions of the *Income Tax Act* that effectively tax back all or part of the old age pension as individual income increases.

Despite the individual nature of the basic old age pension entitlement, two supplemental aspects of the *Old Age Security Act* do rely on relational criteria: the "monthly allowance" and the "guaranteed income supplement" (GIS). Both are attempts to provide additional financial support to older adults since the basic old age pension entitlement is not sufficient to meet subsistence needs.

The GIS is designed to supplement the income of low-income persons over the age of 65 who are receiving the basic old age security benefits. The amount of the GIS benefit depends on the claimant's income, and, regardless of income, there are different benefit rates for conjugal couples and others. For conjugal couples – including married persons and common-law partners – entitlement to benefits is determined by reference to the joint income of the couple. For others, entitlement is based on an individual income test. Moreover, conjugal couples receive a significantly lower benefit than they would if they were living alone or with others in non-conjugal relationships. For example, for the three-month period from July to September 2001, the maximum GIS for a single individual was $518.82, while the maximum benefit for each member of a conjugal couple was $337.94, a difference of 35 percent.

The Monthly Allowance, formerly known as the Spouse's Allowance, is available to low-income persons aged 60 to 64 who are widowed or have a conjugal relationship with a low-income person over the age of 65. In the case of claimants in a conjugal relationship with a pensioner, eligibility and the amount of the benefit is based on an income test that takes into account the combined income of the conjugal couple. Low-income persons aged 60 to 64 who have never married or are separated, divorced or married to a person who has not yet reached age 65 are not eligible for the monthly allowance.

There are three issues raised by the manner in which the GIS and Monthly Allowance provisions take into account personal adult relationships. First, should eligibility for the benefits be determined by an income test that takes into account the combined income of conjugal couples, while, for others, entitlement is based on individual income? Second, should the amount of the benefit be reduced for conjugal couples, but not for others sharing accommodation? Third, is it justifiable to restrict the Monthly Allowance to widows and to spouses or common-law partners of old age pensioners?

The first two issues were raised in our discussion of the GST tax credit.[158] We concluded, first, that the inequities that arise when the state presumes that economies occur in some kinds of relationships but not others, and the administrative difficulties of identifying all sharing relationships between co-residents, support the conclusion that conjugal relationships should not be used as a proxy for reduced needs in the design of income security programs. Second, we concluded that using the combined income of conjugal couples to determine entitlement to benefits should be rejected in favour of an individual income test. Individual income testing promotes the values of gender equality and autonomy.

It avoids the disincentive to the formation and maintenance of family relationships that can result from family income testing. It also avoids the intractable definitional problems that plague family income testing, currently manifest in the uncertain and unprincipled distinction between conjugal and non-conjugal relationships. Finally, individual income testing is by far the simplest and least intrusive approach to administer. These arguments lead to conclusions regarding the *Old Age Security Act* similar to those reached above regarding the GST credit. Removing the penalties imposed on conjugal living would have a significant impact on the cost of these important government programs. The government should explore the cost implications of making these changes to the rules governing entitlement to the GIS and Monthly Allowance and bring forward amendments to the *Old Age Security Act* as soon as resources permit.

Recommendation 26

Income security programs should not assume that consumption and production economies always arise in conjugal relationships and never in other relationships. Parliament should amend the *Old Age Security Act* so that the amount of the Guaranteed Income Supplement or Monthly Allowance is not reduced if a claimant is married or cohabiting in a conjugal relationship.

Recommendation 27

Income security programs should not assume that the benefits of individual income are always shared with others in conjugal relationships and that sharing never occurs in other relationships. Parliament should amend the *Old Age Security Act* so that the amount of the Guaranteed Income Supplement or Monthly Allowance is determined by reference to individual income without reference to the income of spouses, common-law partners or other cohabitants.

Monthly Allowance

The third relational issue raised by the provisions of the Old Age Security Act is whether the restriction of the Monthly Allowance to widows and spouses or common-law partners of pensioners is justifiable. The Allowance is available to low-income persons aged 60 to 64 if they are widowed or have a spouse or common-law partner who is 65 or older. The Act's provision of a guaranteed annual income to old age pensioners is thus extended to persons approaching age 65, but only so long as they are widowed or have a spouse or partner who is a pensioner.

The first task is to clarify the objective of the Monthly Allowance. If the objective is legitimate, we can proceed to asking whether relationships ought to be relevant. Our task is complicated by the fact that the objective of the Monthly

Allowance has not been clearly articulated, and the objectives that have been offered have shifted over time.

When it was enacted in 1975, the Monthly Allowance was presented as a measure designed to enable opposite-sex spouses to retire together. Married women are usually younger than their spouses, and individuals are not eligible for old age security benefits until they reach age 65. At the time, CPP retirement benefits were not payable until age 65 either. A married man who retired at age 65 would be able to claim both OAS and CPP benefits, and perhaps also benefits from an employment pension plan. But if his wife were younger, she would not yet be eligible for basic old age security benefits or the GIS. If she had been in the paid work force, she also would not have been eligible for CPP and might have had to continue working, even though her husband had retired.

The introduction of a special benefit, roughly equivalent to old age security benefits and GIS combined, was intended to alleviate financial hardship for low-income couples, allowing both spouses to "retire" at the same time, even though the younger spouse – generally the wife – had not yet reached age 65.[159] The Honourable Marc Lalonde, who was Minister of Health and Welfare when the Spouse's Allowance was introduced, said "this measure is aimed at the couple which, at present, is expected to live on the pension of one".[160] He had earlier repeated the Liberal promise, made during the 1974 election campaign, that "we will help spouses in cases where both pensioners would be forced to live on one pension".[161]

Since the enactment of the Spouse's Allowance, the need to support early retirement has been attenuated somewhat by changes made in the 1980s to the Quebec Pension Plan and Canada Pension Plan that allowed contributors to choose early retirement and start receiving a reduced benefit at age 60. Take-up rates of the early retirement option were higher than anticipated, and, as a result, claims to the Spouse's Allowance have diminished.[162]

If the objective of the Monthly Allowance is to allow people to retire at an adequate income prior to age 65, then relationships ought not to be relevant. There is no reason why government should support this option for widows, married persons and others in conjugal relationships, but not for others. Relationship status is not relevant to determining the age at which entitlement to retirement with a government pension ought to arise.

Another plausible characterization of the objective of the monthly allowance is to alleviate financial hardship among poor older adults aged 60 to 64 by providing them with an early old age pension entitlement. This is an important objective, but relationships are not relevant to its attainment since the presence (or absence) of a particular relationship is a poor marker of financial need. The denial of the monthly allowance to persons who are not widowed or living in a conjugal relationship with a pensioner is not justifiable. If their financial needs are equivalent or more pressing, it is unfair to deny benefits to persons who are separated, divorced, living on their own, living with non-conjugal cohabitants or living conjugally with non-pensioners.[163]

Recommendation 28

Parliament needs to clarify the objectives of the Monthly Allowance provisions of the *Old Age Security Act*. If the objective is to promote early retirement, or to direct benefits to persons in need, then Parliament should amend the Act so that benefits are not limited to widows and spouses or common-law partners of pensioners.

Relationships clearly do not matter if the objective of the Monthly Allowance is to enable widows or conjugal couples to retire early at an adequate income, or to direct benefits to persons with the greatest financial need among the near-elderly poor. However, the objective could be characterized differently, in a way that suggests relationships may matter. It could be argued that the objective of the monthly allowance is *not* to respond to the financial needs of *all* of the poor older adults aged 60 to 64. Arguably, the monthly allowance reflects a more specific objective. By compensating for the financial hardship that results from the loss of an older breadwinner's income upon retirement, the Act seeks to respond to the distinct needs and contributions of persons, the vast majority of them women, who have supported their families through unpaid caregiving. The spouse who has devoted much of her life to caring for her family, and who is widowed or dependent on the income of her spouse or partner, deserves income support in her own right in recognition of the valuable contributions she has made to society. On some occasions, the government has relied on this reasoning to justify the extension of old age pension entitlements to widows, spouses and partners under the age of 65. For example, when the Spouse's Allowance was extended to widowed persons in 1985, the Honourable Jake Epp, Minister of National Health and Welfare at the time, claimed that the purpose of the Allowance was to support women who were financially dependent because of the roles they assumed in their marriages:

Societal norms dictated that the husband would enter the labour force and earn the money while the wife stayed in the home and performed the unpaid role of mother, housekeeper, companion, nurse, guidance counsellor and community worker, the list is endless… the Bill before us today [extending old age monthly allowances to widows and widowers] recognizes this contribution…the contribution these people have made to our society goes beyond financial measure.[164]

If the objective of the monthly allowance is to recognize the valuable work performed by caregivers by providing them with an early old age pension entitlement, then relationships do matter. The problem with the monthly allowance provisions of the *Old Age Security Act* is that, by employing widowed, spousal or partnership relational status as a precondition to entitlement, they are poorly tailored to achieving this objective. The allowance can be claimed by widows and widowers and by husbands, wives and common-law partners of pensioners, whether or not they raised children and regardless of how long they were married or living in a common-law partnership (so long as the latter has existed for at least one year). But, the allowance cannot be claimed by persons who are living alone or who are separated, divorced, living with others in non-conjugal relationships or living conjugally with non-pensioners, even though these persons may have performed valuable unpaid caregiving work for most of their lives. Any persons who have performed the kind of unpaid caregiving to which the law seeks to respond should be able to claim the early old age pension entitlement made available by the monthly allowance.

...adult siblings [like Matthew and Marilla from the Anne of Green Gables stories]...and friends who live together and have economically interdependent lives, may or may not qualify for benefits under one or other of these programs, depending on their age, the age difference between them, and their individual marital status. Some examples...

➤ If Matthew is aged 65, while Marilla is only 63, for example, Matthew will qualify for OAS and – assuming his income is below the relevant threshold – probably also GIS (at the single rate). But Marilla will not be entitled to any benefits under the monthly Allowance program because she is not "married to a low-income pensioner".

➤ If either Matthew or Marilla (or both) had previously been involved in a conjugal relationship with someone who was now dead, either or both might qualify for a monthly Allowance to the Survivor, based on their own individual income, and assuming they are aged 60-64. However, if the previous conjugal relationship had ended in divorce or separation, they would not be entitled to any benefits under this program, even if their income were low enough otherwise to qualify.

➤ At age 65, assuming their individual income is low enough to qualify, they will each be able to qualify for GIS as individuals, giving them considerably higher benefits than would each receive if they were conjugal partners.

M. Townson, *Reconsidering the Relevance of Relationships in Income Security Programs* (Ottawa: Law Commission of Canada, August 2001) at 8-9.

Given that relationships matter if the objective of the monthly allowance is to compensate for unpaid caregiving, could the law be reformulated to allow individuals to determine for themselves whether they formed the kinds of relationships that ought to qualify for benefits? Since individuals must apply for the monthly allowance, a certain element of self-selection is involved in the application process itself. However, since financial benefits are at stake, self-selection alone cannot provide an answer since the potential for abuse is too great. The criteria of eligibility must be set out in the legislation and applications considered by public employees.

This brings us to the fourth question: since relationships matter to the objective of compensating unpaid caregiving work, and public policy requires that the law delineate the relevant relationships to which it applies, can the monthly allowance provisions be revised to more accurately capture the relevant range of caregiving relationships? We think so. Widowed, spousal and partner status are not accurate means of identifying the relevant relationships. The objective of compensating unpaid caregiving work could be better accomplished if the relational eligibility requirements for the monthly allowance were revised.

Early pension entitlement for persons under the age of 65 – and perhaps enhanced pension entitlements for persons over 65 – could be made available to those who can demonstrate that they have performed unpaid caregiving work. Unpaid work could be defined as childcare, personal care of elderly and family members with disabilities, and volunteer work of a caregiving nature in the community. The amount of benefits could depend on the number of persons for whom a claimant has been a caregiver, adjusted for the length of time during which these responsibilities were undertaken. The main advantage of such a reform is that it would better accomplish the objective of compensating the socially valuable caregiving work performed primarily by women.[165] In such a scheme, claimants would be entitled to a pension prior to the age of 65 – and perhaps enhanced pension entitlement after the age of 65 – if they can show that they provided unpaid care to others. The scheme would, however, likely be costly to design and implement, and its administration would involve at least some invasion of privacy. As such, it is a less attractive option than amending the monthly allowance so that entitlement is determined by financial need alone, without reference to relationships. While the objective of compensating unpaid caregiving is certainly an important one, there may be better ways of accomplishing it.

Recommendation 29

> If the objective of the Monthly Allowance provisions of the *Old Age Security Act* is to support unpaid caregiving, Parliament should consider revising the relational eligibility requirements or replacing the Monthly Allowance with new programs to more closely target benefits to caregivers.

X. The *Canada Pension Plan*: Survivor's Benefits

The *Canada Pension Plan*,[166] together with the *Quebec Pension Plan*, establishes a national scheme of old age pensions and supplementary benefits related to employment. It is a contributory scheme financed by employers and payroll deductions from employees. The Plans provide retirement benefits to contributors over the age of sixty. Relational criteria are taken into account on the death of an employee contributor. In that case, spouses and common-law partners are entitled to claim a pension as survivors.[167] Factors such as age, responsibility for dependent children and disability determine a claimant's entitlement to, and the amount of, the survivor's pension.

When the CPP first came into force in 1966, the survivor's pension was called a "widow's pension".[168] It was a gender-specific benefit that was not generally available to widowers. Limited discretionary recognition was granted to dependent common-law spouses. A widow's pension would terminate if she remarried. CPP survivor's benefits, in their original form, were premised on the assumption that married women were homemakers who were financially dependent on their breadwinner husbands.

The CPP survivor's pension has evolved considerably in the ensuing years in a manner that mirrors changing social attitudes to conjugal relationships. In 1974, the widow's pension became a survivor's pension available to the wife or husband of a deceased contributor.[169] By 1986 and 2000, respectively, opposite-sex and same-sex common-law partners were entitled to a survivor's pension if they had cohabited with the deceased for at least one year, even if the deceased also left a surviving wife or husband.[170]

As the survivor's pension has evolved over time, becoming available to widowers, common-law opposite-sex couples and eventually same-sex couples, the objectives have also evolved. The aim of the 1966 widow's pension was to address the consequences of the presumed dependency of wives on their husbands.[171] The dependency rationale can no longer be the sole purpose underlying the survivor's pensions. Dependency has been rejected as an explicit or implicit requirement of the legislative design. Survivor's pensions now recognize the consequences of relationships characterized by either economic dependence or interdependence. More specifically, they are intended to pursue the original objective of responding to spousal need when dependent spouses suddenly find themselves without their spouses' income. And they are intended to compensate interdependent spouses for the contribution that they have made to their spouses' careers. These are both important government objectives.

One might argue that the objective of responding to income support needs, whether a result of dependency or some other cause, would be better served by an approach to income security that did not take relationships into account, along the lines discussed above in relation to the GST credit and other income security programs. However, the dependency and compensation objectives continue to be important ones. Individuals in economically dependent or interdependent relationships have a strong claim to compensation for the years that they spent contributing to their spouses' careers through various forms of unpaid labour. In response to the first question, then, there is a strong argument that relationships do matter, and that survivor's pensions do continue to serve important relational objectives.

However, there is reason to be concerned about whether the current definition of survivors entitled to claim benefits under the Canada Pension Plan is under-inclusive. The survivor's benefit is available only to spouses and common-law partners.[172] It is not available to persons who had other, non-conjugal relationships with a deceased contributor. But the dual objectives of addressing dependency and compensation may also be relevant to a person who was living with a contributor in a non-conjugal relationship at the time of death.

It would be better to allow individuals to choose their beneficiaries for the purposes of survivor's pensions under the *Canada Pension Plan* or other employment pensions. Rather than restricting benefits to spouses or common-law partners, pensioners could be allowed to designate their chosen beneficiaries. Contributors in non-conjugal relationships should be able to designate the persons with whom they live in close personal relationships as their beneficiaries for the survivor's pension.

What about individual contributors who did not live in conjugal or non-conjugal relationships? Should they not also be able to designate a person of their choice to receive their survivor's benefits? The principle underlying self-designation would suggest that the type of relationship is irrelevant; that is, an individual should be able to decide who is most important to them. However, the existence of a certain kind of relationship is not irrelevant here. The objective of survivor's benefits is to recognize the consequences of relationships of economic dependence or interdependence. Neither the dependency nor compensatory objectives of survivor's benefits fit the situation of single employees.

As a result, the right to designate a beneficiary for survivor's benefits would need to be restricted by a functional test. It would not be open to all individuals to simply designate any beneficiary of their choice for their survivor's benefits. Rather, individuals could designate a person with whom they live in an economically interdependent relationship. Some consideration would need to be given to imposing a limitation on intergenerational designation, since the cost of allowing such designation may be prohibitive to the CPP. The survivor's benefit is currently limited by age. To be eligible for the full survivor's pension at the time of the contributor's death, the survivor must be over the age of 45, have a disability or be supporting dependent children of the deceased. Able-bodied survivors without dependent children receive a reduced survivor's pension if they are between the ages of 35 and 45 at the time of death, and they have no entitlement if the contributor dies before they reach the age of 35.[173] Similar restrictions based on a combination of age, disability and parental status could be imposed on a scheme that allowed self-designation.

An individual could be allowed to select a survivor with whom he or she lives in an economically interdependent relationship and who meets the criteria based on age, disability or parental status. Such an approach would broaden the range of relationships that would be recognized and widen the range of choices available to Canadians. In so doing, it would advance the objectives of promoting individual choice and autonomy, and respecting the diversity and equality of relationships. However, as with immigration, the choice of beneficiary would not be completely open-ended, but rather, restricted to those persons who would meet the functional requirement of economic interdependency and the other criteria of entitlement. In this way, it would be possible to ensure that survivor's benefits continued to serve their specific objectives of recognizing and compensating economic dependency and interdependence. It would not, however, artificially restrict the choice based on the status of relationship – that is, it would no longer restrict the choice to individuals in conjugal relationships. Any relationship that could fit the underlying requirement of economic interdependency and the criteria based on age, disability or parental status could qualify.

One further limitation on the designation of a survivor beneficiary needs to be discussed. It would be important not to undermine the reliance interests of persons in economically interdependent relationships who this scheme is designed to protect. Consider the following scenario. Sam and Asha were married for 30 years. During the marriage, Asha stayed at home to care for the children and provide for the family's needs. They separate, and Sam moves in with a common-law partner, Maria, who is 50 years old.[174] Sam now wants to designate Maria as the beneficiary of his survivor's benefits. Maria would certainly fit within the suggested functional definition of individuals who live in an economically interdependent relationship with a contributor and, being over the age of 45, she would be entitled to a full survivor's pension if Sam dies. But, allowing Sam to designate Maria could disentitle Asha to any survivor's pension. This would be inconsistent with the objectives of survivor's benefits of compensating individuals within relationships of economic dependency and interdependence.

The law would need to be revised to find an appropriate balance between promoting individual choice and protecting the reliance interests of individuals within long-term relationships. The CPP does not currently contain a provision allowing for the apportionment of a survivor's pension where a contributor leaves both a separated spouse and a common-law partner, even if the common-law partnership was brief and the marriage long. The absence of a just apportionment scheme raises the stakes too high in the contests that can arise between two survivors.[175] Indeed, the denial of a survivor's pension to a separated spouse when the deceased spouse had formed a new common-law partnership is clearly inconsistent with the basic compensatory objective of the survivor's benefit. This is a problem that needs to be addressed in the law as it currently stands and in any reform to the CPP survivor's benefit along the lines that we are advocating here. Returning to our scenario, a self-designation scheme would need to be designed to allow for an apportionment between Asha, the ex-spouse, and Maria, the designated beneficiary living with the contributor in an economically interdependent relationship (as in the apportionment provisions that already exist in federal employment pension laws other than the CPP). It might put some limits on the ability of individuals with ex-spouses or former common-law partners to designate their beneficiaries. Sam, for example, would be allowed to designate Maria as a beneficiary of his survivor's benefits, but he could designate only a portion of those benefits.

Recommendation 30

Governments should amend the *Canada Pension Plan* and laws governing employment pensions and veterans' pensions, to permit a contributor, employee or veteran to designate a person with whom they are living in an economically interdependent relationship as a beneficiary of their survivor's benefits.

Conclusion

In this chapter, we have been considering the question of how state regulation can recognize and support close personal relationships in a more principled and coherent manner. We have suggested that the first task is to clarify the objectives of laws that take relationships into account. If these laws are pursuing valid objectives, the next question is whether relationships are even relevant to those objectives. If not, then the law should eliminate reliance on relational considerations altogether, by individualizing the rights and responsibilities in question. For example, some tax and pension laws currently provide a lower level of benefits to persons in conjugal relationships. Since relationship status is not a reliable indicator of need, and because such laws have a negative impact on equality and autonomy, we argued that these laws should deliver benefits without taking relationships into account.

In those areas where relationships are relevant to the legislative objectives, our analysis turns to whether it is possible to allow individuals rather than governments to choose the relevant relationships. Our discussion suggested some ways in which the importance of relationships in Canadians' lives could be taken into account without the government artificially restricting its recognition and support of the relationships that may be of importance to individuals. We considered the possibility of reframing some laws so that individuals, rather than governments, would be in a position to decide who is most important to them, and relationship recognition could then be extended on the basis of that choice. We suggested that laws establishing bereavement leave and caregiving leave, as well as laws dealing with the right to sue for relational harm, were good examples of contexts where governments should make room for individuals to identify the relationships most important to them.

In other contexts, we suggested that some limits be placed on the choices, that is, that individuals be granted the ability to select or designate within a limited range of relationships. In immigration law, we suggested that persons "known and emotionally important" to a sponsor would be the appropriate limit. In pension laws, we suggested that "economic interdependency" would be the appropriate limit for designating relationships for the purposes of survivor's benefits. In both of these examples then, the ability to choose would be limited by a functional definition. It would, in our view, be better for individual Canadians to be able to make these choices from among their relationships that fit these functional definitions than to have governments insist that the choices be limited on the basis of relationship status.

If, however, self-selection is not workable, we turned to a consideration of whether there is a better way for governments to include relationships. We considered a number of examples in which relational definitions could be redrawn to better focus on the full range of relevant relationships. The laws regarding testimonial privilege, and those regarding conflicts of interest, are examples in which the law should apply to all close personal relationships, not just relationships between persons related by blood, marriage, common-law partnership or adoption.

1   An excellent review of the common law and civil law approaches to compensating relational harm can be found in Shauna Van Praagh, *Compensation for Relational Harm* (Ottawa: Law Commission of Canada, 2001), which includes a detailed analysis of the relevant statutory provisions.

2   The common law had not allowed wrongful death claims since 1808, when it was decided in *Baker* v. *Bolton*, (1808) 1 Camp. 493, 170 E.R. 1033 (K.B.) that "in a civil Court, the death of a human being could not be complained of as an injury".

3   *An Act for Compensating the Families of Persons Killed by Accidents*, 1846, 9 & 10 Vict., c.93.

4   Article 1457, *Civil Code of Quebec*.

5   In *Augustus* v. *Gosset*, [1996] 3 S.C.R. 268, the Supreme Court held that grief *(solatium doloris)* could be recognized as a relational loss in the civil law.

6   [1929] S.C.R. 650 (interpreting article 1053 of the *Civil Code of Lower Canada*, the precursor to Article 1457 of the new *Civil Code of Quebec, supra* note 4).

7   See, e.g., *Augustus, supra* note 5 at paras.50-51.

8   Van Praagh, *supra* note 1 at 25.

9   *Ibid.*, at 25-7.

10 R.S.C. 1985, c.C-26, Schedule 2, s.1.

11 S.C. 2001, c.6

12 R.S.C. 1985, c.S-9.

13 *Ordon Estate* v. *Grail*, [1998] 3 S.C.R. 437 at 508.

14 *Marine Liability Act, supra* note 11, s.4.

15 *Ibid.*, s.6(3)(a). This provision codifies a change to maritime law made earlier by the Supreme Court in *Ordon, supra* note 13.

16 *Ibid.*, s.6. In this respect, too, the legislation is codifying a change to maritime law made by the Supreme Court in *Ordon, supra* note 13.

17 R.S.C. 1985, c.L-2, s.210.

18 *Canada Labour Standard Regulations*, C.R.C., c.986, s.33, online: http://laws.justice.gc.ca/en/L-2/C.R.C.-c.986/29630.html#rid-29753.

19 Jody Freeman, "Defining Family in *Mossop* v. *DSS*: The Challenge of Anti-Essentialism and Interactive Discrimination for Human Rights Litigation" (1994) 44 U.T.L.J. 41 at 64.

20 *An Act respecting Labour Standards*, R.S.Q., c.N-1.1, s.81.2.

21 British Columbia, *Rights and Responsibilities in a Changing Workplace: A Review of Employment Standards in British Columbia* (Victoria: Ministry of Skills, Training and Labour, 1994) (Chair: M. Thompson); *Report of the Advisory Group on Working Time and the Distribution of Work* (Ottawa: Minister of Supply and Services Canada, 1994) (Chair: A. Donner).

22   Pat Armstrong and Olga Kits, *One Hundred Years of Caregiving* (Ottawa: Law Commission of Canada, 2001); Roeher Institute, *Personal Relationships of Support Between Adults: The Case of Disability* (Ottawa: Law Commission of Canada, 2001); Fraser Valentine, *Enabling Citizenship: Full Inclusion of Children with Disabilities and their Parents* (Ottawa: Canadian Policy Research Networks, 2001) at 43-4; Caroline Beauvais and Jane Jenson, *Two Policy Paradigms: Family Responsibility and Investing in Children* (Ottawa: Canadian Policy Research Networks, 2001).

23   *Employment Standards Act*, R.S.B.C. 1996, c.113, s.52.

24   *Ibid.*, s.1(1). See also *Employment Standards Act*, S.N.B. 1982, c.E-7.2, s.44.022 as am. by an *Act to Amend the Employment Standards Act*, S.N.B. 2000, c.55, S.5 (an employee is entitled to up to 3 days of unpaid family responsibility leave per year to meet responsibilities related to the health, care or education of a person in a close family relationship with the employee).

25   *Employment Standards Act*, S.O. 2000, c.41, s.50.

26   *Ibid.*, s.50(2).

27   *Labour Standards Act*, R.S.S. 1978, c.L-1, s.44.2.

28   *Ibid.*, s.29.3.

29   *Employment Standards Act, supra* note 24, s.1 (definition of "close family relationship").

30   Government of Canada, *Speech from the Throne to Open the First Session of the 37th Parliament of Canada* (2001), online: http://www.sft-ddt.gc.ca.

31   Roeher Institute, *supra* note 22.

32   For example, 20 percent of all persons providing informal care to seniors are friends or neighbours and they experience many of the same stresses as family caregivers: see N.J. Keating, J.E. Fast, L. Oakes and S. Harlton, *Defining Eldercare: Components and Perspectives* (Ottawa: Health Canada, 1996).

33   R.S.C. 1985, c.I-2.

34   Citizenship and Immigration Canada, *Into the 21st Century: A Strategy for Immigration and Citizenship Canada* (1994) (Ottawa: Minister of Supply and Services Canada, 1994) at 36.

35   Citizenship and Immigration Canada, *Planning Now for Canada's Future: Introducing a Multi-Year Planning Process and the Immigration Plan for 2001 and 2002* (2001) (Ottawa: Minister of Public Works and Government Services Canada, 2001) at 1.

36   Citizenship and Immigration Canada, *Building on a Strong Foundation for the 21st Century: New Directions for Immigration and Refugee Policy and Legislation* (Ottawa: Minister of Public Works and Government Services Canada, 1998) at 22.

37   *Immigration Act, supra* note 33, s.6(1); *Immigration Regulations*, SOR/78-172, s.6(1), online: http://laws.justice.gc.ca/en/I-2/SOR-78-172/index.html.

38   *Immigration Act, supra* note 33, s.6(2); *Immigration Regulations, ibid.*, s.5(1).

39   *Immigration Regulations, supra* note 37, s.2(1) (definition of "member of family class").

40   *Ibid.* (definition of "spouse").

41   Section 114 of the *Immigration Act, supra* note 33.

42   Bill C-11, the *Immigration and Refugee Protection Act*, 1st Sess., 37th Parl., 2001 (passed the House of Commons June 13, 2001, online: http://www.parl.gc.ca/37/1/parlbus/chambus/house/bills/government/C-11/C-11_3/C-11_cover-E.html.; currently awaiting 3rd reading in the Senate). Section 13(1) of Bill C-11 provides that "A Canadian citizen or permanent resident may, subject to the regulations, sponsor a foreign national who is a member of the family class." Section 12(1) defines the family class as including a "spouse, common-law partner, child, parent or other prescribed family member". Regulations to be passed pursuant to the new legislation will define what other relationships will be included within the family class.

43   Immigration Legislative Review Advisory Group, *Not Just Numbers: A Canadian Framework for Future Immigration* (Ottawa: Citizenship and Immigration Canada, 1997).

44   *Ibid.*, at 43.

45   *Ibid.*, at 43.

46   *Ibid.*, at 48.

47   *Ibid.*, at 45.

48   The statutory exceptions are set out in subsections 4(2) and 4(4) of the *Canada Evidence Act*, R.S.C. 1985, c.C-5.

49   Section 4(1) of the *Canada Evidence Act* provides that a spouse of the accused is a competent witness for the defence. It does not alter the common law rule that a spouse is not compellable for the defence: see *R. v. Amway Corp.*, [1989] 1 S.C.R. 20 at 29.

50   The marital communications privilege is set out in s.4(3) of the *Canada Evidence Act*.

51   See, e.g, Hamish Stewart, "Spousal Incompetency and the Charter" (1996) 34 Osgoode Hall L.J. 411; Allan Manson, *Spousal Testimony in Criminal Cases in Canada* (Ottawa: Law Commission of Canada, 2001); Jeffrey Schnoor, "Evidence by Spouses in Criminal Proceedings" (Uniform Law Conference of Canada, 1998), online: www.law.ualberta.ca/alri/ulc/criminal/espouse.htm; J. Sopinka, S.N. Lederman and A.W. Bryant, *The Law of Evidence in Canada* (Toronto: Butterworths, 2nd ed. 1999) at 704; *R. v. Czipps*, (1979) 101 D.L..R. (3d) 323 (Ont. C.A.) per Morden J.A. at 329 ("the general law relating to spousal competency and compellability is marked with significant inconsistencies and is in serious need of rationalization at the legislative level.").

52   *R. v. Salituro*, [1991] 3 S.C.R. 654, 678; *R. v. Hawkins*, [1996] 3 S.C.R. 1043, 1071.

53   Stewart, *supra* note 51 at para.1; J.H. Wigmore, *Evidence in Trials at Common Law*, rev. by John T. McNaughton (Boston: Little Brown, 1961) vol. 8 at 213-22.

54   "Both of these thoroughly discredited rationales are, of course, based on archaic notions of a woman's role in society and within marriage." Per L'Heureux-Dubé J. in *Hawkins, supra* note 52 at para.120.

55   See section 3 of the *Canada Evidence Act, supra* note 48.

56   Australian Law Reform Commission, *Evidence, Volume 1* (Interim Report No. 26) (Canberra, 1985) at 289; *Hawkins, supra* note 52 at para.38 (per Lamer C.J. and Iacobucci J.); *Salituro, supra* note 52 at 672-673; Stewart, *supra* note 51 at 416-417.

57   *Hawkins, supra* note 52.

58   *R. v. Bailey*, (1983) 4 C.C.C. (3d) 21 (Ont. C.A.).

59   *Salituro, supra* note 52.

60   Sopinka et al., *supra* note 51, at 699.

61   R. v. *McGinty,* [1986] 4 W.W.R. 97 (Yukon C.A.).

62   *Ibid.,* at 122.

63   As for the defence, section 4(1) provides that spouses are competent witnesses. It has not altered the common law rule that a spouse is not a compellable witness for the defence. This provision probably also alters the common law position that a witness is not competent for a co-accused in any case where the witness's spouse is also a co-accused. Therefore, a co-accused can call a witness who is a spouse of a person jointly charged if he or she is willing, but cannot compel testimony if he or she is not willing.

64   Canada's first *Criminal Code,* enacted in 1893, did not permit husbands or wives to testify regarding marital communications even if they wished to do so. See 56 Vict., c.31, s.4 (no husband or wife "shall be competent to disclose any communication" made to the other "during their marriage").

65   There has been some debate regarding whether the marital communications privilege can be invoked when a spouse is a competent and compellable witness for the Crown, or only when a witness chooses to testify for the defence. The case law, and the rationale for the privilege, suggest that it should be applicable in both situations. See R. v. *Zylstra,* (1995) 95 C.C.C. (3d) 477 (Ont. C.A.); R. v. *Jean and Pisinger,* (1979) 46 C.C.C. (2d) 176 (Alta. C.A.). *Contra,* R. v. *St. Jean,* (1976) 32 C.C.C. (2d) 438 (Que. C.A.).

66   Section 4(3) of the *Canada Evidence Act.*

67   See, e.g., *Zylstra, supra* note 65.

68   R. v. *Lloyd,* [1981] 2 S.C.R. 645. The decision was based on a provision of the *Criminal Code,* now s.189(6), that provides that privileged information that is intercepted by wiretap "remains privileged and inadmissible as evidence."

69   The objective of promoting candour and trust in close personal relationships by protecting confidential communications suggests that it is the state of the relationship at the time of the communication that is relevant, not the state of the relationship at the time of the trial. For this reason, the privilege should not be terminated by divorce, separation or death. The law is not yet clear on this point. See R. v. *Bailey,* (1983) 4 C.C.C. (3d) 21, 23-4 (Ont. C.A.), and the discussion in Sopinka et al, *supra* note 51 at 774-775.

70   *Salituro, supra* note 52 at 673. See also R. v. *Edelenbos,* [2000] O.J. No. 2147 (Sup. Ct. J.), declaring the rule of spousal incompetence to be of no force and effect on the grounds that it discriminated on the basis of marital status. McIsaac J. commented (at para.9) that "Family harmony does not constitute a sufficient basis to provide a reasonable limit to the principle of fundamental justice that the criminal trial process is entitled to the evidence of everyone, at least when the witness expresses a willingness to testify for the Crown."

71 See Manson, *supra* note 51; Schnoor, *supra* note 51. The Supreme Court of Canada, in *Salituro*, *supra* note 52 at 677-8, noted that respecting the dignity of spousal witnesses "would appear to favour abolishing the rule entirely", though such "a far-reaching change" was best left to Parliament to consider. See also *Hawkins, supra* note 52 at 1071 per Lamer C.J. and Iacobucci J., and at 1095 per La Forest J. The United States Supreme Court took the position in *Trammel* v. *U.S.*, 445 U.S. 40 (1980) that spouses are competent but not compellable witnesses for the prosecution in federal criminal cases. The law in many states treats spouses the same as any other witnesses: see *McCormick on Evidence*, 5th ed. (West Group: St. Paul, 1999) at 281. Spouses are competent witnesses for the prosecution in the United Kingdom pursuant to s.80 of the *Police and Criminal Evidence Act*, 1984, c.33. Legislation in Australia places limits on the compellability, but not the competence, of witness spouses.

72 *Modernization of Benefits and Obligations Act*, S.C. 2000, c.12.

73 See, e.g., *R.* v. *McClure*, [2001] 1 S.C.R. 445 (solicitor-client privilege is not absolute; it may have to yield to protect an accused's right to make full answer and defence).

74 *R.* v. *Gruenke*, [1991] 3 S.C.R. 263; *A.(M.)* v. *Ryan*, [1997] 1 S.C.R. 157.

75 Law Reform Commission of Canada, *Report on Evidence* (Ottawa, 1975)

76 Australian Law Reform Commission, dissent of Michael Kirby, *supra* note 56.

77 *Crimes Act* 1958 (Vic.), ss.399-400.

78 Australian Law Reform Commission, *Evidence, Volume 1 (Interim Report No. 26)* (Canberra, 1985) at 135 and 289-91, online: http://www.austlii.edu.au/au/other/alrc/publications/reports/26/; Australian Law Reform Commission, *Evidence (Final Report No. 38)* (Canberra, 1987) at para.79, online: http://www.austlii.edu.au/au/other/alrc/publications/reports/38/ALRC38.html.

79 No. 2 of 1995, online: http://www.austlii.edu.au/au/legis/cth/consol_act/ea199580/.

80 *Ibid.*, s.12.

81 *Ibid.*, s.18(1).

82 *Ibid.*, s.18(6). The balancing required here is similar to the fourth stage of the Wigmore test adopted by the Supreme Court of Canada for the determination of "case-by-case privileges" in *Gruenke, supra* note 74. According to the Wigmore test, privilege should be accorded to statements only if "the injury that would inure to the relation by the disclosure of the communications" is "greater than the benefit thereby gained for the correct disposal of litigation." J.H. Wigmore, *Evidence in Trials at Common Law*, vol. 8 revised by J.T. McNaughton. (Boston: Little, Brown, 1961) at 527.

83 *Ibid.*, s.18(7).

84 In its 1987 report, *supra* note 78, the Australian Law Reform Commission noted (at para.81) that "Enquiries have been made in Victoria and South Australia, where similar legislation has applied for several years, about the operation of that legislation. Information obtained indicates general satisfaction with the approach and that the issue rarely arises and when it does rarely occupies much time."

85 See Schnoor, *supra* note 51 at text accompanying footnote 28.

86 Manson, *supra* note 51 at 31.

87   *Ibid.* In *R. v. Khan*, [1990] 2 S.C.R. 531 and *R. v. Smith*, [1992] 2 S.C.R. 915 the Court created a new discretionary exception to the hearsay rule: evidence could be admitted so long as it was reliable and necessary. Later, in *R. v. K.G.B.*, [1993] 1 S.C.R. 740, the Court applied this line of reasoning to the prior statements made by a witness who had recanted in the stand. The Court ruled that the prior inconsistent statements could be admitted for their truth if there were sufficient guarantees of trustworthiness. Similarly, out-of-court statements taken from a person close to an accused may be admissible on the "reliable and necessary" test. The necessity part of the test is certainly easier to satisfy if the witness is ruled non-compellable. See *Hawkins, supra* note 52.

88   R.S.C. 1985, c.B-3.

89   *Ibid.*, s.138.

90   *Ibid.*, s.136(1)(d).

91   S.C. 1996, c.23.

92   *Ibid.*, s.5(2)(i).

93   *Ibid.*, s.3(2), incorporating by reference s.251(1)(a) of the *Income Tax Act*.

94   *Ibid.*, s.251(1)(b) of the *Income Tax Act*.

95   S.C. 1990, c.40.

96   This provision is now s.3(2)(c)(ii) of the *Employment Insurance Act, supra* note 91.

97   Dozens of appeals are heard by the Tax Court each year by claimants denied unemployment insurance on the grounds that they were employed by relatives. The vast majority of these appeals fail because the claimant has failed to establish an arbitrary or capricious exercise of discretion by the Minister. In contrast, there are few reported cases finding employment between unrelated persons to be uninsurable.

98   For examples of cases where the female claimant's denial of a common-law relationship with her employer was rejected after the court examined the details of the personal relationship, see *Sparkes* v. *Canada (Minister of National Revenue)*, [1999] T.C.J. No. 660 at para.39; *Boisvert* v. *Canada (Minister of National Revenue)*, [1999] T.C.J. No. 222 at paras.20-2; *Kitchen* v. *Canada (Minister of National Revenue)*, [1998] T.C.J. No. 169; *Sampson* v. *Canada (Minister of National Revenue)*, [1997] T.C.J. No. 1061; *Falardeau* v. *Canada*, [1997] T.C.J. No. 203. See also *Hollett* v. *Canada (Minister of National Revenue)*, [1998] T.C.J. No. 724 (considering whether separation of claimant from her husband employer meant they were at arm's length).

99   R.S.C. 1985, c.B-2.

100   Section 138 deals with the wage claims of relatives (discussed above); s.100 deals with reviewable non-arm's length transactions (discussed below); s.137(2) provides that spouses or common-law partners cannot claim a dividend for wages until all claims of other creditors have been satisfied; and sections 95 and 96 provide a transaction between an insolvent person and a creditor who is a related person, entered into during the year before the initial bankruptcy event, is deemed to be fraudulent and void if it has the effect of giving that creditor a preference (discussed below).

101   *Ibid.*, s.100(2).

102   *Ibid.*, s.3(1).

103   *Ibid.*, s.3(3) and 4(2).

104 *Ibid.*, s.3(2).

105 R.C.C. Cuming, "Transactions at Undervalue and Preferences under the Bankruptcy and Insolvency Act: Rethinking Outdated Approaches" (31st Annual Workshop on Commercial and Consumer Law, Faculty of Law, University of Toronto, 19-20 October 2001) at 213 [unpublished].

106 *Bankruptcy and Insolvency Act*, *supra*, note 99 s.95.

107 *Ibid.*, s.96.

108 R.C.C. Cuming, *supra* note 105 at 228.

109 R.C.C. Cuming, *supra* note 105 at 228-229.

110 *Bank Act*, S.C. 1991, c.46, s.489(1).

111 *Ibid.*, s.486(1)(c).

112 *Income Tax Act*, R.S.C. 1985, c.1 (5th supp).

113 See House of Commons, Sub-Committee on Tax Equity for Canadian Families with Dependent Children, *For the Benefit of Our Children: Improving Tax Fairness* (June 1999) at 10 ("Many witnesses came before the Committee with numerical examples that compared the tax position of one-earner and two-earner families. They noted the discrepancy in taxes paid, and often suggested income-splitting as a solution to this discrepancy.").

114 Cathal O'Donoghue and Holly Sutherland, "Accounting for the Family in European Income Tax Systems" (1999) 23 Cambridge Journal of Economics 565 at 573.

115 In seeking to draw lessons for Canada from the United States experience with family-based income tax, it is important to note that the adoption by the United States government of family-based taxation in 1948 was the result of an accident of history and not a principled decision that equal tax should be imposed on equal-income families instead of equal-income individuals. Family-unit taxation was a way of dealing with the problem that arose when the courts held that, in states that had enacted a form of community family property law regime, families could split their incomes for tax purposes even though the basic system was individual-based. It was also a politically expedient way for a Republican Congress to provide a large tax cut after the war to wealthy families. Finally, by providing a large tax break to one-earner families, it was a deliberate attempt by Congress to encourage women, many of whom had taken employment in factories during the war, to leave the paid work force and return to work in the home.

116 For a review of this literature, see E.J. McCaffery, *Taxing Women* (Chicago: University of Chicago Press, 1997).

117 See, e.g., Shelley A. Phipps and Peter S. Burton, "Sharing Within Families: Implications for Measurement of Poverty Among Individuals in Canada" (1995) 28 Canadian Journal of Economics 177; Frances R. Woolley and Judith Marshall, "Measuring Inequality Within the Household" (1994) 40 Review of Income and Wealth 415; Carolyn Vogler and Jan Pahl, "Money, Power and Inequality within Marriage" (1994) Sociological Review 263 at 285 ("The orthodox model of households as egalitarian decision making units, within which resources are shared equally, applied to only one fifth of the households in the sample.").

118 There are other ways in which the tax system may penalize dual earner families. Additional cash income earned by the secondary earner might result in the loss of income-tested benefits such as the child tax benefit. And, because many in-kind employee benefits provide coverage to spouses and common-law partners, when secondary earners begin paid employment they are likely to be taxed on the value of in-kind fringe benefits that have no value to them.

[119] Section 251(2).

[120] For a description and classification of many of these rules, see Kathleen A. Lahey, *The Benefit/Penalty Unit in Income Tax Policy: Diversity and Reform* (Ottawa: Law Commission of Canada, 2000); Claire Young, *What's Sex Got to Do With It? Tax and the "Family"* (Ottawa: Law Commission of Canada, 2000).

[121] Section 118(1)(b).

[122] Section 118(1)(c.1). Eligible relatives include children, grandchildren, parents, grandparents, siblings, aunts, uncles, nephews and nieces: section 118(1)(c.1)(B).

[123] Section 118(1)(d). A "dependant" is defined in s.118(6) as a child, grandchild, parent, grandparent, sibling, uncle, aunt, niece or nephew of the taxpayer or the taxpayer's spouse or partner. Unlike the "caregiver credit," the "infirm dependant" credit does not require co-residence.

[124] The need to develop a range of policies to support caregivers is a theme in the literature. See, e.g., Pat Armstrong and Olga Kits, *One Hundred Years of Caregiving* (Ottawa: Law Commission of Canada, 2001); Caroline Beauvais and Jane Jenson, *Two Policy Paradigms: Family Responsibility and Investing in Children* (Ottawa: Canadian Policy Research Networks, 2001); Janet E. Fast and Norah C. Keating, *Family Caregiving and Consequences for Carers: Towards a Policy Research Agenda* (Ottawa: Canadian Policy Research Networks, 2000); Fraser Valentine, *Enabling Citizenship: Full Inclusion of Children with Disabilities and their Parents* (Ottawa: Canadian Research Policy Networks, 2001).

[125] For further discussion, see The Roeher Institute, *Personal Relationships of Support Between Adults: The Case of Disability* (Ottawa: Law Commission of Canada, March 2001) at 61-65.

[126] *Ibid.*, at 63.

[127] Section 118(1)(a).

[128] These are the values of the federal basic and "spouse and common-law partner" tax credits. In addition, all of the provinces provide analogous credits in their income taxes. The value of these credits varies considerably from province to province. In Nova Scotia, to take one example, the value of the basic personal credit is $706, and the value of the spouse and common-law partner credit is $600 in 2001.

[129] Canada, Department of Finance, *Tax Expenditures and Evaluations 2000* (Ottawa), Table 1.

[130] Lahey, *supra* note 120 at 78-9.

[131] Neil Brooks, "The Irrelevance of Conjugal Relationships in Assessing Tax Liability" in Richard Krever and John Head eds., *Tax Units and the Tax Rate Scale* (Melbourne: Australian Tax Research Foundation, 1996) at 73.

[132] Ontario Fair Tax Commission, *Fair Tax in a Changing World: Report of the Ontario Fair Tax Commission* (Toronto: University of Toronto Press, 1993) at 268.

[133] See CCH, *British Tax Reporter* (London: CCH looseleaf) at paras.210-250.

[134] Because the CCTB is currently delivered as a refundable tax credit, it is not claimed by a significant number of parents who do not file tax returns: Young, *supra* note 120 at 64-5.

[135] See Monica Townson, *Reducing Poverty Among Older Women: The Potential of Retirement Income Policies* (Ottawa: Status of Women Canada, 2000).

[136] Section 122.5.

137 The government wanted to make this additional credit unavailable to single individuals who were dependent upon their parents. The way the government attempted to exclude students (and other dependant adults) from the extra credit was to deny it to individuals whose incomes were under $6,169 (the income sheltered from tax by the basic personal credit). The GST credit is phased in at a rate of 2 percent for incomes above this amount, reaching a maximum of $107 at a net income of $13,175.

138 The credit is calculated annually, based on the individual's previous year's adjusted income.

139 Lahey, *supra* note 120 at 107.

140 See Statistics Canada, "Population 15 Years and Over by Marital Status, Showing Selected Age Groups and Sex, for Canada, Provinces and Territories", online: http://www.statcan.ca/english/census96/oct14/mar1.htm.

141 Leaving aside the significant numbers of single parents and adult children living with their parents, the number of persons who did not have a spouse or opposite sex common-law partner who lived with others in 1996 was 1.86 million. See Statistics Canada, "Population in private households, showing living arrangements, 1996 Census", online: http://www.statcan.ca/english/Pgdb/People/Families/famil52a.htm.

142 *Income Tax Act*, s.180.2.

143 See section 122.5 (the GST credit), section 122.61 (the child tax benefit), and section 122.51 (the medical expense supplement). Some commentators have noted that it appears inconsistent to use the individual as the basic taxpaying unit but to use the combined income of conjugal couples in phasing out tax credits such as the GST credit. See Peter W. Hogg, Joanne E. Magee and Ted Cook, *Principles of Canadian Income Tax Law* 3rd ed. (Toronto: Carswell, 1999) at 100. However, all of the provisions in the *Income Tax Act* that phase out benefits on the basis of a conjugal couple's income are tax expenditures. They are designed to provide income support to individuals in need. Hence, conceptually, since these provisions serve a very different purpose than determining individuals' ability to pay tax, there is no inconsistency in the fact that the technical tax system is based upon the individual and these transfer payments are phased out based upon the combined income of the parties to a conjugal relationship.

144 The discriminatory effects of the "tax on marriage" or "tax on conjugal cohabitation" may go beyond different treatment of similarly situated conjugal and non-conjugal cohabitants. In a recent empirical study, Kathleen Lahey demonstrates that the burden of family income tests falls disproportionately on women with children, lesbian couples and low-income couples. See Kathleen A. Lahey, *The Impact of Relationship Recognition on Lesbian Women in Canada: Still Separate and Only Somewhat "Equivalent"* (Ottawa: Status of Women Canada, 2001), online: http://www.swc-cfc.gc.ca/publish/research/010914-0662659406-e.html.

145 It might include, however, a consideration of income derived from investments or assets.

146 For this reason, several reports have recommended against using individual income as the basis for income-tested benefits: Social Assistance Review Committee, *Transitions: Report of the Social Assistance Review Committee* (Toronto: Queen's Printer, 1988) at 161; Quebec, Ministry of Finance, *White Paper on the Personal Tax and Transfer System* (Quebec: Department of Finance, 1984). On the other hand, others argue that the "wealthy banker's wife" is an inappropriate scenario on which to base social policy. The "inequality" costs of maintaining the economic dependency must be considered. Family income testing may create additional barriers to the exercise of a choice to leave abusive situations. See Gwen Brodsky and Shelagh Day, *Determining Entitlement to Income Security* (Ottawa: Law Commission of Canada, July 2001).

147 The cost implications of replacing the family income test by an individual income test must not take place in a vacuum; the government must also take into account the costs to Canadians of retaining the status quo, which include the costs of maintaining economic dependency. It must be remembered that the costs of maintaining family income testing are borne by the poorest members of our society.

148 K. Battle and S. Torjman, *The Post-Welfare State in Canada: Income Testing and Inclusion* (Ottawa: Caledon Institute of Social Policy, 2001) at 10.

149 If Parliament decides to retain the family income test in its current form, it should consider alleviating its negative impact on conjugal couples. Some of the unfairness of the GST credit phase-out arises since the phase-out is the same for individuals and couples. For individuals who are married or living in common-law partnerships, the phase-out is based on the combined income of the couple, but the phase-out rate and therefore the range over which the phase-out occurs is identical for couples and individual taxpayers. Thus the income level at which a couple loses all entitlement to the credit is the same as the income level at which an individual loses entitlement to the credit, $41,884. One partial response to this penalty on couples would be to base the phase-out on the combined income of couples, but to impose the phase-out on them at half the rate (and therefore twice the range) applicable to individual taxpayers. While a phase-out based solely on individual income would be preferable, a delayed family-income phase-out would at least temper the inequities of the current approach. It would be more consistent, for example, with the empirical evidence demonstrating that full and equal sharing of income is uncommon, even in conjugal relationships. See sources cited in *supra* note 117.

150 Section 73(1).

151 Section 70(6).

152 Claire Young, *What's Sex Got to Do With It? Tax and the "Family"* (Ottawa: Law Commission of Canada, 2000) at 82.

153 *Ibid.*, at 83.

154 *Ibid.*, at 82-85.

155 These so-called "spousal" trusts are extremely common in the wills of husbands and male common-law partners. This aspect of the rollover would appear to be inconsistent with its justification and, in practice, likely results in men being able to constrain the ability of their wives or common-law partners to control their wealth even after the death of the husband or male partner in heterosexual relationships. It allows the deceased partner to obtain a deferral of tax liability for property in which the surviving partner only has an income interest for life (which might have little value), in which the surviving partner has no power of disposition or control, and for which the deceased partner has designated the ultimate beneficiary. The fundamental justification for this rollover is that the property is likely to be beneficially owned by both partners. This being the case, it arguably should not apply to property in which one partner is only prepared to transfer a life interest to the other. If both beneficially own the property, then the surviving spouse should have a claim to the property outright. Moreover, the effect and even intent of the "spousal" trust provision would appear to be to prevent widows from controlling the devolution of property beneficially owned during the relationship. Indeed, it would appear to be a potent, if subtle, technique for permitting the disinheritance of widows.

156 In order to operationalize these recommendations, governments will have to set out and make public the criteria that will be used; factors such as cohabitation for a certain length of time, the existence of marriage or a registered relationship may all be considered.

157 R.S.C. 1985, c.O-9.

158 Pages 78 to 87.

159 In Holland's words, the objective was "to compensate for the hardships that would result in dependency relationships when the breadwinner retired and the couple was forced to live on a single pension". Winifred H. Holland, *Ascription of Spousal Status: Identifying Legislative Objectives in Ascribing Spousal Status to Cohabitants* (Ottawa: Law Commission of Canada, 2001) at 26.

160 *House of Commons Debates,* June 6, 1975, at p.6520.

161 *House of Commons Debates,* May 22, 1975, at p.6041.

162 Since 1987, when the number of claimants of the Spouse's Allowance reached a peak of almost 140,000, the number of beneficiaries has dropped by more than 30 percent to just over 97,000 in 1999. At the same time, the number of people aged 60 to 64 receiving a CPP retirement pension has more than tripled. Monica Townson, *Reconsidering the Relevance of Relationships in Income Security Programs* (Ottawa: Law Commission of Canada, August 2001) at 7.

163 See *Collins* v. *Canada,* [2000] 2 F.C.R. 3 (T.D.) (monthly allowance provisions of the *Old Age Security Act* discriminate on the basis of marital status in violation of s.15 of the Charter).

164 *House of Commons Debates,* February 4, 1985, at p.1941.

165 See Monica Townson, *Reducing Poverty Among Older Women: The Potential of Retirement Income Policies* (Ottawa: Status of Women Canada, 2000) at pp.50-52.

166 R.S.C. 1985, c.C-8.

167 *Ibid.,* s.44(1)(d).

168 *Canada Pension Plan,* S.C. 1964-65, c.51, s.56.

169 *An Act to amend the Canada Pension Plan,* S.C. 1974-75-76, c.4, s.29.

170 R.S.C. 1985, c.30 (2nd Supp.), s.1 (adding a definition of spouse to s.2 of the CPP); *Modernization of Benefits and Obligations Act,* S.C. 2000, c.11, s.42(2) (adding definition of common-law partner to the CPP) and s.44(3) (adding definition of survivors that includes common-law partners).

171 Holland, *supra* note 159 at 21-22.

172 *Canada Pension Plan,* R.S.C. 1985, c.C-8, s.42(1).

173 *Ibid.,* s.44(1)(d) and s.58(1).

174 In our example, Maria could instead be Sam's sister; the same problem arises.

175 See, for example, *Fraser* v. *Canadien National,* [1999] J.Q. No. 2286 and *Smades* v. *Canada (Minister of Employment and Immigration),* [1995] F.C.J. No. 544 (C.A.), where surviving wives argued that their husbands' cohabitants were not spouses for the purposes of entitlement to survivor's benefits.

Chapter Four

The Legal Organization of Personal Relationships

In this chapter, we set out to address the nature of the state's role and interest in assigning rights and responsibilities within committed personal adult relationships. What should the state's role be in relation to committed relationships? What is the nature of the state's obligation in providing legal mechanisms to support relationships and to assist in the legal organization of such relationships?

We begin by suggesting that the state does indeed have a role in creating legal mechanisms for people to express their commitments to one another. Such a role must be carried out in light of the plurality of relationships that exist in Canadian society as well as the values of equality and autonomy that should characterize governmental action. How can the state adequately respond to the variety of needs that people have in organizing their personal relationships? How can it ensure that the values of autonomy are respected while ensuring that the risks of exploitation are minimized? These are the questions discussed in this chapter.

The Role of the State

Many people long for stability and certainty in their personal relationships just as they do in other areas of their lives, at work or in business. The state does have a role in providing legal mechanisms for people to be able to achieve such private understandings. It must provide an orderly framework in which people can express their commitment to each other and voluntarily assume a range of legal rights and obligations.

In attempting to provide for adequate legal structures or mechanisms that may support the relationships that people develop, the state must respect the values that we outlined earlier: equality, autonomy and choice.

For a long time, the state has focused on marriage as the vehicle of choice for adults to express their commitment. Marriage provides parties with the ability to state publicly and officially their intentions toward one another. It is entered voluntarily. It also provides for certainty and stability since the marriage cannot be terminated without legal procedures. Marriage as a legal tool demonstrates characteristics of voluntariness, stability, certainty and publicity that made it attractive as a model to regulate relationships.

But it is no longer a sufficient model to respond to the variety of relationships that exist in Canada today. Whether we look at older people living with their adult children, adults with disabilities living with their caregivers, or siblings cohabiting in the same residence, the marriage model is inadequate. Some of these other relationships are also characterized by emotional and economic interdependence, mutual care and concern and the expectation of some duration. All of these personal adult relationships could also benefit from legal frameworks to support people's need for certainty and stability.

Throughout our consultations, it became clear that simply allowing people the option to enter into private contracts, such as cohabitation agreements or caregiving arrangements, was insufficient because it did not always have the official or public aspect that was needed, nor did it offer sufficient guarantee of certainty. In addition, the lack of official record of such private arrangements prevents the efficient administration of laws and programs where relationships could be relevant. For example, it might be easier to prove that one is in a close personal relationship according to our proposed *Evidence Act*, if one benefits from an already publicly acknowledged relationship.

We must therefore examine ways for the state to offer all Canadians appropriate legal frameworks that respond to their needs for certainty and stability in their personal relationships. This role of providing sufficient legal mechanisms for people to carry out their private and personal commitments is an important one. It is just as important as insuring that the corporate world has the legal tools to respond to its needs for stability and certainty. These legal frameworks must keep pace with the ways in which adults organize their lives.

It is in this context that one must look at the mechanisms currently developed to allow Canadians to organize their private lives.

> The sole traditional model, once accepted by most couples, has given way to a variety of models. These models are determined by the people involved based on their specific expectations. As the chair of the Conseil de la famille et de l'enfance du Québec stated:
>
> The values emerging from the surveys show a society that is primarily individualistic and pluralistic, a society that is looking for new models. There is a lack of the common, clearly defined reference points that people once used to guide them in their search for happiness. [...] Increasingly, individuals rather than major institutions are defining reference points and guideposts.
>
> A. Roy, *Le contrat en contexte d'intimité* (Ottawa: Law Commission of Canada, June 2001) at 15.

Legal Frameworks for Personal Relationships

In this section, we review four legal models of regulation of personal relationships. The first, the private law model, is one that operates by default. When governments do not provide any legal framework, parties resort to traditional private law concepts to organize their lives. This is the current case for non-conjugal relationships in Canada in which people may choose to be regulated privately. For conjugal relationships, there are three models to regulate personal relationships that have been used around the world: ascription, registration and marriage. In this section, we explore the advantages and disadvantages of the four mechanisms with a view to suggesting possible avenues for governments to better reflect the diversity of personal relationships.

Private Law

People are always at liberty to express their commitments through contracts. Whether written or oral, contracts do regulate personal relationships. Expressly or implicitly, people who reside together, who help each other or who have an intimate relationship organize their lives around shared expectations that are more or less well defined. When such expectations are not fulfilled, they may seek remedy in court under various theories of private law, unjust enrichment, constructive trust, or the creation of an implicit partnership,[1] to name a few.

Parties may choose to state explicitly in a written document their shared expectations and demand execution of such a contractual arrangement through the civil courts. The ability to forge one's own contractual regime and negotiate the terms of one's commitment is a valued tool in a free society and one which must always be available.

But it is a tool beyond the reach of many people. Leaving the parties to design their own contractual or private law arrangements imposes too high a burden on people who do not have time, energy or the requisite knowledge to do so. The possible involvement of a lawyer to design such arrangements is also too costly or inconvenient for the majority of people. Furthermore, there is also a concern that the stronger or wealthier party may impose unfavourable terms on the poorer or weaker party.

Although contracts will continue to remain an important method for individuals to determine their mutual rights and obligations, they are not a sufficient remedy in and of themselves.[2] The contractual model may respect the value of autonomy but often falls short of fulfilling other values such as equality or efficiency since too few individuals are prepared to negotiate the terms of their close personal relationships.

In the absence of a contract, people will also continue to use the courts and private law remedies to respond to various ways in which their expectations have not been met or to remedy the exploitation that they have suffered. However, this mechanism, used in the aftermath of a relationship, is uncertain, expensive and requires that people be able to afford and endure costly and difficult court proceedings.

In the case of conjugal relationships, governments have long recognized the limitations of the contractual and private law models and have moved to a presumptive model for most of these relationships, a model that we describe as ascription.

Ascription

Ascription refers to treating unmarried cohabitants as if they were married, without their having taken any positive action to be legally recognized. In most Canadian provinces and at the federal level, governments have moved to extend policies and legislation aimed at married couples to common-law partners. For example, the *Modernization of Benefits and Obligations Act*[3] extended to both same-sex and opposite-sex couples living in a conjugal relationship for at least one year, a wide array of rights and obligations previously available only to married couples.

Ascription is generally heralded as a way for governments to prevent the risks of exploitation inherent in a contractual model. It imposes a set of obligations on people in conjugal relationships which are presumed to correspond to the expectations of the majority of people. It has hence allowed governments to respond to the changes in Canadian society, particularly with respect to the regulation of the relationships of unmarried conjugal relationships. It also supplies a default arrangement for couples who have not provided for any arrangements[4] and who would otherwise have to resort to cumbersome traditional private law models.

However, ascription as a model has limits. First, it is a blunt policy tool in that it treats all conjugal relationships alike, irrespective of the level of emotional or economic interdependency that they may present. Second, it infringes upon the value of autonomy. Although people may opt out of certain statutory provisions governing their relationships, they are not always aware of this possibility. In addition, ascription is not the best way to respond to the needs of non-conjugal relationships.[5] It would be inappropriate to presume that all older parents living with their adult children have the same needs or that adults with disabilities have equally similar patterns of caring and support. Although ascription may serve the particular purpose of preventing exploitation,[6] it is a tool that must be used sparingly, where there is evidence of exploitation. Governments should continue to use the model of ascription but they should also provide Canadians with appropriate tools to define for themselves the terms of their relationships.

It is in that context that governments should look at a system that would affirm the capacity of people to establish for themselves the terms of their relationships while providing models for doing so. Registration models would serve that purpose.

Registration

Recently, there has been a move toward the creation of a new status, often called registered partnership (or Registered Domestic Partnership or RDP). A domestic partnership scheme was first adopted in Denmark in 1989,[7] and since then has been adopted in other European countries,[8] Hawaii[9] and Vermont.[10] Often RDPs were introduced as a means of recognizing same-sex relationships. However, as these schemes developed in other jurisdictions, they have been extended to also allow opposite-sex couples to register their relationships. For example, in the Netherlands, the registration scheme is open to both same-sex and opposite-sex partners.[11] Belgium, France and the Spanish province of Catalonia have also enacted registration schemes open to two persons of the opposite or same sex.[12] In what is the first registration scheme in Canada, the province of Nova Scotia has introduced a registration scheme that is open to both same-sex and opposite-sex couples.[13]

The objective of these registration schemes is to provide an alternative way for the state to recognize and support close personal relationships. When people register their relationships, they are then included within a range of rights and responsibilities often similar to marriage.[14] It is a regime that has begun to develop as a parallel to marriage, in which the state is promoting a similar set of objectives in the recognition and support of personal relationships. Like marriage, registrations have the characteristics of voluntariness, stability, certainty and publicity. They provide an orderly framework in which people can express their commitment to each other, receive public recognition and support, and voluntarily assume a range of legal rights and obligations. These regimes also provide for an orderly and equitable resolution of the registrants' affairs if their relationships break down. These are the advantages to a registration scheme. Such schemes allow individuals to express their commitment publicly and voluntarily choose to be included within a range of legal rights and responsibilities. These schemes affirm the basic principles and values that ought to guide the regulation of personal adult relationships, including equality and respect for diversity on one hand, and autonomy and freedom of choice on the other.

First, a registration scheme is worthy of consideration because it would enable a broader range of relationships to be recognized. It would therefore provide both conjugal and non-conjugal unions with a way to formalize their relationship and to voluntarily assume rights and responsibilities toward each other. In this way, a registration system would promote the equality of non-conjugal relationships. The second major advantage of a registration scheme is that it affirms the autonomy and choices of Canadians in their close personal relationships. There is value in encouraging people to make their relationship commitments clear and in recognizing the choices that people make in their close personal relationships. A registration scheme provides a way in which a broad range of relationships, including non-conjugal relationships, can be recognized, while also promoting and respecting the value of autonomy. A registration scheme has a number of advantages specifically related to the value of autonomy and choice. In such a scheme, rights and responsibilities are based on the mutual and voluntary decisions of the individuals in the relationship. It thereby avoids many of the problems with functional definitions that impose relationship status on individuals whether or not they so desire.

A registration scheme could play an important role in broadening the range of options available for people (conjugal and non-conjugal alike) to voluntarily assume rights and responsibilities. The ability to formalize a relationship through a public declaration of commitment is important to Canadians. A registration scheme provides a way in which individuals in close personal relationships can choose to make such a public declaration of commitment, which would then be respected by government.

A registration system may also promote the values of equality and autonomy within relationships without compromising the value of privacy. The ascription model described above, if it were to use more functional definitions, would require that governments examine individual relationships to decide whether they fit the definition. It is an approach that necessarily involves some degree of invasion of privacy. A registration scheme, on the other hand, by leaving the choice entirely up to the individuals within relationships and then respecting that choice, provides a way of recognizing conjugal and non-conjugal relationships without compromising the values of autonomy or privacy. Within a registration scheme there would be no uncertainty about the legal status of the close personal relationship and no reason for the government to subject the relationship to scrutiny. Ascription, however, should continue to be used where there is evidence of exploitation.

Designing a Registration Scheme

There are many challenging questions that governments will have to address in deciding how a registration scheme should be designed and implemented. In this section, we review some of these questions and, drawing on the insights that can be gleaned from developments in other jurisdictions, we suggest how a registration system should be designed.

Formal Attributes

The first question that must be addressed in designing a registration scheme involves its formal attributes, that is, who may register? Should there be any limits on who may register?

One of the greatest advantages of a registration scheme is that it provides an opportunity to recognize the formal commitment of individuals in any relationship. There is no reason for governments to restrict a registration scheme to conjugal couples or to same-sex couples[15] or, indeed, only to couples.[16] Some models of registration developed in Europe have been restricted to conjugal unions or even to same-sex relationships.[17] Many other jurisdictions that have introduced registration schemes have limited these schemes to conjugal couples. For example, in the first registration scheme to be introduced in Canada, the province of Nova Scotia limits domestic partner declarations to "two individuals who are cohabiting in a conjugal relationship".[18] In the Nordic countries, because the registration schemes were introduced to give some form of legal recognition to same-sex couples, they tend to have the same kind of restrictions as those imposed on marriage. Most commonly, individuals cannot register if they are related too closely by blood. While none of these schemes specify that individuals must have a sexual relationship,[19] the restriction on not entering into a registration within a "close family relationship" means that registration is not available for non-conjugal couples who are related too closely by blood. For example, then, two adult siblings

---

We are thirty-six-year-old twin sisters who have never been married or had children and who live together… Our lives are inextricably linked: aside from being related and having known each other all of our lives, we have co-habited continuously for the last seventeen years (since leaving our parental home), rely on each other for emotional support, and are entirely dependent on each other financially – we co-own all of our possessions and share all of our living expenses. A more stable relationship cannot be found. Yet, because we are sisters, rather than husband and wife, and because we are not a couple in a presumably sexual relationship, we are denied tax benefits, "family" health coverage, and a multitude of other advantages constructed upon sexist and heterosexist ideas about what constitutes meaningful relationships.

We find this situation incredibly frustrating. It seems to us that we are being penalized for not marrying or living with men – or even with women in a presumably sexual relationship. Should the possibility of sexual relations between two co-habitating[sic] adults, whether heterosexual or homosexual, really be the yardstick by which the government, the law, and the corporation measure a citizen's entitlement to social and economic rights? This notion is completely absurd, and yet our entire social structure is premised upon it.

Law Commission of Canada Comments Board, website, June 2000 - January 2001,
posted with permission.

---

who live together could not enter into a registration in these regimes.[20]

A few jurisdictions have introduced registration schemes which include non-conjugal couples. In Hawaii, the "reciprocal beneficiaries" scheme extends certain rights and benefits to couples who are legally prohibited from marrying.[21] Under this scheme, same-sex couples as well as non-conjugal couples are permitted to register their relationship. A study by the British Columbia Law Institute recommended that registrations be made available to conjugal and non-conjugal couples alike.[22]

Finally, a number of jurisdictions have considered whether registrations should be limited to couples who live together. In the Netherlands, domestic partners have an obligation to cohabit. However, in Denmark and Sweden, there is no obligation for the partners to live together. In our view, there is no reason to impose a residential requirement on registrations. There is no similar restriction on marriage: married couples do not have to live together for the marriage to be valid. There is, then, no compelling reason to impose such a restriction on registered relationships.[23]

Another question that governments will have to address is how registrations should be terminable; that is, how can partners decide to end their registration? In our view, registrations should be terminable by mutual agreement. Registered partners should be able to make a mutual declaration that their partnership has ended. Furthermore, given that married spouses can end their marriage unilaterally by making an application for divorce after living separate and apart for one year,[24] it would not be justifiable to impose a more rigorous standard on domestic partners. Partners in a registered relationships should similarly be able to register a dissolution of their registration.[25]

In addition, the regulation of the dissolution of registrations must ensure that the legal obligations between the registrants are respected upon relationship breakdown. Restructuring financial relationships on relationship breakdown remains an important state objective. The state should ensure that the reasonable expectations of partners are not undermined on the breakdown of the relationship.

Legal Implications of Registrations

In the Nordic European jurisdictions and Vermont, registrations have been created as a parallel to marriage. In these regimes, people can choose to enter into a registration and are then subject to a predetermined set of rights and responsibilities. While these are not always the identical set of rights and responsibilities as marriage, the legal consequences are similar.

Governments could enact a registration regime based on this model, whereby people could formally enter into a registration and then be entitled to predetermined rights and responsibilities. The possibility of choosing the same rights and responsibilities as spouses or common-law partners could be offered.

It might also be possible to design more flexible arrangements that may respond better to the variety of caregiving relationships that exist. Models of caregiving arrangements could be proposed which parties could modify, if they so wish.[26]

The legal consequences of registration might be limited to the private rights and responsibilities within the relationship. It could involve such issues as property and support obligations both during and after the relationship. It could involve determinations for care arrangements, consent to treatment or other aspects of the relationship. The commitment of entering into a registration would be about the voluntary assumption of mutual responsibilities. It would be about clarifying this commitment of mutual responsibility in law, both for the parties themselves and for potentially interested third parties.

Intergovernmental and International Implications

There are significant intergovernmental implications of introducing a federal registration scheme. The jurisdiction of the federal government to implement a registration scheme is limited. The federal government has jurisdiction over marriage and divorce (s. 91(26) of the *Constitution Act, 1867*), which includes the corollary issues of support and custody. However, it is unlikely that this jurisdiction would allow the federal government to enact a registration regime that regulated the private legal obligations between domestic partners. Federal jurisdiction over marriage and divorce is not sufficiently broad to empower Parliament to pass legislation regulating entry into, and exit from, this new civil arrangement that, like marriage, would then be possibly employed in federal, provincial and territorial laws. The best scenario would be for a coordinated initiative, such as a model Uniform Act for the registration of relationships.[27]

Governments will also need to consider the international implications of a registration scheme. If individuals entered into a registration, would that relationship be recognized abroad? What if these two individuals were non-conjugal? What if they were of the same sex? What if they were persons of the opposite sex living together in a conjugal relationship, but decided to forgo marriage in favour of a registered status? These questions all raise serious and not easily answerable foreign recognition and conflict of laws issues. First, it is worth noting that the law regarding the recognition of foreign marriages is itself a controversial and confusing area. Notwithstanding efforts to harmonize this law, through the *Hague Convention on Celebration and Recognition of the Validity of Marriage*, different countries adopt different approaches to the recognition of foreign marriages. Canada, among other countries, has not signed the Convention and follows its own rules on the recognition of foreign marriages.[28] Potential registrants in Canada would have to be educated about the effects and limitations of their registered status in other countries. Secondly, there are the new and distinctive problems associated with the creation of a civil status in some states but not others, a status that is itself not uniform in scope as between these different states. European countries that have enacted registration schemes have begun to grapple with some of these issues. But, to date, there is little uniformity in approach.[29] The Hague Conference on Private International Law (which works towards the unification of the rules of private international law) is currently considering the issues related to unmarried couples, including registered partnership. The Council of Europe has also expressed interest in the private international law aspects of registered partnerships.

Canada should participate in the efforts toward international recognition of registration systems. It should also attempt to design its international arrangements on the basis of the existence of a variety of relationships and move toward an international recognition of registrations.

Recommendation 31

Parliament and provincial/territorial legislatures should pass laws enabling adults to register their relationship.

Considerations:

- The registration should not be restricted only to conjugal relationships.
- It should provide for a set of commitments, which could include caring arrangements, consent to treatment dispositions, support and sharing in property from which the parties may opt out.

Recommendation 32

Governments should attempt to design their international arrangements on the basis of the existence of a variety of relationships and move toward an international recognition of registrations.

Registration schemes are not a panacea: the number of people who choose to register their relationships may not be significant.[30] It also seems clear that registration schemes could not completely replace the ascription model which has taken root in Canadian law, particularly when the care of children is involved. Nevertheless, they offer the following significant advantages to complement and nuance such ascriptive models: they offer people the possibility of voluntarily assuming responsibilities toward another; they may provide models of arrangements that could be helpful in framing negotiations between parties; and they provide for an expression of commitment outside of conjugal and intimate relationships. This is a feature that distinguishes them from the fourth legal instrument for the regulation of close personal adult relationships: marriage.

Marriage

Our marriage laws are the product of a long history and they date to the early days of Confederation.[31] A review of the role of the state toward the organization of personal relationships in Canada would not be complete without an assessment as to whether our marriages laws continue to meet the needs of our evolving society.[32] This is the purpose of this section.

We begin with a fundamental question as to whether there needs to be marriage laws at all. One could imagine that in order to achieve equality toward the range of relationships that exist in Canada, the state could simply institute a system of registration as recommended above that could replace marriage, for all legal purposes. What would be the implications of such a model? Would it better serve the objectives of the state?

Registration Instead of Marriage

Creating a registration scheme that would permit all relationships, conjugal and other, to benefit from the characteristics of voluntariness, publicity, certainty and stability now afforded only to marriage could eliminate the need for marriage. It would not prevent people from marrying religiously or calling themselves "married" in addition to "registering" their unions. However, the religious marriage would not carry legal connotations nor would the public identification as "married" be of any legal consequence. In order to have legal consequences, people would have to register their relationship. Legal consequences would accompany only the additional and separate step of registering the relationship for civil purposes. The system of civil registration would be open to all, married couples and others, who want to obtain public recognition and support of their relationships while voluntarily subscribing to a range of legal rights and obligations.[33]

This idea has many advantages. By removing the link between marriage and legal consequences, the spheres of religious and secular authority would be more clearly delineated. By establishing a civil registration scheme open to all persons in committed relationships, the state could focus more clearly and effectively on accomplishing the underlying objective currently accomplished incompletely by marriage, namely, recognizing and supporting committed personal adult relationships by facilitating an orderly regulation of their affairs.

However, one disadvantage of leaving the solemnization of marriage to religious authorities is that the option of marrying in a secular ceremony would be lost. This may be a serious disadvantage given that civil marriage ceremonies constitute a growing proportion of marriages solemnized in many Canadian jurisdictions. Nevertheless, this would not prevent couples from calling "marriage" the registration of their unions and celebrating this commitment.

It should also be noted that under this model, married persons would have the choice, currently unavailable to them, whether or not to have their relationship status formally recognized by the state. There are both advantages and disadvantages to this choice. On the one hand, it promotes the value of autonomy for married and unmarried persons alike since they all will be able to choose whether or not to register their relationships. On the other hand, it may create the undesirable situation of undermining individuals' reasonable expectations. If individuals do not understand that a religious marriage unaccompanied by a registration does not result in any legal consequences, they may be lulled into a false sense of security having entered only a religious marriage. This would have to be understood and reinforced particularly by the religious organizations currently empowered to marry.

It should also be noted that this option may require substantial provincial and territorial co-operation. The complexities of divided jurisdictions would pose a challenge to the replacement of marriage with civil registration.

While there are many principled advantages to this model, it is not likely an option that would appear very attractive to a majority of Canadians. Replacing marriage with a system of registration undermines choice in the regulation of close personal relationships. Removing marriage as a choice for conjugal couples prevents them from continuing to use a legal mechanism that many regard as fundamental to their commitment. While further debate about the appropriate role of the state in marriage, including the possibility of removing the state from the marriage business, is worthwhile, we do not believe that this is a viable reform option at this time.

We are left with attempting to determine whether our marriage laws continue to respond to the needs of society.

Adequacy of Current Marriage Laws

The history of marriage laws in Europe has been characterized by a struggle between religious organizations and the state to control the institution. We begin by briefly reviewing this history since it helps explain the presence of religious denominations in the administration of marriage laws in Canada. This historical overview is limited to the evolution of marriage in the Western world and is offered as a background to understand the current mix of religious and state administration of marriage in Canada. In a subsequent section, we discuss the appropriateness of religion in the administration of marriage laws versus a system comprised solely of civil marriages. In the final section, we address the issue of same-sex marriages.

A Brief History of Marriage Laws

In Roman law, marriage was considered to be largely a private matter, regulated by custom more than law. Marriage did have legal consequences: it was indirectly significant when the law "had to deal with problems involving membership of the 'houses' of which the body politic was composed, with succession on death, or with allocation of responsibility for civil wrongs".[34] But the formation and dissolution of marriage was governed primarily by custom. As Mary Ann Glendon concludes, in Roman times, "the law took little notice of the social institution of marriage…marriage was not a legal institution".[35]

The fall of the Roman Empire and the rise of the Christian church brought about a fundamental transformation in the regulation of marriage, as the church claimed exclusive jurisdiction over marriage. This claim to exclusive jurisdiction, and "the novel idea that marriage was indissoluble," were "both closely connected to the new Christian idea that marriage was a sacrament".[36] The idea of indissolubility did not take hold easily. For several centuries, the Church had to tolerate local customs in which divorce and remarriage were common, as it slowly acquired its control over marriage. The authority of the ecclesiastical courts and the basics of canon law were in place in France and the Germanies by the end of the 10th century, and in England by the 12th century. Canon law established the indissolubility of marriage and, along with it, a complex web of regulations for more precisely defining marriage.[37] Up to the Council of Trent in the mid-16th century, the church had continued to recognize local, informal marriage customs. But, with the Decree *Tametsi* in 1563, no marriage would be valid unless it had been publicly celebrated in the presence of a priest.[38]

From the 16th century onwards, the Catholic Church began to lose its exclusive jurisdiction over marriage, as the state began to take an interest in its regulation. In parts of continental Europe, the Catholic Church lost its jurisdiction due to the Protestant Reformation. But, as jurisdiction was slowly transferred to the secular authorities, there was little change in the rules governing marriage. Rather, the secular authorities "simply took over much of the ready-made set of rules of the canon law".[39] The 18th century witnessed the rise of the codification of private law, including the extensive regulation of the formation, dissolution and content of marriage, as well as the emergence of the compulsory civil marriage ceremony, according to which only a civil marriage would be recognized as a valid marriage. The compulsory civil marriage was the product of the French Revolution. While the royal courts had already assumed control over marriage from the church, the introduction of the civil marriage completed the state's exclusive jurisdiction over

> Marriage [is like] …an archaeological site on which the present is constantly building over the past, letting history's many layers twist and tilt into today's walls and floors…many people believe theirs is the one true claim to this holy ground. But…marriage has always been a battleground, owned and defined first by one group and then another. While marriage…may retain its ancient name, very little else in this city has remained the same, not its boundaries, boulevards, or daily habits – except the fact that it is inhabited by human beings. And yet, marriage has outlasted its many critics…and has outlasted as well, the doomsayers of so many eras who post marriage's obituary notice every time society talks about changing its marriage rules.
>
> E.J. Graff, *What is Marriage For?* (Boston: Beacon Press, 1999) at xi.

marriage and, with it, the separation of church and state.[40]

In England, the church retained its ecclesiastical jurisdiction over marriage well into the 19th century. Informal marriages continued to be valid until *Lord Hardwicke's Act*[41] in 1753, which, like the Decree *Tametsi*, banned clandestine marriages and made an ecclesiastical ceremony compulsory. Civil marriage was introduced only in 1836 with the *Marriage Act*.[42] Unlike France and other countries in Europe, however, civil marriage did not displace religious marriages.

These two different approaches to the role of church and state in relation to marriage continue in contemporary Western Europe. In some countries – including Belgium, France, Germany, the Netherlands, and Switzerland – a civil marriage ceremony is mandatory. It is the only type of marriage recognized by law. A religious ceremony may be held following the civil ceremony, but no legal consequences attach to it. The respective roles of church and state are thus clearly separated. In other countries – including Denmark, the United Kingdom, Greece, Ireland, Italy, Norway, Portugal, Spain and Sweden – civil and religious ceremonies are alternate routes to the same legal consequences. Church and state both have the authority to solemnize a marriage for the purposes of legal recognition.[43] This is the approach that was inherited from England and has since been maintained in both Canada and the United States.

As this brief historical review reveals, state jurisdiction over marriage is a relatively recent phenomenon. And the state's interest in marriage has also continued to change. Indeed, as opinions and values have continued to change, so too have the state objectives underlying marital regulation. While the state's interest in establishing the requirements of a valid marriage and the legal consequences that attach to marriage partners has been a constant over the course of Canadian history, the nature of state regulation of marriage has undergone profound change. Consider the differences between the contemporary regulation of marriage and the situation a century ago.

In the late 19th century, the law continued to enforce the Christian understanding of marriage as a lifelong, indissoluble union of one man and one woman to the exclusion of all others.[44] Legal regulation supported a division of labour along gender lines: in urban areas at least, wives were to provide a range of domestic services in exchange for their husbands' economic support. The law worked together with other social practices to place its weight behind the Christian conception of marriage. Intimate relations within marriages were protected from state scrutiny, while sexual activity outside of marriage was heavily discouraged. Unmarried mothers and their children were penalized. Divorce was so difficult and costly to obtain that formal dissolution of marriages was not an option that could be contemplated by Canadians of ordinary means. Limitations on women's civil and political rights were seen as extensions of wives' legal and financial dependency on their husbands. We now see the nineteenth century model of marital regulation as one that was deeply implicated in structures of gender inequality.

The contemporary law of marriage is very different.[45] Women have achieved recognition of their independent legal personalities and equal political rights. Gender-neutral laws have replaced legislation that accorded different legal rights and responsibilities to husbands and wives. Contemporary family laws recognize marriage as a partnership between equals.[46] Sexual assault within marriage[47] and other forms of domestic abuse can give rise to criminal prosecution. Marriages are no longer legally indissoluble: the availability of no-fault divorce makes the continuation of a marital union a matter of mutual consent.[48] The decision whether or not to procreate and raise children is an issue of fundamental personal choice. The heavy legal and social penalties imposed on non-marital cohabitation or children born out of wedlock have been removed. The law has had to recognize that children formerly known as "illegitimate" are part of society – not recognizing their existence does not make them less so and fails to protect their basic interests. Now federal legislative policy and constitutional norms dictate equal treatment of married spouses and unmarried conjugal cohabitants.[49]

Further, although many people marry to have children, and marriage is, in many cases, the legal arrangement that supports parenting, marriage is not the only place where parenting is performed. While the overall childbearing rate has been on the decline, the non-marital childbearing rate has increased sharply. The percentage of non-marital births was one-third of all children born in 1994, compared with only 6 percent in 1974.[50] The fact that marriages occur when people are no longer able to have children and the fact that many children are born and live outside marriage indicates that parenting and marriage are not interchangeable concepts although, in the lives of many Canadians, the two concepts continue to be inter-related.

Borrowing the term from the history of church and state, Nancy Cott has described the transformation in the relationship between marriage and the state in the United States as "disestablishment". Just as the state does not recognize a single, officially established church, no longer is any single, official model of adult intimate relationship supported and enforced by the state.[51]

Nevertheless, Canadian laws have long recognized that marriage can be formalized either through a religious or civil ceremony. Provincial and territorial laws draw a clear distinction between religious and secular means of formalizing marriage. Religious marriage ceremonies are performed by religious authorities pursuant to a state-issued licence or pursuant to the publication of banns. Civil marriage ceremonies are performed in a secular context by designated state authorities. The preconditions of each type of marriage may differ. For example, the Roman Catholic Church does not permit divorce and will not perform a religious ceremony if one of the intending spouses has been divorced. Nonetheless, Canadian law permits both a civil divorce and a civil remarriage, whatever the religion of the parties. While the rate of civil marriage is increasing in many jurisdictions, it remains the case that the majority of marriages in Canada are formalized pursuant to a religious ceremony (except in British Columbia where the civil form of marriage is more popular).[52]

In Canada, therefore, we currently have a complex regime where both the religious authorities and state authorities are present. Does this regime continue to be adequate for the evolving Canadian society? Would it be appropriate to revisit the role of the religious authorities as state-delegates for the purposes of marriage celebrations and adopt the regime of civil marriages that exist in numerous countries?

The Case for Civil Marriage

In many countries, only a civil marriage has legal consequences. Religious institutions conduct religious marriages. However, a couple must enter a civil marriage in order for the marriage to have legal consequences. This model of civil marriage has been in effect in France since the French Revolution.[53] The religious celebration of marriage has no legal effect: couples must first have a secular marriage ceremony.[54] A similar model of civil marriage is followed in Belgium, Germany, the Netherlands and Switzerland. This model of civil marriage is one that completely separates the respective roles of church and state. Churches continue to have authority over the religious aspects of marriage, but the state alone has jurisdiction over the civil aspects of marriage. Only civil marriages have legal consequences.

The only disadvantage to adopting a model of civil marriage as it exists in France and other European countries is the duplication it entails. While the rate of civil marriage is increasing in many jurisdictions, the majority of marriages in Canada are formalized pursuant to a religious ceremony. A mandatory civil ceremony would require the additional visit to state officials, and the appropriate personnel and facilities for such celebrations.

Nevertheless, the option of moving toward a civil marriage should be considered because it would clarify the respective roles of the state and religious organizations. The current situation, in which the state and religious denominations are both involved and have different rules governing marriage, creates confusion that often increases the difficulty and polarization of public policy debates. This is the case for the issue of same-sex marriages.

The Case for Same-Sex Marriage

Marriage, from the point of view of secular state authority, is a means of facilitating in an orderly fashion the voluntary assumption of mutual rights and obligations by adults committed to each other's well-being.[55]

A review of the history of state regulation of marriage helps illuminate that the state interest in marriage is not connected to the promotion of any particular conception of appropriate gender roles. Nor is the state reserving marriage to procreation and the raising of children. People may marry even if they cannot or do not intend to have children. The purposes that underlie contemporary state regulation of marriage are to provide an orderly framework in which couples can express their commitment to each other and voluntarily assume a range of legal rights and obligations. The law also attempts to provide for an orderly and equitable resolution of married spouses' affairs if their relationships break down.

There are diverse views on same-sex marriage, with strong feelings on each side of the issue. For those same-sex couples who wish to marry, the prohibition on same-sex marriage represents a rejection of their personal aspirations and the non-recognition of their personhood. They feel that without equal access to the institution of marriage, their ability to celebrate their love and their lives on equal terms is undermined. They feel that they are denied a fundamental personal choice.[56]

On the other side are those who argue, equally passionately, that marriage has always been defined as, and should remain limited to, the union of a man and a woman. For the opponents of same-sex marriage, it is a matter of preserving a time-tested and even sacred institution. Although a number of religious institutions are now celebrating same-sex commitment ceremonies, some of the opposition to expanding the entitlement to marry to include same-sex couples stems from religious beliefs. Many feel that Parliament should not redefine a concept that they consider inseparable from its societal and religious meanings and origins. Others point to the universality of the recognition of the heterosexual aspects of marriage and find it difficult to accept that marriage be extended to same-sex couples.[57]

In its public consultations, the Law Commission received many submissions both for and against same-sex marriage. Public polls indicate that Canadians are increasingly accepting of the idea of same-sex marriage[58] although there remains strong opposition to it in certain segments of the population.

Nevertheless, the issue of same-sex marriage cannot be avoided. Several cases challenging the current exclusion are now before the courts.[59] The status quo or even the creation of a registration system will not prevent the Charter challenges. The introduction of a registration scheme should not be seen as a policy alternative to reforming marriage. Registration schemes in lieu of allowing same-sex couples to access marriage are seen, by those in favour of same-sex marriage, as creating a second-class category of relationships.[60]

The enactment of a registration scheme, however, would allow the diversity of relationships to be expressed. This may, in turn, diffuse the opposition to same-sex marriage, which as the polls suggest, is waning. Therefore, an option might be a two-part response to the issue of same-sex marriage by first enacting a registration scheme to permit same-sex couples to have access to a legal framework to organize their affairs and, as the population becomes more receptive to it or as they become pressed by international or judicial developments, governments could then pass legislation that would allow same-sex couples to marry. This has been the pattern in the Netherlands.[61]

Nevertheless, the argument that marriage should be reserved to heterosexual couples cannot be sustained in a context where the state's objectives underlying contemporary state regulation of marriage are essentially contractual ones, relating to the facilitation of private ordering. There is no justification for maintaining the current distinctions between same-sex and heterosexual conjugal unions in light of current understandings of the state's interests in marriage. The secular purpose of marriage is to provide an orderly framework in which people can express their commitment to each other, receive public recognition and support, and voluntarily assume a range of legal rights and obligations. The current law does not reflect the social facts: as the Supreme Court of Canada has recognized, the capacity to form conjugal relationships characterized by emotional and economic interdependence has nothing to do with sexual orientation.[62] Furthermore, whether or not denial of same-sex marriage infringes the Charter, adherence to the fundamental values of equality, choice and freedom of conscience and religion requires that restrictions on same-sex marriage be removed; the status quo reinforces the stigmatization felt by same-sex couples. If governments are to continue to maintain an institution called marriage, they cannot do so in a discriminatory fashion.

It is important to recognize that the removal of restrictions on same-sex marriages does not eliminate the need for the enactment of registration schemes for several reasons. First, international developments in the recognition of registration schemes may justify the establishment of Canadian registration schemes to provide conjugal and non-conjugal unions with legal mechanisms that are recognized internationally. Second, establishing registration schemes provides choices for Canadians. The ability to choose how one wants to regulate one's personal relationships is an important feature of living in a democracy. This ought to be preserved and enhanced.

Finally, it is also important to emphasize that civil recognition of same-sex marriage does not alter the right of religious denominations to perform wedding ceremonies without state interference according to the values and traditions of their faith. While the state could recognize same-sex marriages for the purposes of civil marriage, it could not take any position on religious marriages. As is the case now, some religious institutions would choose to sanctify same-sex unions as marriages, while others would not. As it does now, the state would recognize the marriage performed during a religious ceremony by a person authorized to do so under provincial and territorial marriage statutes. The preconditions for each type of marriage, religious and secular, could differ as it often does today. For example, as mentioned earlier, the Roman Catholic Church does not permit divorce and will not perform a religious ceremony if one of the intending spouses has been divorced. Nonetheless, Canadian law permits both a civil divorce and a civil remarriage, whatever the religion of the parties. This is a result that should be celebrated in a society that values religious pluralism.

Recommendation 33

> Parliament and provincial/territorial legislatures should move toward removing from their laws the restrictions on marriages between persons of the same sex.

Conclusion

The state has a role in providing a legal framework to help people fulfill the responsibilities and rights that arise in close personal relationships. However, any involvement by the state should honour the choices that people make. Instead of focusing mainly on married couples and couples deemed to be "marriage-like," governments should establish registration schemes to facilitate the private ordering of both conjugal and non-conjugal relationships. While the state's interest in marriage is primarily focused on contractual issues, Canadians continue to value the importance of a marriage ceremony, whether civil or religious. To the extent that the state continues to have a role in legally recognizing marriage, fundamental Canadian values and the secular nature of the state's interest in marriage require that the state not discriminate against same-sex couples.

[1]   A constructive trust is used as a vehicle to compensate for unjust enrichment in appropriate cases...the plaintiff is found to have an interest in property. *Peter v. Beblow*, [1993] 1 S.C.R. 980 at 995. The doctrine of unjust enrichment is an equitable concept created to remedy injustices that occur where one person makes a substantial contribution to the property of another. *Peter v. Beblow*, [1993] 1 S.C.R. 980 at 987. An implied partnership arises in the absence of an express agreement between parties, where the court finds that the parties were carrying on a business in common with a view to profit. Provincial statutory law, for example, *The Partnership Act*, R.S.S. c.P-3, as amended, set out the factors that determine the existence of a partnership and the interests and duties of the partners. For a discussion in Quebec civil law of tacit partnerships in the context of unmarried cohabitants, see *Beaudoin – Daigneault v. Richard*, [1984] 1 S.C.R. 2. Unmarried couples may also opt into contractual arrangements equivalent to marriage, see *S.C. v. P.G.* [2001] J.Q. No 3817 (Qué. C.A.).

[2]   C. Davies, "The Extension of Marital Rights and Obligations to the Unmarried: Registered Domestic Partnerships and Other Methods" (1999) 17 Canadian Family Law Quarterly 247 at 257 cited in Nicole LaViolette, *Registered Partnerships: A Model for Relationship Recognition* (Ottawa: Law Commission of Canada, August 2001) at 23.

[3]   S.C. 2000, c.12.

[4]   Professor Winifred Holland, in "Intimate Relationships in the New Millenium: The Assimilation of Marriage and Cohabitation?" (2000) 17 Can. J. Fam. L. 114 at 152, described it this way: "people don't engage in 'crystal-ball' gazing at the inception of the relationship".

[5]   Currently, they may be covered by federal statutes that employ terms such as "dependant" or "related person" where those terms are defined broadly to include non-conjugal cohabitants. At the moment, federal statutes that embrace non-conjugal cohabitants are relatively few in number and most apply to individuals who are related in some way. See B. Cossman and B. Ryder, *The Legal Regulation of Adult Personal Relationships: Evaluating Policy Objectives and Legal Options in Federal Legislation* (Ottawa: Law Commission of Canada, May 2000) at 161.

[6]   The courts have rejected the argument that since the couple made a "choice" not to marry, there should be no rights or obligations. There is too much potential for the stronger party to take advantage of the weaker party by denying responsibility for dependencies once the relationship is over. N. Bala, "Alternatives for Extending Spousal Status in Canada" (2000) 17 Can. J. Fam. L. 169 at 193. Bala suggests that factors favouring ascription might include protection of the interests of children, protection of vulnerability or dependence, and compensation for contribution. See also LaViolette, *supra* note 2 at 21.

[7]   Lov. nr. 372 af 7.6.1989 om registreret partnerskab [Act No. 372 of June 7, 1989 on Registered Partnership]. See Nielsen, "Family Rights and the 'Registered Partnership' in Denmark" (1990) 4 Int'l J. L. & Fam. 297; Lund-Andersen, "Moving Towards the Individual Principle in Danish Law" (1990) 4 Int'l J. L. & Fam. 328; Pedersen, "Denmark: Homosexual Marriages and New Rules Regarding Separation and Divorce" (1991/92) 30 J. Fam. L. 290; Dupuis, "The Impact of Culture, Society and History on the Legal Process: An Analysis of the Legal Status of Same-sex Relationships in the United States and Denmark" (1995) 9 Int'l J.L. & Fam. 86.

[8]   Including Norway (1993), Sweden (1994), Iceland (1996) and the Netherlands (1998). For a discussion and further references, see Brenda Cossman and Bruce Ryder, *supra* note 5 at 130-132, and Ingrid Lund-Andersen, "Cohabitation and Registered Partnership in Scandinavia: The Legal Position of Homosexuals" in John M. Eekelaar and Thandabantu Nhlapo eds., *The Changing Family: Family Forms & Family Law* (Oxford: Hart Publishing, 1998) at 397-404.

9   *An Act relating to Unmarried Couples*, 1997 HI H.B. 118. For descriptions of the Act, see Bailey, "Hawaii's Same-sex Marriage Initiatives: Implications for Canada" (1998) 15 Can. J. Fam. L. 153; Martha Bailey, *Marriage and Marriage-Like Relationships* (Ottawa: Law Commission of Canada, 1999) at 125-127; Cossman and Ryder, *ibid.* at 132-134.

10   Act 91, 2000, *An Act Relating to Civil Unions*. See Cossman and Ryder, *supra* note 5 at 135-136.

11   Act of July 5, 1997, Staatsblad 1997, 324. See Schrama, "Registered Partnership in the Netherlands" (1999) 13 Int'l J.L.P. & Fam. 315.

12   For a description of these schemes, see N. LaViolette, *supra* note 2, Annex 1.

13   *Law Reform (2000) Act*, S.N.S. 2000, c.29, ss.32-45.

14   The particular rights and responsibilities that attach to domestic partners vary from jurisdiction to jurisdiction. Only in Vermont, and then only for the purposes of state law, are the rights of domestic partners equivalent to those of married spouses. In other jurisdictions, domestic partners have a similar, but not identical, set of rights and responsibilities.

15   See N. Bala, "Alternatives for Extending Spousal Status in Canada" (2000) 17 Can. J. Fam. L. 169.

16   It is too early in the process to determine the full implications of a registration scheme. As seen in the discussion that follows, governments will have a number of decisions to make regarding the form and legal implications of such a system. However, in principle, the Law Commission sees no reason to limit registration to two people. Registration should capture situations involving three siblings or four housemates, so long as the relationships are characterized by economic or emotional interdependence of some duration. The values and principles of autonomy and state neutrality require that people be free to choose the form and nature of their close personal adult relationships. This issue, however, requires further consideration of factors, such as potential for abuse and exploitation, conflicting interests and claims, and potential costs to third parties.

17   In Denmark, the first country to adopt a registered partnership regime, registation was limited to two persons of the same sex. However, the two persons did not have to share a sexual relationship or even live together. A number of other Nordic countries followed the Denmark model, including Norway, Sweden and Iceland. In the state of Vermont, a recently introduced registration scheme is limited to same-sex couples. For example, in the Netherlands, the registration scheme is open to both same-sex and opposite-sex partners. Belgium, France and the Spanish province of Catalonia have also enacted registration schemes open to two persons of the opposite or same sex. Nova Scotia has recently introduced a registration scheme that is open to both same-sex and opposite-sex couples.

18   *Law Reform (2000) Act*, S.N.S. 2000, c.29, s.53(1).

19   (In fact, in Sweden, the law says that the individuals do not have to have a sexual relationship).

20   In contrast to the Nordic European model, the Hawaii "reciprocal beneficiaries" statute is open only to persons who are prohibited from marrying because they are of the same sex or within the prohibited degrees of consanguinity.

21   Hawaii Revised Statutes 1999, s.572C-1.

22   British Columbia Law Institute, *Report on Recognition of Spousal and Family Status* (Vancouver: British Columbia Law Institute, 1998).

23   This was the position taken by the British Columbia Law Institute in its report, *ibid.*, at 12.

24   *Divorce Act*, R.S.C. 1985, c.3 (2nd Supp.), s.8.

25 Governments may want to consider whether it was appropriate to apply a similar waiting period of one year on domestic partners.

26 In general, governments should be encouraged to develop a variety of model agreements which could serve as the basis for negotiations between the parties. The literature seems to support the view that parties should "contract out" of responsibilities as opposed to be in the position to spell out their responsibilities. Such contracting out may prevent the exploitation of the most vulnerable party: W. Holland, *supra* note 4 at 166-167.

27 Governments should work with Aboriginal communities regarding the design and implementation of registration schemes. In particular, First Nations must be consulted regarding any impact of a registration scheme on the *Indian Act*.

28 According to Martha Bailey in "Private International Law Issues Relating to Registered Partnerships: A Canadian Perspective" (Domestic Partnerships Conference, Faculty of Law, Queen's University, 21-23 October 1999) [unpublished], the essential validity of marriage is governed by the law of the domicile of each of the spouses at the time of marriage, or by the law of the parties intended post-marriage domicile.

29 William Duncan, "The Recognition of Foreign Registered Partnerships in European States: the Existing Situation and the Prospects for the Future" (Domestic Partnerships Conference, Faculty of Law, Queen's University, 21-23 October 1999) [unpublished] has described this "European patchwork" as follows: "In certain countries registered partnerships are not recognised (Germany, France, Lithuania and Luxembourg). In many others the position is uncertain depending in part on the scope of the public policy doctrine (for example, Spain and the United Kingdom). In some countries, such as Portugal, a same sex partnership abroad could possibly be recognised under general conflict principles, even when one of the partners is a national of the recognising State. In Hungary, in accordance with the principle that civil status is governed by nationality, a foreign partnership registered between two persons whose national laws recognise registered partnership, would be entitled to recognition provided that there is no conflict with Hungarian law. It is also possible that in certain countries (for example Switzerland), despite the absence of explicit recognition principles, courts may be prepared to recognise some of the incidental effects of a registered partnership."

30 Nicole LaViolette, in *Registered Partnerships: A Model for Relationship Recognition* (Ottawa: Law Commission of Canada, August 2001) at 29-30, points out that there has been some concern about low utilization rates of available registration systems around the world. Authors have suggested the following factors: reluctance to disclose a same-sex relationship, benefits are already received from another source, unwillingness to take on financial responsibility for a partner, or discouraging formalities. Statistics, however, are often non-existent and incomplete.

31 K. Arnup, *Close Personal Relationships between Adults: 100 Years of Marriage in Canada* (Ottawa: Law Commission of Canada, March 2001) at 6.

32 In this Report, the Law Commission of Canada does not address the issue of polygamy. Further study is required on the effects of polygamy and the appropriate governmental response, for example, around inequality and balance of power issues which may exist within the relationship. However, it is reasonable to question whether use of the *Criminal Code* is the best way to respond to these issues. See Law Reform Commission of Canada, *Bigamy* (Working Paper 42, 1985). The previous Commission recommended that the offences against conjugal unions, apart from bigamy,

be repealed (at 22-23). There is a strong case that the consequences of bigamy are also better addressed through civil sanctions. Criminal prosecutions of bigamy are rare, and the penalties imposed on conviction modest: see *R. v. Sauve*, [1997] A.J. No. 525 (Alta. Prov. Ct.); *R. v. Moustafa*, [1991] O.J. No. 835 (Ont. C.J. Prov. Div.); *R. v. Young*, [1965] O.J. No. 498 (C.A.).

[33] It should be emphasized that the disentanglement of the state from the marriages of the nation would have no impact on the rights and obligations of married spouses who choose to take advantage of civil registration. The legal formalities to be followed in obtaining civil status would be changed by this proposal, not the content of legal regulation of registered relationships. The civil consequences of marriage would flow from the additional step of registering as committed partners, not from the conclusion of the marriage ceremony itself. The vast majority of married persons would likely choose to register their committed relationship for civil purposes. The additional step of registration would likely become a routine formality followed after the solemnization of marriages, replacing the current practice of filing marriage documents with provincial registries.

[34] Mary Ann Glendon, *The Transformation of Family Law: State, Law and Family in the United States and Western Europe* (Chicago: University of Chicago Press, 1989) at 21.

[35] *Ibid.*

[36] Mary Ann Glendon, *State, Law and Family: Family Law in Transition in the United States and Western Europe* (New York: North-Holland Publishing, 1977) at 309.

[37] Glendon, *supra* note 34, at 27.

[38] Glendon, *supra* note 36, at 314.

[39] Glendon, *supra* note 34, at 31.

[40] *Ibid.*

[41] 1753, 26 Geo. II, c. 33.

[42] 1836 (U.K.), 6&7 Will.4, c.85.

[43] Carolyn Hamilton and Kate Standley eds., *Family Law in Europe* (London: Butterworths, 1995).

[44] See Peter Ward, *Courtship, Love and Marriage in Nineteenth-Century English Canada* (Montreal and Kingston: McGill-Queen's University Press, 1990) at 38: "through its use of law, government reinforced the stability of marriage. It defined the range of acceptable spouses, it established the terms under which men and women married, it empowered the agents authorized to perform wedding ceremonies, it frustrated the dissolution of marriage, and it punished those who transgressed its bounds. In these ways the state put its weight behind the traditional Christian concept of marriage." See also James G. Snell, *In the Shadow of the Law: Divorce in Canada 1900-1939* (Toronto: University of Toronto Press, 1991); Cossman and Ryder, *supra* note 5 at 6-13; Arnup, *supra* note 31, at 3-24.

[45] Arnup, *supra* note 31, at 25 and following.

[46] For example, the preamble to the Ontario *Family Law Act*, R.S.O. 1990, c. F.3, states that "…it is necessary to recognize the equal position of spouses as individuals within marriage and to recognize marriage as a form of partnership…". See also the preamble to Manitoba's *Marital Property Act*, R.S.M. 1987, c. M45: "Whereas marriage is an institution of shared responsibilities and obligations between parties recognized as enjoying equal rights…".

47 Prior to 1983, rape was defined in s.143 of the Code as a male person having non-consensual "sexual intercourse with a female person who is not his wife". Now, rape has been replaced with the crimes of sexual assault in sections 271-3 of the *Criminal Code*, R.S.C. 1985, c. C-46. Section 278 provides that a husband or wife may be charged with sexually assaulting his or her spouse.

48 Judges may grant a divorce if spouses have been living separate and apart for at least one year: *Divorce Act*, R.S.C. 1985, c. 3 (2nd Supp.), s.8.

49 *Modernization of Benefits and Obligations Act*, S.C. 2000, c.12; *M* v. *H*, [1999] 2 S.C.R. 3; *Miron* v. *Trudel*, [1995] 2 S.C.R. 418; *Walsh* v. *Bona*, (2000) 186 D.L.R. (4th) 50 (N.S.C.A.), leave to appeal to S.C.C. granted, 15 February 2001.

50 David Ford and François Nault, "Changing Fertility Patterns, 1974 to 1994" (1996) 8 Health Report 39-46.

51 Nancy F. Cott, *Public Vows: A History of Marriage and the Nation* (Cambridge: Harvard University Press, 2000) at 212.

52 The national trend is that civil marriages make up an increasing proportion of a declining marriage rate. There are significant provincial variations in marriage ceremony preferences. In 1999, the proportion that civil marriages constituted of all marriages was 57 percent in British Columbia (http://www.health.gov.bc.ca/vs/stats/annual/1999/m_summ.html), 29 percent in Quebec (http://www.stat.gouv.qc.ca/donstat/demograp/mariage/513.htm), and 24 percent in Nova Scotia (source: Nova Scotia Vital Statistics). In contrast, the rate of civil marriage in Ontario has declined from a high of 16 percent in 1983 to less than 5 percent in 1998 (source: Ontario Office of the Registrar General).

53 Canon law was replaced by the Constitution Civile du Clergé in 1790, which gave the secular courts jurisdiction over some aspects of marriage. The Civil Code of 1804 completely secularized marriage, denying all legal effect to religious marriages. See Mary Ann Glendon *State, Law and Family: Family Law in Transition in the United States and Western Europe* (New York: North-Holland Publishing 1977) 56-57.

54 According to Glendon, *ibid.* at 56, "..the practice of having two marriage ceremonies (the civil one required by law to precede any religious one) is still followed by a great many French couples".

55 Glendon, *supra* note 36 at 321: "Now the law is… leaving questions of who marries whom and how, what rights and duties the spouses have toward each other, as well as how such unions are terminated, increasingly in the private order."

56 EGALE Canada, *Division of Powers and Jurisdictional Issues Relating to Marriage* (Ottawa: Law Commission of Canada, June 2000) at 73-75 and *Egale Inc. et al.* v. *The Attorney General of Canada* (3 October 2001), Vancouver L002698 and L003197 (B.C.S.C.) (Submission of Petitioner, EGALE at paras. 115-137, available online at http://www.egale.ca/documents/BC-Final.htm) [accessed October 20, 2001].

57 *Ibid.*, Submission of the Intervenor, The Interfaith Coalition for Marriage, at pages 7-14, available online at http://www.evangelicalfellowship.ca/resources/resource_viewer.asp?Resource_ID=117 [accessed October 20, 2001].

58 According to a Gallup Poll analysis of March 7, 2000, the percentage of Canadians in favour of same-sex marriage has nearly doubled from 24 percent in 1992 to 43 percent in 2000, while over the same period the percentage that oppose has decreased from 61 percent to 48 percent. A number of other recent polls, conducted between June 1999 and June 2001, indicate that between 40 percent and 65 percent of Canadians favour recognition of same-sex marriages. Support is consistently strongest among women, younger people (18-34), residents of Quebec, those with

post-secondary education and those with higher annual household incomes. Support is weakest among males, people over age 55, residents of the Prairies, and those with less than a high school education. See Angus Reid, Media Release, "Majority (55%) Agree With Supreme Court Decision That Definition of 'Spouse' Apply to Same-Sex Couples" (9 June 1999); Gallup Canada Inc., News Release, "About Four-in-Ten Canadians Accepting of Same Sex Marriages, Adoption" (7 March 2000); Centre for Research and Information on Canada and The Association for Canadian Studies, *Destination 2025 – National Survey of Young Canadians*, December 2000 at 3-4 http://www.cric.ca/en_html/sondages/cric.html (date accessed: 10 October 2001); R. Sheppard, "We Are Canadian" *Maclean's*, Maclean's/Global Television 17th annual year-end poll, (25 December 2000); Decima Research Inc., "Canadians Split on Same Sex Marriage" (22 January 2001); Environics Research Group, "Most Canadians Favour Gay Marriage; Approval of Homosexuality Continues to Increase" (10 May 2001); Léger Marketing, "Canadian Perceptions of Homosexuality – Executive Report" (22 June 2001).

[59] In the recently released *Egale Inc. et al.* v. *The Attorney General of Canada* (3 October 2001), Vancouver L002698 and L003197 (B.C.S.C.), Mr. Justice Pitfield concluded that restricting marriage to opposite-sex relationships infringes s.15 of the Charter, but that it is saved by section 1 as a reasonable and demonstrably justified limit in a free and democratic society. The Court also ruled that Parliament does not have the jurisdiction to change the legal meaning of marriage without amending the meaning of marriage in s. 91(26) of the Constitution. One of the petitioners, EGALE Canada (Equality for Gays and Lesbians Everywhere), has indicated that they will appeal the decision: EGALE Canada, Press Release, "B.C. Court Releases Decision in Same-Sex Marriage Case" (3 October 2001). There are also currently cases pending in Ontario and Quebec.

[60] Kathleen A. Lahey, *Are We 'Persons' Yet? Law and Sexuality in Canada* (Toronto: University of Toronto Press, 1999) at 328. See also McCarthy and Radbord, "Family Law for Same-Sex Couples: Charter(ing) the Course" (1998) 15 Can. J. Fam. L. 101, 123 ("Separate is not equal. Registered domestic partnerships create a second class category of relationships for those deemed less worthy of recognition. The introduction of registered domestic partnerships prevents access to the fundamental social and cultural institution of marriage in an attempt to privilege heterosexuality.").

[61] K. Waaldijk, *Civil Developments: Patterns of Reform in the Legal Position of Same-Sex Partners in Europe* (2000) 17 Can. J. Fam. L. 62 at 62-66 and 86-88. On April 1, 2001, the Same-Sex Marriage Act came into force in the Netherlands. See that country's Department of Justice factsheet at http://www.minjust.nl:8080/a_beleid/fact/same-sexmarriages.htm (last modified: 8 May 2001).

[62] *M* v. *H*, [1999] 2 S.C.R. 3 at para.73.

Conclusion

In this Report, the Law Commission of Canada has questioned the role of the state in the regulation of personal adult relationships. The Law Commission has argued that governments have tended to rely too heavily on conjugal relationships in accomplishing what are otherwise important state objectives. Focusing only on spousal or conjugal relationships is simply not the best way to promote the state's interests in close personal relationships since it excludes other relationships that are also important. But, instead of simply arguing that some relationships that are currently excluded (such as non-conjugal relationships) should be included, the Law Commission is of the view that it is time for governments to re-evaluate the way in which personal adult relationships are regulated.

The Law Commission has suggested a new methodology for addressing the legal regulation of personal adult relationships. First, are the objectives of the legislation, currently aimed at spousal or conjugal relationships, legitimate? Second, are relationships relevant to the objective at hand? Third, assuming that relationships are relevant, could the law or program allow individuals to decide for themselves which of their close personal relationships should be subject to the law or policy? Fourth, assuming that relationships do matter, and self-selection of relationships will not work, is there a better way for governments to include relationships?

If this methodology were implemented to systemically reform laws and programs, the reliance on relationships and relational status would be much diminished. Sometimes the government objective is no longer a legitimate one; it is rooted in archaic assumptions about gender or society generally. In many areas – particularly in income security programs – governments should allocate rights and responsibilities on a more individualized basis. In other areas, where relationships continue to matter, such as immigration, the law should try to facilitate the choices of individuals by allowing those individuals to decide which of their relationships is most important to them. Finally, in other areas, governments should rely on relationships that are relevant to the objectives, as defined by their function rather than their status.

While reliance on the relational status of marriage and conjugality should be restricted to a few contexts, this is not to say that there is no longer a need for marriage or for a legal framework for personal relationships. Indeed, there is a role for the state to provide an orderly framework to facilitate the voluntary assumption of rights and obligations between the parties. Law has an important role to play in both facilitating the choices of individuals in the private relationships and preventing exploitation or abuse within these relationships. And it should do so by broadening the range of relationships that receive this kind of state recognition and support through the legalization of same-sex marriage and the creation of a registration scheme for conjugal and non-conjugal relationships. Although the use of ascription to regulate conjugal couples may be appropriate in certain circumstances, it ought to be used sparingly and only where exploitation is a significant concern.

In conclusion, the message is clear. Canadians enter into a wide variety of close personal adult relationships that matter greatly to them, and it is important to Canadians that governments respect their choices in the legal treatment of personal relationships. In order to do so, governments have to both recognize and support a broader range of caring personal adult relationships and rethink the way in which they regulate these relationships. They must move beyond conjugality.

Summary of Recommendations

Recommendation 1 (page 31)

Governments should review all of their laws and policies that employ relational criteria to ensure that they are pursuing objectives that respond to contemporary social realities in a manner consistent with fundamental values.

Recommendation 2 (page 32)

Governments should review all of their laws and policies that employ relational terms to determine whether relationships are relevant to, or an effective means of accomplishing, each law's objectives. If not, legislation should be revised to remove the unnecessary relational references.

Recommendation 3 (page 33)

Governments should review all of their laws and policies to consider whether legislative objectives could be better accomplished if individuals were entitled to choose which of their close personal relationships they want to be subject to particular laws or policies. If so, legislation should be revised to permit self-designation of included relationships.

Recommendation 4 (page 36)

Governments should review all of their laws and policies to determine whether they could more accurately capture the range of relationships relevant to their particular legislative objectives. If so, laws should be revised to more precisely target relationships by reference to the factual or functional attributes relevant to those particular legislative objectives.

Recommendation 5 (page 36)

Governments should apply this four-step methodology in the development and implementation of all future laws and programs. Before they initiate any new laws or programs that employ relational criteria, governments should ensure that they are pursuing legitimate objectives and they should consider whether relationships are relevant to, or an effective means of accomplishing, those legislative objectives. If so, governments should consider whether individuals should be permitted to designate the relationships most important to them. If this is not a feasible option, governments should precisely target relationships by reference to the factual or functional attributes relevant to particular legislative objectives.

Recommendation 6 (page 40)

Parliament should amend laws like the *Marine Liability Act* that confer a right to sue for negligently caused harm to relationships, to permit recovery by any individual who can prove that the defendant's fault caused a recognized kind of relational loss.

Recommendation 7 (page 41)

Parliament should amend the *Canada Labour Code* to permit employees to designate the relationships most meaningful to them for the purposes of bereavement leave or place a cap on the number of days that an employee can take for bereavement leave.

Recommendation 8 (page 43)

Parliament should amend the *Canada Labour Code* to provide employees with the right to take caregiving leave and to permit employees to designate the relationships most meaningful to them for the purposes of caregiving leave. To control the risk of abuse, the legislation could place a cap on the number of days that an employee could take for caregiving leave, or it could permit employees to provide a list to employers of those persons with whom they have relationships that may give rise to the need to provide care.

Recommendation 9 (page 46)

Parliament should amend the sponsorship provisions of the *Immigration and Refugee Protection Act* and regulations to permit individuals to sponsor persons with whom they have a close personal relationship, even if that relationship does not involve ties of blood, marriage, common-law partnership or adoption.

Recommendation 10 (page 50)

Parliament should amend the *Canada Evidence Act* to repeal the common law rule that a spouse of the accused is not a competent witness for the Crown.

Recommendation 11 (page 55)

Parliament should replace the spousal non-compellability rules with an amendment to the *Canada Evidence Act* that enables judges to excuse a witness from having to testify if he or she objects to testifying, has an ongoing close personal relationship with the accused, and the judge finds that the harm that would be caused to the witness or to the relationship by having to testify outweighs the desirability of admitting the testimony.

Recommendation 12 (page 55)

Parliament should replace the marital communications privilege with an amendment to the *Canada Evidence Act* that enables judges to prevent the divulgence of a confidential communication if the witness had a close personal relationship with the accused at the time the communication was made, and the need to protect and promote candour and trust in close personal relationships outweighs the desirability of admitting the testimony.

Recommendation 13 (page 56)

Parliament should amend laws seeking to prevent fraudulent transactions to remove irrebuttable presumptions based on relationship status.

Recommendation 14 (page 57)

Parliament should amend laws seeking to prevent fraudulent transactions to remove rebuttable presumptions based on relationship status. The objectives of these laws would be better accomplished if they prohibited fraudulent transactions and required disclosure of conflicts of interest without relying on relational presumptions.

Recommendation 15 (page 59)

The *Employment Insurance Act* should be amended so that employment by a relative is not treated as presumptively uninsurable. All employment contracts manufactured for the purpose of claiming benefits, whether the parties are in a close personal relationship or not, should be excluded from the definition of insurable employment.

Recommendation 16 (page 61)

Parliament should amend the *Bankruptcy and Insolvency Act* so that all transactions entered into by a bankrupt may be set aside if the transaction was entered into at a time when the bankrupt was insolvent, and the effect of the transaction was to diminish the assets that would otherwise vest in the bankrupt's estate.

Recommendation 17 (page 62)

Parliament should amend the *Bankruptcy and Insolvency Act* so that the extended one-year period for setting aside preferences would not depend on relationships but would apply whenever a creditor knew of the bankrupt's insolvency at the time of the preference.

Recommendation 18 (page 63)

> Parliament should amend the *Bank Act*, and other legislation regulating financial institutions, so that the special rules regulating transactions with related parties apply to any prospective customer with a close personal relationship with a director, officer or significant shareholder of the institution.

Recommendation 19 (page 71)

> The individual, rather than the conjugal couple or some other definition of the family unit, should remain the basis for the calculation of Canada's personal income tax.

Recommendation 20 (page 73)

> Parliament should extend the tax credits for dependent relatives so that they can be claimed by any taxpayer who has provided financial or caregiving support to a person who is dependent by reason of age, disability or illness, without reference to relationship status. Consideration should be given to extending income assistance to caregivers by making the dependants' credits refundable or by delivering direct grants outside of the tax system.

Recommendation 21 (page 74)

> Parliament should consider providing income support, by way of direct grants or refundable tax credits, to persons with disabilities to enable them to hire or purchase the supports they require.

Recommendation 22 (page 77)

> Parliament should replace the *Income Tax Act*'s spouse and common-law partner tax credit with enhanced or new programs that more carefully target caregivers and children for direct income support.

Recommendation 23 (page 82)

> Income security programs should not assume that consumption and production economies always arise in conjugal relationships and never in other relationships. Parliament should amend the *Income Tax Act* so that the amount of the Goods and Services Tax credit to which individuals are entitled is not reduced if they are married or cohabiting in a conjugal relationship.

Recommendation 24 (page 87)

Income security programs should not assume that the benefits of individual income are always shared with others in conjugal relationships, and that sharing never occurs in other relationships. Parliament should amend the *Income Tax Act* so that the amount of the Goods and Services Tax credit (and other income-tested benefits) to which individuals are entitled is determined by reference to individual income without reference to the income of spouses, common-law partners or other cohabitants.

Recommendation 25 (page 89)

Parliament should amend the *Income Tax Act* so that the provisions that allow capital property to be transferred tax-free between spouses and common-law partners apply to all persons who are living together in economically interdependent relationships.

Recommendation 26 (page 91)

Income security programs should not assume that consumption and production economies always arise in conjugal relationships and never in other relationships. Parliament should amend the *Old Age Security Act* so that the amount of the Guaranteed Income Supplement or Monthly Allowance is not reduced if a claimant is married or cohabiting in a conjugal relationship.

Recommendation 27 (page 91)

Income security programs should not assume that the benefits of individual income are always shared with others in conjugal relationships and that sharing never occurs in other relationships. Parliament should amend the *Old Age Security Act* so that the amount of the Guaranteed Income Supplement or Monthly Allowance is determined by reference to individual income without reference to the income of spouses, common-law partners or other cohabitants.

Recommendation 28 (page 93)

Parliament needs to clarify the objectives of the Monthly Allowance provisions of the *Old Age Security Act*. If the objective is to promote early retirement, or to direct benefits to persons in need, then Parliament should amend the Act so that benefits are not limited to widows and spouses or common-law partners of pensioners.

Recommendation 29 (page 95)

If the objective of the Monthly Allowance provisions of the *Old Age Security Act* is to support unpaid caregiving, Parliament should consider revising the relational eligibility requirements or replacing the Monthly Allowance with new programs to more closely target benefits to caregivers.

Recommendation 30 (page 99)

Governments should amend the *Canada Pension Plan* and laws governing employment pensions and veterans' pensions, to permit a contributor, employee or veteran to designate a person with whom they are living in an economically interdependent relationship as a beneficiary of their survivor's benefits.

Recommendation 31 (page 122)

Parliament and provincial/territorial legislatures should pass laws enabling adults to register their relationship.

Considerations:
- The registration should not be restricted only to conjugal relationships.
- It should provide for a set of commitments, which could include caring arrangements, consent to treatment dispositions, support and sharing in property from which the parties may opt out.

Recommendation 32 (page 122)

Governments should attempt to design their international arrangements on the basis of the existence of a variety of relationships and move toward an international recognition of registrations.

Recommendation 33 (page 131)

Parliament and provincial/territorial legislatures should move toward removing from their laws the restrictions on marriages between persons of the same sex.

Appendix A

Bibliography

Contents

I. Discussion Documents and Background Research Papers Published by the Law Commission of Canada

Law Commission of Canada, *Close Personal Relationships between Adults: 100 Years of Marriage in Canada* by K. Arnup (Ottawa: Law Commission of Canada, March 2001). Available in French: *Rapports de nature personnelle entre adultes : 100 ans de mariage au Canada.* Available in hard copy from the Law Commission of Canada and online: http://www.lcc.gc.ca.

Law Commission of Canada, *Division of Powers and Jurisdictional Issues Relating to Marriage* by J. Fisher, K. Lahey and L. Arron (Equality for Gays and Lesbians Everywhere – EGALE) (Ottawa: Law Commission of Canada, June 2000). Available in French: *Le partage des pouvoirs et l'analyse des compétences en matière de mariage.* Available in hard copy from the Law Commission of Canada and online: http://www.lcc.gc.ca.

Law Commission of Canada, *Marriage and Marriage-Like Relationships* by M. Bailey (Ottawa: Law Commission of Canada, 1999). Available in French: *Le mariage et les unions libres.* Available in hard copy from the Law Commission of Canada and online: http://www.lcc.gc.ca.

Law Commission of Canada, *Personal Relationships of Support between Adults: The Case of Disability*, Roeher Institute (Ottawa: Law Commission of Canada, March 2001). Available in French: *Relations personnelles de soutien entre adultes – Le cas de l'invalidité.* Available in hard copy from the Law Commission of Canada and online: http://www.lcc.gc.ca.

Law Commission of Canada, *Recognizing and Supporting Close Personal Relationships Between Adults* (Discussion Paper) (Ottawa: Law Commission of Canada, May 2000). Available in French: *La reconnaissance et le soutien des rapports de nature personnelle entre adultes.* Available in hard copy from the Law Commission of Canada and online: http://www.lcc.gc.ca.

Law Commission of Canada, *Spousal Testimony in Criminal Cases in Canada* by Allan Manson (Ottawa: Law Commission of Canada, August 2001). Available in French: *Témoignage d'un conjoint dans les causes criminelles au Canada.* Available in hard copy from the Law Commission of Canada and online: http://www.lcc.gc.ca.

Law Commission of Canada, *The Benefit/Penalty Unit in Income Tax Policy: Diversity and Reform* by K. Lahey (Ottawa: Law Commission of Canada, September 2000). Available in French: *La politique fiscale et l'unité d'imposition : diversité et réforme.* Available in hard copy from the Law Commission of Canada and online: http://www.lcc.gc.ca.

Law Commission of Canada, *The Evolution and Diversity of Relationships in Canadian Families* by T. Janz (Ottawa: Law Commission of Canada, September 2000). Available in French: *Évolution et diversité des relations au sein des familles canadiennes.* Available in hard copy from the Law Commission of Canada and online: http://www.lcc.gc.ca.

Law Commission of Canada, *The Legal Regulation of Adult Personal Relationships: Evaluating Policy Objectives and Legal Options in Federal Legislation* by B. Cossman and B. Ryder (Ottawa: Law Commission of Canada, May 2000). Available in French: *L'assujettissement juridique des rapports personnels entre adultes : Évaluation des objectifs des politiques et des alternatives juridiques dans le cadre de la législation fédérale.* Available in hard copy from the Law Commission of Canada and online: http://www.lcc.gc.ca.

Law Commission of Canada, *What's Sex Got to do With it? Tax and the "Family"* by C. Young (Ottawa: Law Commission of Canada, May 2000). Available in French: *La fiscalité, la «famille» et le sexe : quel rapport?* Available in hard copy from the Law Commission of Canada and online: http://www.lcc.gc.ca.

2. Background Research Papers Prepared for the Law Commission of Canada

Anderson, T., "Personal Relationships – Federal Statutes Database Project" [a database developed by the British Columbia Law Institute for the Law Commission of Canada] (Vancouver: British Columbia Law Institute and Law Commission of Canada, May 2000) [unpublished research archived at the Law Commission of Canada].

Anderson, T. and British Columbia Law Institute, "Report on the Personal Relationships – Federal Statutes Database Project" [report on a database developed by the British Columbia Law Institute for the Law Commission of Canada] (Vancouver: British Columbia Law Institute and Law Commission of Canada, May 2000) [unpublished research report archived at the Law Commission of Canada].

Commission du droit du Canada, *Le contrat en contexte d'intimité* by A. Roy (Ottawa: Commission du droit du Canada, June 2001) [publication forthcoming].

Commission du droit du Canada, *Le traitement juridique des unions de fait en droit québécois* by B. Lefebvre (Ottawa: Commission du droit du Canada, August 2001) [unpublished research report archived at the Law Commission of Canada].

Law Commission of Canada, *Adult Relationships Involving Disabled Persons in Canadian Statutory Law: Language and Meaning* by C. Frazee (Ottawa: Law Commission of Canada, August 2001) [unpublished research report archived at the Law Commission of Canada].

Law Commission of Canada, *Ascription of Spousal Status: Identifying Legislative Objectives in Ascribing Spousal Status to Cohabitants* by Winifred H. Holland (Ottawa: Law Commission of Canada, July 2001) [unpublished research report archived at the Law Commission of Canada].

Law Commission of Canada, *Compensation for Relational Harm* by S. Van Praagh (Ottawa: Law Commission of Canada, July 2001) [publication forthcoming].

Law Commission of Canada, *Determining Entitlement to Income Security* by G. Brodsky and S. Day (Ottawa: Law Commission of Canada, July 2001) [unpublished research report archived at the Law Commission of Canada].

Law Commission of Canada, *One Hundred Years of Caregiving* by P. Armstrong and O. Kits (Ottawa: Law Commission of Canada, April 2001) [unpublished research report archived at the Law Commission of Canada].

Law Commission of Canada, *Reconsidering the Relevance of Relationships in Income Security Programs with Reference to Federal Income Support Programs* by Monica Townson (Ottawa: Law Commission of Canada, August 2001) [unpublished research report archived at the Law Commission of Canada].

Law Commission of Canada, *Registered Partnerships: A Model For Relationship Recognition* by Nicole LaViolette (Ottawa: Law Commission of Canada, August 2001) [publication forthcoming].

Law Commission of Canada, *The Impact of Legislation on First Nations Women* by C. Dieter (Ottawa: Law Commission of Canada, August 2001) [unpublished research report archived at the Law Commission of Canada].

3. Reports

Australian Law Reform Commission, *Evidence (Final Report No. 38)* (Canberra, 1987).

Australian Law Reform Commission, *Evidence, Volume 1 (Interim Report No. 26)* (Canberra, 1985).

British Columbia, *Rights and Responsibilities in a Changing Workplace: A Review of Employment Standards in British Columbia* (Victoria: Ministry of Skills, Training and Labour, 1994) (Chair: M. Thompson).

British Columbia Law Institute, *Report on Recognition of Spousal and Family Status* (Vancouver: British Columbia Law Institute, 1998).

Canada, Citizenship and Immigration Canada, *Building on a Strong Foundation for the 21ˢᵗ Century: New Directions for Immigration and Refugee Policy and Legislation.* (Ottawa: Minister of Public Works and Government Services Canada, 1998). Available in French: *De solides assises pour le 21ᵉ siècle : Nouvelles orientations pour la politique et la législation relatives aux immigrants et aux réfugiés.*

Canada, Citizenship and Immigration Canada, *Into the 21ˢᵗ Century: A Strategy for Immigration and Citizenship Canada* (Ottawa: Minister of Supply and Services Canada, 1994). Available in French: *Vers le 21ᵉᵐᵉ siècle : une stratégie pour l'immigration et citoyenneté.*

Canada, Citizenship and Immigration Canada, *Planning Now for Canada's Future: Introducing a Multi-Year Planning Process and the Immigration Plan for 2001 and 2002* (Ottawa: Minister of Public Works and Government Services Canada, 2001). Available in French: *Planifier dès maintenant l'avenir du Canada : présentation d'un processus de planification pluriannuelle et du plan d'immigration pour 2001 et 2002.*

Canada, Department of Finance, *Tax Expenditures and Evaluations* (Ottawa: Minister of Public Works and Government Services Canada, 2000). Available in French: *Dépenses fiscales et évaluations 2000.*

Canada, Human Resources Development Canada, Advisory Group on Working Time and the Distribution of Work, *Report on Working Time and the Distribution of Work* (Ottawa: Minister of Supply and Services Canada, 1994) (Chair: A. Donner). Available in French: *Rapport du Groupe consultatif sur le temps de travail et la répartition du travail.*

Canada, Nineteenth Report of the Standing Committee on Finance, Sub-Committee on Tax Equity for Canadian Families with Dependent Children, *For the Benefit of Our Children: Improving Tax Fairness* (June 1999). Available in French: *Rapport 19, Dans l'intérêt de nos enfants : une plus grande équité fiscale.*

Canada, Royal Commission on the Status of Women in Canada (Ottawa: Information Canada, 1970).

Chambre des notaires du Québec, *Répertoire de droit*, «Famille», Formulaire – Document 1.1, Montréal, 1996.

Coalition for Lesbian and Gay Rights in Ontario, *Systems Failure: A Report on the Experiences of Sexual Minorities in Ontario's Health-Care and Social Services System* (Toronto: CLGRO, 1997).

Immigration Legislative Review Advisory Group, *Not Just Numbers: A Canadian Framework for Future Immigration* (Ottawa: Citizenship and Immigration Canada, 1997).

Law Reform Commission of Canada, *Bigamy* (Working Paper) (Ottawa: Law Reform Commission of Canada, 1985). Available in French: *La bigamie*.

Law Reform Commission of Canada, *Report on Evidence* (Ottawa: Law Reform Commission of Canada, 1975). Available in French: *Rapport sur la preuve*.

Law Reform Commission of Canada, *Report on Family Law* (Ottawa: Law Reform Commission of Canada, 1976). Available in French: *Rapport, Le droit de la famille*.

Law Reform Commission of Nova Scotia, *Final Report on Reform of the Law Dealing with Matrimonial Property in Nova Scotia* (Halifax: Law Reform Commission of Nova Scotia 1997).

Ontario Fair Tax Commission, *Fair Tax in a Changing World: Report of the Ontario Fair Tax Commission* (Toronto: University of Toronto Press, 1993).

Ontario Fair Tax Commission, Women and Taxation Working Group, *Women and Taxation: Working Group Report* (Toronto: Ontario Fair Tax Commission, 1992).

Ontario, Ministry of Community and Social Services, *Transitions: Report of the Social Assistance Review Committee* (Toronto: Queen's Printer for Ontario, 1988).

Québec, Conseil de la famille et de l'enfance, *Démographie et famille : Les impacts sur la société de demain — les actes du colloque tenu les 28 et 29 novembre 2000* (Québec : Conseil de la famille et de l'enfance, 2001).

Québec, Conseil de la famille et de l'enfance, *Et si on parlait des familles et des enfants... de leur évolution, de leurs préoccupations et de leurs besoins!*, Rapport 1999-2000 sur la situation et les besoins des familles et des enfants (Québec : Conseil de la famille et de l'enfance, 2000).

Quebec, Ministry of Finance, *White Paper on the Personal Tax and Transfer System* (Quebec: Department of Finance, 1984). Available in French: *Livre blanc sur la fiscalité des particuliers*.

Saskatchewan, Ministry of Labour, *Towards More Work-Family Balance in Saskatchewan: Report of the Public Task Force on Balancing Work and Family* (Regina: Government of Saskatchewan, 1998).

The Vanier Institute of the Family, *Profiling Canada's Families II* (Canada: The Vanier Institute of the Family, 2000). Available in French: *Profil des familles canadiennes II.*

4. Books and Chapters

Allahar, A. and Côté, J., *Richer and Poorer: The Structure of Inequality in Canada* (Toronto: James Lorimer & Company, 1998).

Armstrong, P., "The Welfare State as History" in R. Blake, P. Bryden and J. Strain, eds., *The Welfare State in Canada: Past, Present and Future* (Concord, Ontario: Irwin Publishing, 1997) 52.

Arnup, K., "In the Family Way: Lesbian Mothers in Canada" in M. Luxton, ed., *Feminism and Families: Critical Policies and Changing Practices* (Halifax: Fernwood Publishing, 1997) 80.

Backhouse, C., *Petticoats and Prejudice. Women and Law in Nineteenth-Century Canada* (Toronto: Women's Press, 1991).

Bahr, S., ed., *Family Research: A Sixty Year Review, 1930-1990*, vol.1 (New York: Lexington, 1991).

Baird, R.M. and Rosenbaum, S.E., *Same-Sex Marriage: The Moral and Legal Debate* (Amherst, New York: Prometheus Books, 1997).

Baker, M., ed., *Canada's Changing Families: Challenges to Public Policy* (Ottawa: Vanier Institute of the Family, 1994). Available in French: *Les politiques gouvernementales face aux familles en transition.*

Baker, M., ed., *Families: Changing Trends in Canada*, 3rd ed. (Toronto: McGraw-Hill Ryerson, 1996).

Baker, M. "Introduction to Family Studies: Cultural Variations and Family Trends" in M. Baker, ed., *Families: Changing Trends in Canada*, 3rd ed. (Toronto: McGraw-Hill Ryerson, 1996) 3.

Barret, M. and McIntosh, M., *The Anti-Social Family*, 2nd ed. (New York: Verso, 1991).

Bedard, M., *Breaking with Tradition: Diversity, Conflict, and Change in Contemporary American Families* (Dix Hills, New York: General Hall, 1992).

Berg, J. and Piner, K. "Social Relationships and the Lack of Social Relationships" in S. Duck and R. Silver, eds., *Personal Relationship and Social Support* (London: Sage Publications, 1990) 140.

Bernardes, J., *Family Studies: An Introduction* (London: Routledge, 1997).

Brooks, N., "The Irrelevance of Conjugal Relationships in Assessing Tax Liability" in J.G. Head and R. Krever, eds., *Tax Units and the Tax Rate Scale* (Melbourne: Australian Tax Research Foundation, 1996) 35-80.

Brown, I. and Percy, M., eds., *Developmental Disabilities in Ontario* (Toronto: Front Porch Publishing, 1999).

Carbone, J., *From Partners to Parents: The Second Revolution in Family Law* (New York: Columbia University Press, 2000).

CCH, *British Tax Reporter* (London: CCH looseleaf).

Chambers, A. and Montigny E., eds., *Family Matters: Papers in Post-Confederation Canadian Family History* (Toronto: Canadian Scholars' Press, 1998).

Comacchio, C.R., *The Infinite Bonds of Family: Domesticity in Canada, 1850-1940* (Toronto: University of Toronto Press, 1999).

Conway, J., *The Canadian Family in Crisis* (Toronto: James Lorimer, 1993).

Cossman, B., "Family Inside/Out" in M. Luxton, ed., *Feminism and Families. Critical Policies and Changing Practices* (Halifax: Fernwood Publishing, 1997) 124.

Cott, N., *Public Vows: A History of Marriage and the Nation* (Cambridge, Mass.: Harvard University Press, 2000).

Cowan, P. and Cowan, C., "New Families: Modern Couples as New Pioneers" in M. Mason, A. Skolnick, and S. Sugarman, eds., *All Our Families: New Policies for a New Century* (New York: Oxford University Press, 1998) 169.

De Silva, E. and Smart C., eds., *The New Family?* (Sage: London, 1999).

Dumas, J. and Péron, Y., *Marriage and Conjugal Life in Canada: Current Demographic Analysis* (Ottawa: Statistics Canada, 1992). Available in French: *Mariage et vie conjugale au Canada*.

Eekelaar, J.M. and Katz, S., eds., *Marriage and Cohabitation in Contemporary Societies: Areas of Legal, Social and Ethical Change* (Toronto: Butterworths, 1980).

Eekelaar, J.M., and Nhlapo, R.T., eds., *The Changing Family: International Perspectives on the Family and Family Law* (Oxford: Hart Publishing, 1998).

Eichler, M., *Family Shifts: Families, Policies and Gender Equality* (Toronto: Oxford University Press, 1997).

Eskridge, W.N., *The Case for Same-Sex Marriage: From Sexual Liberty to Civilized Commitment* (New York: Free Press, 1996).

Estlund, D.M. and Nussbaum, M.C., eds., *Sex, Preference and Family: Essays on Law and Nature* (New York: Oxford University Press, 1997).

Finch, J., *Family Obligations and Social Change* (Cambridge: Polity Press, 1989).

Fineman, M., *The Neutered Mother, the Sexual Family and Other Twentieth Century Tragedies* (New York: Routledge, 1995).

Fraser, N., "After the Family Wage: A Postindustrial Thought Experiment" in *Justice Interruptus: Critical Reflections on the "Postsocialist" Condition* (New York: Routledge, 1997) 41-66.

Gittens, D., *The Family in Question: Changing Households & Familiar Ideologies*, 2nd ed. (London: Macmillan Press, 1985).

Glendon, M.A., *State, Law and Family: Family Law in Transition in the United States and Western Europe* (New York: North-Holland Publishing, 1977).

Glendon, M.A., *The Transformation of Family Law: State, Law and Family in the United States and Western Europe* (Chicago: University of Chicago Press, 1989).

Goodwin, R., *Personal Relationships Across Cultures* (New York: Routledge, 1999).

Gordon, R. and Verdun-Jones, S., *Adult Guardianship Law in Canada.* (Toronto: Carswell, 1992).

Govier T., *Dilemmas of Trust* (Montreal: McGill-Queen's University Press, 1998).

Govier T., *Social Trust and Human Communities* (Montreal: McGill-Queen's University Press, 1997).

Graff, E.J., *What is Marriage For? The Strange Social History of Our Most Intimate Institution* (Boston: Beacon Press, 1999).

Grand'maison, J., "Les différents types de famille et leurs enjeux" in B. Lacroix, ed., *Vive la Famille* (Montreal: Éditions Fides, 1993) 17.

Graycar, R. and Morgan, J., *The Hidden Gender of Law* (Leichhardt, Australia: Federation Press, 1990).

Hackstaff, K., *Marriage in a Culture of Divorce* (Philadelphia: Temple University Press, 1999).

Hamilton, C. and Standley, K., eds., *Family Law in Europe* (London: Butterworths, 1995).

Hobart, C., "Intimacy and Family Life: Sexuality, Cohabitation and Marriage" in M. Baker, *Families: Changing Trends in Canada*, 3rd ed. (Toronto: McGraw-Hill Ryerson, 1996) 143.

Hogg, P. W., Magee, J. E. and Cook, T., *Principles of Canadian Income Tax Law*, 3rd ed. (Toronto: Carswell, 1999).

Huston, M. and Schwartz, P., "The Relationship of Lesbians and of Gay Men" in J. Wood and S. Duck, eds., *Under-Studied Relationships: Off the Beaten Track – Understanding Relationship Processes Series* vol. 6 (Thousand Oaks, California: Sage Publications, 1995) 89.

Jagger, G. and Wright, C., eds., *Changing Family Values* (New York: Routledge, 1999).

Kasirer, N., "What is vie commune? Qu'est-ce que living together?" in Centre de recherche en droit privé et comparé du Québec, *Mélanges Paul-André Crépeau* (Cowansville: Éditions Yvon Blais, 1997) 487-534.

Kinsey, A.C., Pomeroy, W.B. and Martin, C.E., *Sexual Behaviour in the Human Male* (Philadelphia: W.B. Saunders, 1948).

Kinsey, A.C., Pomeroy, W.B., Martin, C.E. and Gebhard, P.H., *Sexual Behaviour in the Human Female* (Philadelphia: W.B. Saunders, 1953).

Lacroix B., ed., *Vive la Famille* (Montreal: Éditions Fides, 1993).

LaFollette, H. *Personal Relationships: Love, Identity and Morality* (Oxford: Blackwell, 1996).

Lahey, K., *Are We 'Persons' Yet? Law and Sexuality in Canada* (Toronto: University of Toronto Press, 1999).

Larson, L., Goltz, J. and Munro, B., *Families in Canada: Social Context, Continuities and Changes,* 2nd ed. (Scarborough: Prentice Hall Allyn and Bacon Canada, 2000).

Laumann, E.O., Gagnon, J.H., Michael, R.T. and Michaels, S., *The Social Organization of Sexuality: Sexual Practices in the United States* (Chicago: University of Chicago Press, 1994).

Lévesque, A., *Making and Breaking the Rules: Women in Quebec, 1919-1939* (Toronto: McClelland & Stewart, 1994).

Little, M. *"No Car, No Radio, No Liquor Permit": The Moral Regulation of Single Mothers in Ontario, 1920-1997* (Toronto: Oxford University Press, 1998).

Lluelles, D. (with the assistance of Benoit Moore), *Droit québécois des obligations*, vol. 1 (Montreal: Éditions Thémis, 1998).

Lund-Andersen, I., "Cohabitation and Registered Partnership in Scandinavia: The Legal Position of Homosexuals" in John M. Eekelaar and Thandabantu Nhlapo, eds., *The Changing Family: Family Forms & Family Law* (Oxford: Hart Publishing, 1998) 397-404.

Luxton, M. "Feminism and Families: The Challenge of Neo-Conservatism" in M. Luxton, *Feminism and Families: Critical Policies and Changing Practices* (Halifax: Fernwood Publishing, 1997) 10.

Maloney, M., "What is the Appropriate Tax Unit for the 1990s and Beyond?" in A. Maslove, ed., *Issues in the Taxation of Individuals* (Toronto: University of Toronto Press and the Ontario Fair Tax Commission, 1994) 116.

Mandell, N. and Duffy, A., eds., *Canadian Families: Diversity, Conflict and Change*, 2nd ed. (Toronto: Harcourt Brace & Co., 2000).

Marsh, L., *Report on Social Security for Canada* (Toronto: University of Toronto Press, 1975).

Martin-Matthews, A., "Change and Diversity in Aging Families and Intergenerational Relations" in N. Mandell and A. Duffy, eds., *Canadian Families: Diversity, Conflict and Change*, 2nd ed. (Toronto: Harcourt Brace & Company, 2000) 323-360.

Mazeaud, J., Mazeaud, L. and Mazeau, H., *Leçons de droit civil – Les obligations – Théorie générale*, 8th edition (Paris: Montchrestien, 1991).

McCaffery, E. J., *Taxing Women* (Chicago: University of Chicago Press, 1997).

McCarthy, B. "Adult Friendships" in G. Graham, and H. LaFollette, eds., *Person to Person* (Philadelphia: Temple University Press, 1989) 32.

McDaniel, S. "The Family Lives of the Middle-Aged and Elderly in Canada" in M. Baker, ed., *Families: Changing Trends in Canada*, 3rd ed. (Toronto: McGraw-Hill Ryerson, 1996) 195.

Minow, M., *Making All the Difference: Inclusion, Exclusion and American Law*. (Ithaca: Cornell University Press, 1990).

Mitchell, B.A., "The Refilled 'Nest': Debunking the Myth of Families in Crisis" in E.M. Gee and G.M. Gutman, eds., *The Overselling of Population Aging: Apocalyptic Demography, Intergenerational Challenges and Social Policy* (Toronto: Oxford University Press, 2000) 80-99.

Morgan, D., *Family Connections: An Introduction to Family Studies* (Cambridge: Polity Press, 1996).

Mossman, M.J. and Maclean, M., "Family Law and Social Assistance Programs: Rethinking Equality" in P.M. Evans and G.R. Wekerle, eds., *Women and the Canadian Welfare State: Challenges and Change* (Toronto: University of Toronto Press, 1997) 117-141.

Neysmith, S.M., *Restructuring Caring Labour: Discourse, State Practice and Everyday Life* (Don Mills: Oxford University Press, 2000).

Nussbaum, M., *Sex and Social Justice* (New York: Oxford University Press, 1999).

Pahl, J., *Money and Marriage* (London: MacMillan, 1989).

Ramu, G. and Tavuchis, N., "Urban Kin Networks" in G. Ramu, ed., *Marriage and the Family in Canada Today* (Scarborough: Prentice-Hall Canada, 1989) 143.

Roy, A., "Mariage et contrat : fiction ou complémentarité?" in Y. Gendreau, ed., *Les fictions du droit – Fictions in the Law* (Montreal: Thémis, 2001).

Ryder, B., "Becoming Spouses: The Rights of Lesbian and Gay Couples" in *Family Law: Roles, Fairness and Equality (Special Lectures of the Law Society of Upper Canada, 1993)* (Scarborough, Ontario: Carswell, 1994).

Sarason, B.R., Sarason, I.G. and Gurung, R.A. "Close Personal Relationships and Health Outcomes: A Key to the Role of Social Support" in S. Duck, ed.,

Handbook of Personal Relationships: Section V. Clinical and Community Psychology (New York: John Wiley & Sons, 2nd ed. 1997) 547-573.

Scanzoni, J. *et al.*, *The Sexual Bond: Rethinking Families and Close Relationships* (London: Sage Publications, 1989).

Schulz, D. and Rodgers, S., *Marriage, the Family and Personal Fulfilment*, 3rd ed. (New Jersey: Prentice-Hall, 1985).

Silva, E.B. and Smart, C., eds., *The New Family?* (London: Sage, 1999).

Simard, M. and Alary, J., ed., *Comprendre la famille – Actes du 5e symposium québécois de recherche sur la famille* (Trois-Rivières: Presses de l'Université du Québec, 2000).

Singer, G., Powers, L. and Olson, A., eds., *Redefining Family Support. Innovations in Public-Private Partnerships* (Baltimore: Paul H. Brookes Publishing, 1996).

Skolnick, A. and Skolnick, J., *Family in Transition: Rethinking Marriage, Sexuality, Child Rearing, and Family Organization*, 4th ed. (Boston: Little, Brown and Company, 1983).

Smart, C. and Neal, B., *Family Fragments?* (Cambridge: Polity Press, 1999).

Snell, J.G., *In the Shadow of the Law: Divorce in Canada 1900-1939* (Toronto: University of Toronto Press, 1991).

Sopinka, J., Lederman, S.N. and Bryant, A.W., *The Law of Evidence in Canada* (Toronto: Butterworths, 2nd ed. 1999).

Stewart, M., ed., *Chronic Conditions and Caregiving in Canada: Social Support Strategies* (Toronto: University of Toronto Press, 2000).

Strasser, M., *Legally Wed: Same-Sex Marriage and the Constitution* (Ithaca: Cornell University Press, 1997).

Strong, J.W., ed., *McCormick on Evidence*, 5th ed. (St. Paul, Minnesota: West Group, 1999).

Sullivan, A., *Same-Sex Marriage: Pro and Con, A Reader* (New York: Vintage, 1997).

Ursel, J., *Private Lives, Public Policy: 100 Years of State Intervention in the Family* (Toronto: Women's Press, 1992).

Ward, P., *Courtship, Love and Marriage in Nineteenth-Century English Canada* (Montreal and Kingston: McGill-Queen's University Press, 1990).

Weeks J., Heaphy B., and Donovan C., *Same Sex Intimacies: Families of Choice and Other Life Experiments* (New York: Routledge, 2001).

Weston, K., *Families We Choose: Lesbians, Gays, Kinship* (New York: Columbia University Press, 1991).

Wigmore, J.H., *Evidence in Trials at Common Law*, vol. 8 by John T. McNaughton (Boston: Little Brown, 1961).

Wintemute, R. and Andenæs, M., eds., *Legal Recognition of Same-Sex Partnerships* (Oxford: Hart Publishing, 2001).

Wu, Z., *Cohabitation: An Alternative Form of Family Living* (Don Mills: Oxford University Press, 2000).

5. Journals and Articles

Adams, W., "Same-Sex Relationships and Anglo-Canadian Choice of Law: An Argument for Universal Validity" (1996) 34 *The Canadian Yearbook of International Law* 103.

Allard, S. *et al.*, "Le concubinage" in Chambre des Notaires du Québec, *Répertoire de droit*, "Famille", Doctrine – Document 3, Montreal, 1993.

Anderson, T., "Models of Registered Partnership and Their Rationale: The British Columbia Law Institute's Proposed Domestic Partner Act" (2000) 17:1 *Can. J. Fam. L.* 89.

Anson, O., "Marital Status and Women's Health Revisited: The Importance of a Proximate Adult" (February 1989) 51 *Journal of Marriage and the Family* 185.

Aronson, J. and Neysmith, S., "The Retreat of the State and Long-Term Care Provision: Implications for Frail Elderly People, Unpaid Family Carers and Paid Home Care Workers" (Summer 1997) 53 *Studies in Political Economy* 37.

Backhouse, C., "Married Women's Property Law in Nineteenth-Century Canada" (1988) 6:2 *Law and History Review* 211.

Backhouse, C., "'Pure Patriarchy': Nineteenth-Century Canadian Marriage" (1985-1986) 31 *McGill Law Journal* 264.

Bailey, M., "Hawaii's Same-Sex Marriage Initiatives: Implications for Canada" (1998) 15 *Can. J. Fam. L.* 153.

Bailey, M., "How Will Canada Respond to Same-Sex Marriage?" (1998) 32 *Creighton Law Review* 105.

Bailey, M., "Private International Law Issues Relating to Registered Partnerships: A Canadian Perspective" (Domestic Partnerships Conference, Faculty of Law, Queen's University, 21-23 October 1999) [unpublished].

Bala, N., "Alternatives for Extending Spousal Status in Canada" (2000) 17:1 *Can. J. Fam. L.* 169.

Bala, N., "The Evolving Canadian Definition of the Family: Towards a Pluralistic and Functional Approach" (1994) 8 *International Journal of Law and the Family* 293.

Bala, N. and Cano, M., "Unmarried Cohabitation in Canada: Common Law and Civilian Approaches to Living Together" (1989) 4:2 *Canadian Family Law Quarterly* 147.

Bala, N. and Jaremko, R., "Context and Inclusivity in Defining Family Obligations: Canada's Functional and Pluralistic Approach" (forthcoming in 2001) 18 *Can. J. Fam. L.*

Baurain, P., "La cohabitation légale : Mariage ou mirage législatif ", (1998) 120 *R. du N. Belge* 618.

Bess, I., "Widows Living Alone" (1999) 53 *Canadian Social Trends* 2. Available in French: *Les veuves qui vivent seules*.

Boily, N., "Monde en mutation, changement de valeurs? Les repères des Québécoises et des Québécois à l'aube de l'an 2000" in M. Simard and J. Alary, eds., *Comprendre la famille – Actes du 5ᵉ symposium québécois de recherche sur la famille* (Trois-Rivières: Presses de l'Université du Québec, 2000) 377.

Boskin, M. and Sheshinski, E., "Optimal Treatment of the Family: Married Couples" (1983) 20 *Journal of Public Economics* 281.

Bouchard, J., Boyd, S. and Sheehy, E., "Canadian Feminist Literature on Law: An Annotated Bibliography" (1999) 11: 1-2 *Canadian Journal of Women and the Law*.

Boyd, M. and Pryor, E., "Young Adults Living in Their Parents' Homes" (1989) 13 *Canadian Social Trends* 17. Available in French: *Les jeunes adultes vivant avec leurs parents*.

Boyd, S., "Best Friends or Spouses? Privatization and the Recognition of Lesbian Relationships in *M. v. H*" (1996) 13 *Can. J. Fam. L.* 321.

Boyd, S., "Expanding the Family in Family Law: Recent Ontario Proposals on Same-Sex Relationships" (1994) 7 *Canadian Journal of Women and the Law* 545.

Brotman, S., "The Incidence of Poverty Among Seniors in Canada: Exploring the Impact of Gender, Ethnicity and Race" (1998) 17:2 *Canadian Journal on Aging* 166.

Buchignani, N. and Armstrong-Esther, C., "Informal Care and Older Native Canadians" (1999) 19 *Ageing and Society* 3.

Burman, D., "Le déclin de la liberté au nom de l'égalité" (1990) 24 *R.J.T.* 461.

Campbell, L. and Martin-Matthews, A., "Caring Sons: Exploring Men's Involvement in Filial Care" (2000) 19:1 *Canadian Journal on Aging* 57.

Chambers, D., "What if? The Legal Consequences of Marriage and the Legal Needs of Lesbians and Gay Male Couples" (1996) 95 *Michigan Law Review* 447.

Chapelle, A., "Les pactes de famille en matière extra-patrimoniale" (1984) 83 *Rev. tr. dr. civ.* 411.

Che-Alford, J. and Hamm, B., "Under One Roof: Three Generations Living Together" (1999) 53 *Canadian Social Trends* 6. Available in French: *Trois générations réunies sous un même toit.*

Coombs, M.I., "Shared Privacy and the Fourth Amendment, or the Rights of Relationships" (1987) 75 *California Law Review* 1593.

Cossman, B. and Ryder, B., "What is Marriage-Like Like? The Irrelevance of Conjugality" (forthcoming 2001) 18 *Can. J. Fam. L.*

Cox, B.J., "The Little Project: From Alternative Families to Domestic Partnerships to Same-Sex Marriage" (2000) 15 *Wisconsin Women's Law Journal* 77.

Cranswick, K., "Help Close at Hand: Relocating to Give or Receive Care" (1999) 55 *Canadian Social Trends* 11. Available in French: *De l'aide à portée de la main : Déménager pour recevoir ou offrir de l'aide.*

Crompton, S. and Kemeny, A. " In Sickness and in Health: The Well-Being of Married Seniors" (1999) 55 *Canadian Social Trends* 22. Available in French: *Le bien-être des personnes âgées mariées, malades ou en santé.*

Cuming, R.C.C., "Transactions at Undervalue and Preferences under the Bankruptcy and Insolvency Act: Rethinking Outdated Approaches" (31st Annual Workshop on Commercial and Consumer Law, Faculty of Law, University of Toronto, 19-20 October 2001) 213 [unpublished].

Davies, C., "The Extension of Marital Rights and Obligations to the Unmarried: Registered Domestic Partnerships and Other Methods" (2000) 17 *Canadian Family Law Quarterly* 247.

Donnelly, M., "The Disparate Impact of Pension Reform on Women" (1993) 6 *Canadian Journal of Women and the Law* 419.

Duclos, N., "Some Complicating Thoughts on Same-Sex Marriage" (1991) 1 *Law and Sexuality* 31.

Dulude, L. *et al.*, "Taxation of the Family: Joint Taxation of Spouses – A Feminist View" (Winter 1979) 1:4 *Canadian Taxation* 8.

Duncan, W., "The Recognition of Foreign Registered Partnerships in European States: the Existing Situation and the Prospects for the Future" (Domestic Partnerships Conference, Faculty of Law, Queen's University, 21-23 October 1999) [unpublished].

Dupuis, M.D., "The Impact of Culture, Society and History on the Legal Process: An Analysis of the Legal Status of Same-sex Relationships in the United States and Denmark" (1995) 9 *Int'l J.L. & Fam.* 86.

Eekelaar, J.M., "Registered Same Sex Partnerships and Marriages – A Statistical Comparison" (1998) 28 *Family Law* 561.

Eichler, M., "Contemporary and Historical Diversity in Families: Comment on Turcotte's and Smart's Papers" (2000) 17:1 *Can. J. Fam. L.* 54.

Eskridge, W.N., "Equality Practice: Liberal Reflections on the Jurisprudence of Civil Unions" (2001) 64 *Albany Law Review* 853.

Frederick, J. and Fast, J., "Eldercare in Canada: Who Does How Much?" (1999) 54 *Canadian Social Trends* 26. Available in French: *Le profil des personnes qui prodiguent des soins aux aînés.*

Freeman, J., "Defining Family in *Mossop* v. *DSS*: The Challenge of Anti-Essentialism and Interactive Discrimination for Human Rights Litigation" (1994) 44 *University of Toronto Law Journal* 41.

Fried, C., "Privacy" (1968) 77 *Yale Law Journal* 475.

Gavigan, S., "Legal Forms, Family Forms, Gendered Norms: What is a Spouse?" (1999) 14 *Canadian Journal of Law and Society* 127.

Gavigan, S., "Paradise Lost, Paradox Revisited: The Implications of Feminist, Lesbian and Gay Engagement to Law" (1993) 31 *Osgoode Hall Law Journal* 589.

Gay and Lesbian Rights Lobby, "The Bride Wore Pink" (1993) 3 *Australasian Gay and Lesbian Law Journal* 67.

Ghalam, N.Z., "Living With Relatives" (1996) 42 *Canadian Social Trends* 20. Available in French: *Vivre avec des parents*.

Glendinning, C., "Dependency and Interdependency: The Incomes of Informal Careers and the Impact of Social Security" (1990) 19:4 *Journal of Social Policy* 469.

Glossop, R., "Families – Yesterday, Today and Tomorrow" (Winter 1999) 29:4 *Transition* 12.

Graycar, R. and Millbanks, J., "The Bride Wore Pink...To The Property (Relationship) Legislation Act 1999: Relationship Law Reform in New South Wales" (2000) 17:1 *Can. J. Fam. L.* 227.

Hafen, B., "The Family as an Entity" (1989) 22:3-4 *University of California Davis Law Review* 865.

Heller, T., Hsieh, K. and Rowitz, L., "Maternal and Paternal Caregiving of Persons with Mental Retardation Across the Lifespan" (1997) 46:4 *Family Relations* 407.

Henson, D., "A Comparative Analysis of Same-Sex Partnership Protections: Recommendations for American Reform" (1993) 7 *International Journal of Law and Family* 282.

Holland, W., "Cohabitation and Marriage – A Meeting at the Crossroads?" (1990) 7 *Canadian Family Law Quarterly* 31.

Holland, W., "Intimate Relationships in the New Millennium: the Assimilation of Marriage and Cohabitation?" (2000) 17:1 *Can. J. Fam. L.* 114.

Karst, K., "The Freedom of Intimate Association" (1980) 89 *Yale Law Journal* 624.

Keefe, J. and Fancey, P., "Financial Compensation or Home Help Services: Examining Differences Among Program Recipients" (1997) 16:2 *Canadian Journal on Aging* 254.

Kitchen, B., "The Patriarchal Bias of the Income Tax in Canada" (1986) 11 *Atlantis* 35.

Knopff, R., "The Case for Domestic Partnership Laws" (June 1999) 20 *Policy Options* 53.

Krause, H.D., "Marriage for the New Millenium: Heterosexual, Same Sex – or Not at All?" (2000) 34 *Fam. L.Q.* 271.

La Novara, P., "Changes in Family Living" (1993) 29 *Canadian Social Trends* 12. Available in French: *La famille en évolution.*

Le Bourdais, C., Neill, G. and Turcotte, P., "The Changing Face of Conjugal Relationships" (2000) 56 *Canadian Social Trends* 14. Available in French: *L'évolution des liens conjugaux.*

LeFebour, P., "Same-Sex Spousal Recognition in Ontario: Declarations and Denial – A Class Perspective" (1993) 9 *Journal of Law and Social Policy* 272.

Lewin, E., *The Real Thing, or Enacting Authenticity in Lesbian and Gay Weddings* (prepared for delivery at the 1999 Domestic Partnership Conference, Faculty of Law, Queen's University, Kingston, Ontario, 21-23 October, 1999).

Lindsay, C., "Seniors: A Diverse Group Aging Well" (Spring 1999) 52 *Canadian Social Trends* 24. Available in French: *Les aînés : un groupe diversifié qui vieillit bien.*

London, J., "Taxation of the Family: The Family as the Basic Tax Unit" (1979) 1:4 *Canadian Taxation* 4.

Lund-Andersen, I., "Moving Towards the Individual Principle in Danish Law" (1990) 4 *Int'l J. L. & Fam.* 328.

MacDougall, B., "The Celebration of Same-Sex Marriage" (2000-01) 32 *Ottawa L. Rev.* 235.

MacDougall, D., "Marriage Resolution and Recognition in Canada" (1995) 29 *Family Law Quarterly* 541.

Maloney, M., "Women and the Income Tax Act: Marriage, Motherhood and Divorce" (1989) 3:1 *Canadian Journal of Women and the Law* 182.

Marcil-Gratton, N., "Growing Up With Mom and Dad?" (Spring 1999) 29:1 *Transition* 4.

McAuley, M., "Human Rights and Sexuality: Help or Hindrance" (International Bar Association 2000 Conference, Amsterdam, 17-22 September 2000) [unpublished].

McCarthy, M. and Radbord, J., "Family Law for Same-Sex Couples: Chart(er)ing the Course" (1998) 15:2 *Can. J. Fam. L.* 101.

McDaniel, S., "Serial Employment and Skinny Government: Reforming Caring and Sharing Among Generations" (1997) 16:3 *Canadian Journal on Aging* 465.

Meekosha, H. and Dowse, L., "Enabling Citizenship: Gender, Disability and Citizenship in Australia" (1997) 57 *Feminist Review* 49.

Michaud, C., "Le mariage et la famille : des réalités dessoudées" in Conseil de la famille, Gouvernement du Québec, *Recueil de réflexion sur la stabilité des couples-parents* (Québec: 1996) at 195

Millbank, J., "The De Facto Relationships Amendment Bill 1998 (NSW): The Rationale for Law Reform" (1999) 8 *Australasian Gay & Lesbian Law Journal* 1.

Minow, M., "All in the Family and In All Families: Membership, Loving and Owing" (1992-93) 95 *West Virginia Law Review* 275.

Minow, M., "Redefining Families: Who's In and Who's Out?" (1991) 62 *University of Colorado Law Review* 269.

Minow, M., "The Free Exercise of Families" (1991) *University of Illinois Law Review* 925.

Nielsen, L., "Family Rights and the 'Registered Partnership' in Denmark" (1990) 4 *Int'l J. L. & Fam.* 297.

Oderkirk, J., "Marriage in Canada: Changing Beliefs and Behaviours, 1600-1990" (Summer 1994) *Canadian Social Trends* 2. Available in French: *Le mariage au Canada : Évolution des croyances et des comportements, 1600-1990.*

O'Donoghue, C. and Sutherland, H., "Accounting for the Family in European Income Tax Systems" (1999) 23 *Cambridge Journal of Economics* 565.

Oldman, O. and McIntyre, M., "Taxation on the Family in a Comprehensive and Simplified Income Tax" (1997) 90 *Harvard Law Review* 1573.

Pahl, J., "Personal Taxation, Social Security and Financial Arrangements Within Marriage" (1986) 13 *Journal of Law and Society* 241.

Paoletti, I., "A Half Life: Women Caregivers of Older Disabled Relatives" (1999) 11:1 *Journal of Women and Aging* 53.

Pedersen, M. H., "Denmark: Homosexual Marriages and New Rules Regarding Separation and Divorce" (1991-92) 30 *J. Fam. L.* 290.

Penning, M., "Self-, Informal and Formal Care: Partnerships in Community-Based and Residential Long-Term Care Settings" (2000) 19:1 *Canadian Journal on Aging* 75.

Phipps, S.A. and Burton, P.S., "Sharing Within Families: Implications for Measurement of Poverty Among Individuals in Canada" (1995) 28 *Canadian Journal of Economics* 177.

Rea, S., "Taxes, Transfers and the Family" (1984) 34 *University of Toronto Law Journal* 314.

Rioux, M.H., "Towards a Concept of Equality of Well-Being: Overcoming the Social and Legal Construction of Inequality" (January 1994) 7:1 *Canadian Journal of Law and Jurisprudence* 127.

Robb, R. *et al.*, "Valuation of Unpaid Help by Seniors in Canada: An Empirical Analysis" (1999) 18:4 *Canadian Journal on Aging* 430.

Rogerson, C., *Couples or Individuals or Parents? Rethinking the Appropriate Unit for the Allocation of Social Benefits* (prepared for delivery at the 1999 Domestic Partnership Conference, Faculty of Law, Queen's University, Kingston, Ontario, 21-23 October, 1999).

Rolland, L., "Les figures contemporaines du contrat" (1999) 44 *R.D. McGill* 903.

Salvatori, P. *et al.*, "Aging with an Intellectual Disability: A Review of Canadian Literature" (1998) 17:3 *Canadian Journal on Aging* 249.

Schnoor, J., "Evidence by Spouses in Criminal Proceedings" (paper presented to Uniform Law Conference of Canada, 1999).

Schrama, W. M., "Registered Partnership in the Netherlands" (1999) 13 *Int'l J.L.P. & Fam.* 315.

Silvers, A., "Reconciling Equality to Difference: Caring (F)or Justice for People with Disabilities" (1995) 10:1 *Hypatia* 30.

Smart, C., "Stories of Family Life: Cohabitation, Marriage and Social Change" (2000) 17:1 *Can. J. Fam. L.* 20.

Smock, P. and Gupta, S., *Cohabitation in Contemporary North America* (2000 Family Issues Symposium Papers, Population Research Institute, The Pennsylvania State University, 2000), online: http://www.pop.psu.edu/events/fisym2000-papers.html.

Snell, J., "Filial Responsibility Laws in Canada: An Historical Study" (1990) 9:3 *Canadian Journal on Aging* 268.

Stewart, H., "Spousal Incompetency and the Charter" (1996) 34 *Osgoode Hall L.J.* 411.

Teitelbaum, Lee, "The Family as a System" (1996) *Utah Law Review* 537.

Vogler, C. and Pahl, J., "Money, Power and Inequality Within Marriage" (1994) *Sociological Review* 263.

Waaldijk, K., "Civil Developments: Patterns of Reform in the Legal Position of Same-Sex Partners in Europe" (2000) 17:1 *Can. J. Fam. L.* 62.

Wakkary, A., "Assessing the Impact of Changing Marital Rights and Obligations: Practical Considerations" (2000) 17:1 *Can. J. Fam. L.* 200.

Wintemute, R., "Sexual Orientation Discrimination as Sex Discrimination: Same-Sex Couples and the Charter in *Mossop, Egan* and *Layland*" (1994) 39 *McGill Law Journal* 429.

Wolfson, C. *et al.*, "Adult Children's Perceptions of Their Responsibility to Provide Care for Dependent Elderly Parents"(1993) 33:3 *The Gerontologist* 315.

Woolley, F., "For a Radical Redesign of Our Tax Treatment of the Family" *Policy Options* (September 1998) 7.

Woolley, F. and Marshall, J., "Measuring Inequality Within the Household" (1994) 40 *Review of Income and Wealth* 415.

Young, C., "(In)visible Inequalities: Women, Tax and Poverty" (1995) 27 *Ottawa Law Review* 99.

Young, C., "Spousal Status, Pension Benefits and Tax" (1998) 6 *Canadian Labour and Employment Law Journal* 435.

Young, C., "Taxing Times for Lesbians and Gay Men: Equality at What Cost?" (1994) 1 / *Dalhousie Law Journal* 534.

Young, P.D., *The Debate Over Same-Sex Relationships in Religious Traditions* (prepared for delivery at the 1999 Domestic Partnership Conference, Faculty of Law, Queen's University, Kingston, Ontario, 21-23 October, 1999).

6. Research Studies

Battle, K., *Relentless Incrementalism: Deconstructing and Reconstructing Canadian Income Security Policy* (Ottawa: Caledon Institute of Social Policy, 2001).

Battle, K. and Torjman, S., *The Post-Welfare State in Canada: Income-Testing and Inclusion* (Ottawa: Caledon Institute of Social Policy, 2001).

Beauvais, C. and Jenson, J., *Two Policy Paradigms: Family Responsibility and Investing in Children* (Ottawa: Canadian Policy Research Networks, 2001).

Cheal, D., Woolley, F., and Luxton, M., *How Families Cope and Why Policymakers Need to Know* (Ottawa: Canadian Policy Research Networks, 1998).

Cossman, B. and Ryder, B., *Gays, Lesbians and Unmarried Heterosexual Couples and the Family Law Act: Accommodating a Diversity of Family Forms. A Research Paper.* (Toronto: Ontario Law Reform Commission, 1993).

Dumas, J., and Peron, Y., *Marriage and Conjugal Life in Canada: Current Demographic Analysis* (Ottawa: Statistics Canada, 1992).

Duxbury, L. and Higgins, C., *Work-Life Balance in Saskatchewan: Realities and Challenges* (Regina: Government of Saskatchewan, 1998).

Fast, J.E. and Keating, N.C., *Family Caregiving and Consequences for Carers: Toward a Policy Research Agenda* (Ottawa: Canadian Policy Research Networks, 2000).

Ford, D. and Nault, F., "Changing Fertility Patterns, 1974 to 1994" (1996) 8 *Health Report* 39-46.

Jenson, J. and Jacobzone, S., *Care Allowances for the Frail Elderly and Their Impact on Women Care-Givers* (Paris: Organization of Economic Co-operation and Development, 2000).

Keating, N.C., Fast, J.E. *et al.*, *Defining Eldercare: Components and Perspectives* (Ottawa: Health Canada, 1996).

Keating, N.C., Fast J.E, Frederick J. *et al.*, *Eldercare in Canada: Context, Content and Consequences* (Ottawa: Statistics Canada, 1999).

Krashinsky, M. and Cleveland, G., *Tax Fairness for One-Earner and Two-Earner Families: An Examination of the Issues* (Ottawa: Canadian Policy Research Networks, 1999).

Lahey, Kathleen A., *The Impact of Relationship Recognition on Lesbian Women in Canada: Still Separate and Only Somewhat "Equivalent"* (Ottawa: Status of Women Canada, 2001). Available in French: *L'effet de la reconnaissance des unions sur les lesbiennes au Canada : encore distincte et presque «équivalentes»*.

Lindsay, C., *Lone-Parent Families in Canada* (Ottawa: Statistics Canada, 1992).

Morris, M., Robinson, J. and Simpson, J., *The Changing Nature of Home Care and Its Impact on Women's Vulnerability to Poverty* (Ottawa: Status of Women Canada, 1999). Available in French: *L'évolution des soins à domicile et la fragilité financière des femmes.*

Myers, T. *et al.*, *The Canadian Survey of Gay and Bisexual Men and HIV Infection: Men's Survey* (Ottawa: Canadian AIDS Society, 1993).

New Zealand Law Commission, *Study Paper 4: Recognising Same-Sex Relationships* (Wellington, New Zealand: Law Commission, 1999).

Prince, M.J., *Governing in an Integrated Fashion: Lessons from the Disability Domain* (Ottawa: Canadian Research Policy Networks, 2001).

Samis, S.M., "'An Injury to One is an Injury to All': Heterosexism, Homophobia, and Anti-Gay/Lesbian Violence in Greater Vancouver" (M.A. Thesis, Simon Fraser University, 1995).

Statistics Canada, *1996 Census: Marital Status, Common-law Unions and Families* (Ottawa: Statistics Canada, 1997).

Statistics Canada, *Characteristics of Dual-Earner Families 1993* (Ottawa: Statistics Canada, 1995).

Statistics Canada, Housing, Family and Social Statistics Division, *Women in Canada: A Statistical Report*, 3rd ed. (Ottawa: Statistic Canada, 1995). Available in French: *Portrait statistique des femmes au Canada.*

Statistics Canada, "Population in private households, showing living arrangements, 1996 Census", online: http://www.statcan.ca/english/Pgdb/People/Families/famil52a.htm.

Statistics Canada, "Population 15 Years and Over by Marital Status, Showing Selected Age Groups and Sex, for Canada, Provinces and Territories, 1996 Census", online: http://www.statcan.ca/english/census96/oct14/mar1.htm.

Statistics Canada, "Population 15 Years and Over Living in Common Law Unions, 1996 Census", online: http://www.statcan.ca:80/english/census96/oct14/mar2.htm.

The Roeher Institute, *Disability-Related Support Arrangements, Policy Options and Implications for Women's Equality* (Ottawa: Status of Women Canada, 2001). Available in French: *Services d'appoint pour les personnes handicapées : options stratégiques et incidences sur l'égalité des femmes.*

Townson, M., *Reducing Poverty Among Older Women: The Potential of Retirement Income Policies* (Ottawa: Status of Women Canada, 2000). Available in French: *Réduire la pauvreté parmi les femmes âgées : le potentiel des politiques en matière de revenu de retraite.*

Valentine, F., *Enabling Citizenship: Full Inclusion of Children with Disabilities and their Parents* (Ottawa: Canadian Policy Research Networks, 2001).

7. Other

Angus Reid, Media Release, "Majority (55%) Agree With Supreme Court Decision That Definition of 'Spouse' Apply to Same-Sex Couples" (9 June 1999).

Centre for Research and Information on Canada and The Association for Canadian Studies, *Destination 2025 – National Survey of Young Canadians*, December 2000 at 3-4 http://www.cric.ca/en_html/sondages/cric.html.

Decima Research Inc., "Canadians Split on Same Sex Marriage" (22 January 2001).

Egale Inc. et al. v. *The Attorney General of Canada* (3 October 2001), Vancouver L002698 and L003197 (B.C.S.C.) (Submission of Petitioner, EGALE Canada), available online at http://www.egale.ca/documents/BC-Final.htm).

Egale Inc. et al. v. *The Attorney General of Canada* (3 October 2001), Vancouver L002698 and L003197 (B.C.S.C.) (Submission of the Intervenor, The Interfaith Coalition for Marriage), available online at http://www.evangelicalfellowship.ca/resources/resource_viewer.asp?Resource_ID=117.

Environics Research Group, "Most Canadians Favour Gay Marriage; Approval of Homosexuality Continues to Increase" (10 May 2001).

Gallup Canada Inc., News Release, "About Four-in-Ten Canadians Accepting of Same Sex Marriages, Adoption" (7 March 2000).

Léger Marketing, "Canadian Perceptions of Homosexuality – Executive Report" (22 June 2001).

Sheppard, R., "We Are Canadian" *Maclean's*, Maclean's/Global Television 17th annual year-end poll, (25 December 2000).